T0330443

Public Pensions and Immigration

Public Pensions and Immigration

A Public Choice Approach

Tim Krieger

NORDAKADEMIE – Hochschule der Wirtschaft, Germany

Edward Elgar
Cheltenham, UK • Northampton, MA, USA

Published by
Edward Elgar Publishing Limited
Glensanda House
Montpellier Parade
Cheltenham
Glos GL50 1UA
UK

Edward Elgar Publishing, Inc.
136 West Street
Suite 202
Northampton
Massachusetts 01060
USA

A catalogue record for this book
is available from the British Library

Library of Congress Cataloguing in Publication Data

Krieger, Tim.
    Public pensions and immigration : a public choice approach / Tim Krieger.
        p. cm.
    Includes bibliographical references.
        1. Pensions–Government policy–European Union countries–Public opinion.
    2. Emigration and immigration–Government policy–European Union
    countries–Public opinion. 3. Alien labor–European Union countries–Public
    opinion. 4. Immigrants–Pensions–European Union countries–Public opinion.
    5. Public opinion–European Union Countries. I. Title.

    HD7164.5.K75 2006
    331.25'2'094–dc22

                                                                    2005049435

ISBN 1 84542 440 9

Printed and bound in Great Britain by MPG Books Ltd, Bodmin, Cornwall

Contents

Figures

Tables

Preface

This book was mainly written while I was working as a lecturer at the Institute for Social Policy Research in Göttingen and at the Seminar for Economic Policy in Munich. Many contacts with members of the Economics Departments at the Georg-August-Universität Göttingen and the Ludwig-Maximilians-Universität München have contributed to the shape of the present study.

I owe sincere thanks to my academic teacher, Professor Andreas Haufler, who constantly supported this work with both general advice and detailed comments and who created within his research unit a stimulating and cooperative environment. Professor Andreas Wagener and Professor Martin Kolmar made a large number of valuable suggestions and shared their expertise on the theory of pension systems and labor mobility with me. I am further grateful to Professor Hans-Werner Sinn for detailed comments on the first draft of this study. I very much appreciate that Professor Sinn and Professor Ray Rees served as members of my thesis committee.

I have further benefited from helpful discussions and suggestions received from several other colleagues, discussants and referees. I am grateful to Christoph Sauer who has been my co-author in a study on eastern European pension systems which is presented in this book. Finally, I thank Alexandra Minton and Kate Emmins at Edward Elgar for answering all my questions regarding the preparation of this book. Last but not least, I thank my wife Frauke for her love and support.

Acknowledgements

The editor and publishers wish to thank the following who have kindly given their permission for the use of copyright material.

- Springer Science and Business Media (the model presented in Section 4.2, parts of the model presented in Chapter 6 including Figures 6.1 and 6.2 as well as Tables 6.1 and 6.2).
- Dr. Martin Werding and Ifo Institute (Figures 3.1 and 8.1).

Every effort has been made to trace all the copyright holders but if any have been inadvertently overlooked the publishers will be pleased to make the necessary arrangements at the first opportunity.

1. Introduction

In the first decade of the new millennium the process of globalization has advanced to new and higher levels. Restrictions to the mobility of the factors of production, capital and labor, have been reduced substantially and the factors have in fact become much more mobile. Due to this western industrialized countries, in particular the European welfare states, face new challenges. It has become increasingly difficult to collect tax revenues and social-security contributions. At the same time welfare systems which are still generous attract poor people from all over the world although these systems are under heavy strain due to the ageing of societies. Therefore, it is not a surprise that immigration is a highly controversial topic in many countries around the world. For some, the perception of immigration is that people entering the country are potential net beneficiaries of the welfare state taking away some of an already shrinking cake. These opponents to immigration believe that past immigration has harmed welfare states and expect this to happen with future immigration as well.

Others, however, believe that – at least in the long run – immigrants will help to stabilize welfare states and particularly the pension systems which suffer from a too small number of contributors due to low population growth rates. There is some truth in the arguments of both opponents and supporters. In many countries the school performance of foreigners is below the average while unemployment is above. Hence, foreigners are more likely to become net beneficiaries of the social system. But, at the same time with well chosen incentives a positive selection of able immigrants may be attracted. Often the share of foreigners founding new enterprises, thereby creating several new jobs, is larger than this share among natives. And – most important for social systems and a more dynamic growth of the economy – immigrants are young and have on average more children than natives. This helps to slow down the ageing of the societies.

The link between immigration on the one hand and demographics and the pension system on the other hand can hardly be disputed, neither in theory nor in practice. However, there is some discussion about the size of this effect. The opponents of immigration acknowledge that immigration may improve demographics. However, in their opinion the effect is insufficiently large to solve the problems of ageing in countries like Germany or Italy. For them, there is no need to change the existing immigration policy as the small positive effect on the pension system is unlikely to outweigh the negative effects expected from immigration. In fact, they often propose further restrictions to immigration. Proponents believe that the positive effects on the social security systems and other parts of the economy will dominate, maybe not immediately but certainly in the long run when pension systems are feared to collapse under the burden of demographic problems.

Given these observations it is not clear a priori how voters in a democratic country decide on pension and immigration issues. There may be a majority either for or against changes of the parameters of the pension system such as contribution rates, pension benefits, retirement age or the relative importance of funding and redistribution. Immigration policy may be inviting, selective or restrictive with different effects on the age structure of the society. The final voting outcome depends on the preferences of individual voters and voter groups in society. Our discussion in this book will deal in detail with these issues. The goal is to investigate the connections between migration, politics and pension systems in order to understand how voting decisions and voting outcomes regarding these topics come about. This will give us some insights into whether immigration – as often argued – can help to solve or at least relax the problem of ageing societies.

Our discussion begins in Chapters 2 and 3 by providing an introduction to basic issues related to pension systems and labor mobility. This information is helpful to better understand the discussion in later chapters. First, we will give some basic information and stylized facts regarding the dramatic ageing process in many countries. We will discuss how many immigrants will be necessary to ameliorate this development. Then, the basic modes of operation of different types of pension systems, such as pay-as-you-go and fully funded systems, will be introduced. We will learn that it is mainly the pay-as-you-go system which is affected by ageing (and immigration). The important concepts of implicit taxes and debt will be introduced which will later be used to evaluate the level of redistribution inherent in a pension system. Finally, we will deal with the effect of immigration on pay-as-you-go systems, thereby arguing that immigrants generate a positive externality on existing members of the pension system. This effect may be weaker or stronger depending on the type of immigrants and the gain from immigration may not accrue to all members equally; some people may even lose. From this problem arises the general political conflict that will be discussed in the chapters to follow.

In Chapters 4 through 6, we will therefore turn to an analysis of public pensions and immigration based on public choice theory. Given that we know how immigration affects the pension system, we can ask how voters decide on immigration issues. What is the optimal immigration policy and which policy is effectively chosen by the electorate if voters are able to anticipate the effects that immigration may have on contribution rates and pension benefits? Public choice theory offers some explanations in this context. Each voter weighs up the positive and negative effects of immigration on his circumstances, before he decides which level of immigration he prefers. Depending on his age, skill level or the pension system he lives in, he will choose to allow more or fewer immigrants into the country. Assuming a median-voter model, the final voting outcome is determined by the characteristics of the median voter. Notice that we will argue mainly in terms of economic theory and put aside arguments like xenophobia or ideology which are more in the field of political science or sociology.

Our discussion will begin in Chapter 4 by introducing the well-known public choice model of Browning (1975), which determines how voters of different ages decide on age-dependent issues such as the parameters of the pension system. The model will be the starting point for the investigation of the so called 'perfect assimilation hypothesis' which is common in models on immigration policy. The hypothesis assumes that immigrants assimilate perfectly in the sense of becoming just like natives as soon as they enter the host country. As a consequence even immigration of persons who will be net beneficiaries of the welfare system induces an unambiguously positive effect on the entire native population due to additional contribution payments. Relaxing this rather strong assumption leads to different and more realistic voting outcomes. A poor school performance by immigrant children, for example, makes native workers more reluctant to allow foreigners into the country. Because the gain from immigration will accrue only to a minority of voters (retirees) immigration may no longer be supported. We will also explain other factors potentially having an impact on the voting decision, for example, social distance, unemployment probabilities or return migration. Anticipating these effects may change the preferences for immigration of different groups in society as well. Finally, we will ask whether the design of pension systems affects voting decisions, that is, whether it will make a difference to either have a Beveridgian or Bismarckian, a fixed-benefit or fixed contribution-rate system. We can show that these differences may turn the natives' incentives regarding the level of immigration upside down for different groups of voters. With fixed contribution rates additional contributors due to immigration lead to higher benefits per capita for a given number of retirees. Workers may suffer from a lower marginal productivity of labor. On the other hand, with fixed benefits any additional contributor allows for falling contribution rates and thus increasing net incomes for the working generation.

Dealing with immigration policy the public choice approach is not in all cases appropriate as the final Chapters 7 through 9 of our book show. Within the EU an important goal is the freedom of movement for all EU citizens. Neither national restrictions on the inflow of citizens from other EU member states nor a discrimination between nationals and EU foreigners are allowed. This leads to very different questions and problems because migration cannot be restricted and therefore effects on the social systems are likely. Mobile workers may move between EU member states in order to look for optimal living conditions, one of their choice criteria possibly being the attractiveness of social and pension systems.

Under these conditions of systems competition national pension policy may need to adjust to increasing labor mobility. Our discussion of this situation begins by introducing a simple static model of a country with a redistribution instrument such as the pension system. With international labor mobility redistribution will no longer be sustainable. The reason is that generous welfare systems attract potential welfare recipients from other member states with less generous systems. At the same time potential contributors want to move to countries with as little redistribution as possible. They hope for higher net incomes due to lower taxation. This situation is feared to induce an incentive to cut back redistribution in order to repel costly beneficiaries and to attract contributors to the social system. In the context of ageing societies, this implies that some people may leave a country with severe financing problems in the pension system. We will show that the existing institutional framework of the EU cannot prevent this danger. While theory predicts that the problem of harmful migration within the EU may be solved by coordination of contribution rates, each EU member state is free to set contribution rates and there is little cooperation between countries.

Fortunately, the willingness to migrate within Europe is rather low but this is expected to change with the EU eastern enlargement which imposes further challenges to western European countries. If substantial east–west migration takes place pension systems may benefit from immigrants but at the same time strong negative effects have to be feared, for example, pressure on lower wage groups. There is also indirect evidence that even before the enlargement systems competition has started to reshape pension systems in various countries by reducing the level of redistribution.

Our discussion ends with Chapter 10 in which some brief conclusions are presented. It will show the importance of the public choice approach towards public pensions and immigration to better understand what immigration can contribute to the solution to the ageing problem. At the same time the limitations of the approach will become clearer. This understanding permits insight into future perspectives.

2. Some basic facts on ageing societies and immigration

Before we begin the theoretical discussion of pension systems, immigration and voting behavior, some basic information and stylized facts on ageing societies and immigration will be given in this chapter. We will present an extensive database for further discussion. Our goal is to make the reader aware of the problems of ageing societies before immigration as a possible solution is presented and evaluated. Furthermore, important concepts will be introduced to which we will often refer back in later chapters.

Our analysis starts with a discussion of reproduction behavior, age structure and life expectancy. We will show that fertility rates have decreased substantially while life expectancy is increasing. As a consequence the age distribution of the populations of industrialized countries is becoming less and less favorable for younger generations. By introducing the concept of the old-age dependency rate we will develop a way of describing the process of ageing in a single variable. This will be very useful for the discussion of pension systems. Then, we will question whether immigration can be a means to stop the shrinking and ageing of societies. The effect of immigration on the age structure will be investigated before we present the numbers of immigrants that would be necessary to keep the population constant. We will demonstrate that immigration alone will hardly be able to solve the ageing problem.

2.1 AGEING SOCIETIES

Today, it is a well-established fact that societies in most industrialized countries are ageing in the sense that (i) reproduction rates are very low and (ii) life expectancy is increasing substantially. The average age of the population is increasing, and the number of retired persons is rising both in absolute and relative terms. For a long time, this development has been neglected although population projections are based on long-term trends and rarely lead to surprises. If one wants to know how many persons aged 60

5

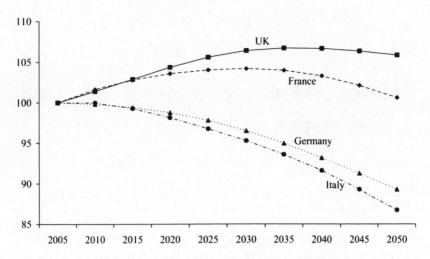

Source: US Census Bureau – International Database; own calculations.

Figure 2.1.   Population projection until 2050 for selected European countries

will be alive in 40 years, one just has to count how many persons aged 20 are alive today and adjust this number according to the mortality table. Only if a country has significant and unsteady in- or outflows of migrants will there be a noticeable element of uncertainty in the prediction. We will turn to the issue of immigration later. First we will take a closer look at the ageing effect alone.

Figure 2.1 presents population projections for four European countries. We index the number of citizens at 100 for the year 2005. The total population in France is approximately 61 million, in Germany 82 million, in Italy 58 million and in the United Kingdom 60 million. The graphs show how the size of the population will change in the future. In France and the UK total population will have increased slightly by 2050. The reasons for this positive development are a rather high fertility rate and immigration in these countries. However, the population increases only until about 2030 or 2035, then it will start to fall slowly. The process of ageing will become visible only at the end of the projection horizon. In the decades to follow the decrease is likely to continue. Then, a development similar to the one in Germany and Italy may occur where the maximum number of citizens has occurred already in the late 1990s. These countries may therefore be characterized as 'rapidly ageing'. The populations will decrease by more than 10 per cent which is equivalent to 8 to 9 million persons despite the fact that in particular Germany is an important immigration country (immigration is accounted for in the projection). In the following we will

Table 2.1.   *Total fertility rates of selected industrialized countries, 1990–2000*

	1990	1992	1994	1996	1998	2000
EU-15	1.57	1.51	1.44	1.44	1.45	1.48
Austria	1.45	1.49	1.44	1.42	1.34	1.34
Belgium	1.62	1.65	1.56	1.55	1.53	1.66
Denmark	1.67	1.76	1.81	1.75	1.72	1.77
Finland	1.78	1.85	1.85	1.76	1.70	1.73
France	1.78	1.73	1.66	1.72	1.75	1.88
Germany	1.45	1.30	1.24	1.32	1.36	1.38
Greece	1.39	1.38	1.35	1.30	1.29	1.29
Ireland	2.11	1.99	1.85	1.89	1.93	1.89
Italy	1.33	1.31	1.21	1.20	1.19	1.24
Luxembourg	1.61	1.64	1.72	1.76	1.68	1.80
Netherlands	1.62	1.59	1.57	1.53	1.63	1.72
Portugal	1.57	1.54	1.44	1.43	1.46	1.52
Spain	1.36	1.32	1.21	1.17	1.15	1.23
Sweden	2.13	2.09	1.88	1.60	1.50	1.54
U.K.	1.83	1.79	1.74	1.72	1.71	1.64
Iceland	2.30	2.21	2.14	2.12	2.05	2.10
Japan	1.54	1.50	1.50	1.44	na	1.41
Norway	1.93	1.88	1.86	1.89	1.81	1.85
Switzerland	1.59	1.58	1.49	1.50	1.46	1.50
USA	2.08	2.07	2.04	2.04	na	2.06

Source: Statistisches Bundesamt (2003, p. 13).

discuss how the shrinking of populations may be explained.

Fertility
Knowing that the future development of the age structure can be derived from past reproduction behavior, it is interesting to look at total fertility rates (TFR) from the past before considering future trends. The TFR measures the number of children that would be born if all women lived to the end of their childbearing years and bore children according to a given fertility rate at each age. Thus, the TFR is the most direct measure of reproduction and has a reference point of 2.1 children per woman. Numbers below the reference point imply that there are too few children to keep the total population at its initial level, given an unchanged life expectancy. If life expectancy is increasing even more than 2.1 children per woman are needed to keep the ratio of old and young persons constant.

Table 2.1 shows numbers for the EU-15 and some other OECD countries.

In the year 2000, the southern European countries Spain (1.23), Italy (1.24) and Greece (1.29) can be found at the lower end of the spectrum, followed by Austria and Germany. Differences between the countries are substantial: France, for example, has a TFR which is about 50 per cent higher than the Spanish (but still 12 per cent below the reference point). Over time, the situation in most countries has not changed much: the relative position among the countries remains mostly the same. Only France, Belgium, Denmark, Luxembourg and the Netherlands improved their TFR slightly during the 1990s; in all other countries and for the entire EU before the eastern enlargement (EU-15) there was a decrease. Remarkable is the decrease in Sweden where the TFR dropped from 2.13 to 1.54 in only one decade. Hardly any industrialized country has a sufficiently high TFR to keep total population constant given life expectancy. Iceland is a notable exception but also the United States has a rather dynamic population growth.

Age structure

How does the age structure look today and how will it develop in the future? Over the last 20 to 30 years the number of new-born children in most countries ranged well below the numbers necessary to replace the parent generation. At the same time, the baby boomer cohorts of the 1950s and 1960s moved upwards in the age pyramid which more and more resembles a tree with a narrow trunk of young cohorts and a relatively broad top of cohorts of retirement age. Table 2.2 shows the projected change in the age structure for Europe over the next 50 years. In many other regions of the world the situation is similar to the European.

Table 2.2.   Projected changes of the age structure in Europe, 2000–2050

Age group	2000		2025		2050	
	millions	%	millions	%	millions	%
0–19	81.74	21.6	67.84	18.3	62.98	18.6
20–39	103.48	27.4	84.78	22.8	70.16	20.7
40–59	106.53	28.2	103.35	27.8	81.06	23.9
60+	86.37	22.8	115.39	31.1	125.11	36.9
65+	66.01	17.5	86.94	23.4	102.95	30.3
80+	16.77	4.4	24.19	6.5	40.18	11.8
Total pop.	378.12		371.36		339.31	

Source: UNECE Demographic Database; own calculations.

Table 2.2 displays the dramatic trend of ageing. According to this projection the number of children in Europe will fall by about 14 million within the next 20 years. A particularly strong decrease can be found among the young working age population aged 20 to 39 years. It is feared that this trend will cause problems for economic growth as this group is considered to be highly productive and dynamic. A decrease by more than 30 million workers until 2050 will necessarily have consequences, in particular when compared to other economic regions such as North America. From the table we can easily see how the effect of today's low birth rates influences the future age structure. Those who are children today (about 80 million persons) will be young workers (aged 20 to 39) in 2025 and old workers (aged 40 to 59) in 2050.[1] A small number of children today will therefore become a problem only in the next decades when contributors to the pension system are needed. The column for the year 2050 shows how continuously low birth rates of yet unborn cohorts are expected to affect future population growth. Each age group is more than 10 per cent smaller than their parent group.

This effect can also be observed when it comes to older groups in society. The number of older workers aged 40 to 59 will hardly change over the next two or three decades. The reason is that today's age group of 20 to 39 year old workers is still relatively large. In 20 years (when these workers have advanced into the next age group) this will hardly have changed. But in 40 years the small group of today's children – and the few children they have themselves – will have replaced all cohorts of working age. This leaves only a rather large group of retirees.

If we consider total population, however, an effect of ageing can hardly be detected in the beginning. Until 2025 the total population in Europe will shrink by only 7 million persons. The dramatic demographic changes are likely to remain disguised for the next one or two decades. The reason is that the size of the baby boomer generations will not diminish substantially during that time. A person born in the late 1950s will just have retired by that time. However, by 2050 many members of the baby boomer cohorts will have ceased. The combination of a large number of deaths in the baby boomer cohorts with low birth rates of small future cohorts will lead to an ever increasing surplus of deaths around the middle of the century. Due to this development the total population will start to decrease substantially. In rapidly ageing countries this decrease will already have occurred between 2020 and 2030; in more fertile countries this effect will happen one or two decades later.

Life expectancy
The ageing process is further aggravated by an increasing life expectancy. Table 2.3 shows how life expectancy of new-born children will develop in the course of the next five decades. During this period life expectancy will on average rise by about four years in western countries. This holds for

Table 2.3. Projected life expectancy at birth in selected countries, 2005–2050

	2005–2010		2020–2025		2035–2040		2045–2050	
	M	F	M	F	M	F	M	F
Austria	76.2	82.3	78.3	84.1	79.8	85.6	80.8	86.6
Belgium	76.5	82.7	78.6	84.2	80.1	85.7	81.1	86.7
Denmark	75.0	79.9	76.8	81.7	78.2	83.1	79.0	83.9
Finland	75.4	82.3	77.8	84.1	79.0	85.3	79.8	86.1
France	76.0	83.3	78.1	84.8	79.6	86.3	80.6	87.3
Germany	76.0	82.0	78.1	83.8	79.6	85.3	80.6	86.3
Greece	76.2	81.4	77.7	82.9	78.9	84.1	79.7	84.9
Ireland	75.2	80.4	76.7	81.9	78.1	83.2	78.9	84.0
Italy	76.0	82.4	77.5	83.6	78.7	84.8	79.5	85.6
Luxembourg	75.9	82.2	78.3	84.0	79.8	85.5	80.8	86.5
Netherlands	76.1	81.5	77.6	82.9	78.8	84.1	79.6	84.9
Portugal	73.4	80.4	75.5	81.9	77.0	83.3	77.9	84.1
Spain	76.7	83.3	78.5	84.8	80.0	86.3	81.0	87.3
Sweden	78.1	83.1	79.6	84.6	81.1	86.1	82.1	87.1
UK	76.5	81.5	78.6	83.6	79.8	84.8	80.6	85.6
Japan	78.7	86.3	80.8	89.4	82.7	91.7	83.7	92.5
USA	74.9	80.6	76.0	82.2	77.7	83.1	79.2	84.1

Notes: M - Males, F - Females.

Source: United Nations (2005).

both men and women. The initial level difference of about six years (life expectancy of men is approximately 76 years, of women 82 years) will remain. The most extreme development is expected to occur in Japan which already has the highest average life expectancy. Here, an increase by another six years is expected for women. Even if we assume that birth rates remain constant, this development will lead to substantially higher average age of populations in industrialized countries.

Dependency rate
The age structure of populations is highly important for analyzing pension systems. However, changes in the age structure result from a combination of two effects, changes of fertility rates and changes of life expectancy. Therefore, it would be helpful to find a single variable that summarizes these changes. For this, the most commonly used variable is the so-called 'old-age dependency rate', that is, the number of dependent persons over the number of contributors to a social security system. In terms of the pension

system the dependency rate tells us how many retirees are supported by 100 young workers who contribute to the pension system.[2] While the size of the labor force seems to be an appropriate measure here, the ratio of those aged 65 and older over those aged (15 or) 20 to 64 years is usually chosen in demography. Sometimes, children below age 20 are counted as dependent persons as well (see, for example, Hauser, 2001), which in fact they are but we will follow the convention and ignore children.

Table 2.4. *Projected old-age dependency rates (65+/15–64) for selected countries, 1990–2050*

	1990	2000	2010	2020	2030	2040	2050
Austria	na	25.1	29.4	34.1	46.5	57.4	58.3
Belgium	na	28.2	29.5	35.7	45.3	51.2	52.1
Denmark	25.9	24.1	28.1	34.7	40.8	46.9	45.1
Finland	21.9	24.7	28.6	40.5	48.8	49.9	51.3
France	24.0	27.3	28.2	36.2	43.2	49.2	50.5
Germany	na	26.4	33.5	37.8	50.0	58.1	57.6
Greece	na	28.5	31.5	36.0	42.9	54.1	63.7
Ireland	21.9	19.4	20.2	25.8	31.7	38.3	47.0
Italy	na	28.7	33.1	38.4	47.7	63.4	67.0
Luxembourg	na	23.4	24.5	27.6	33.3	36.3	36.0
Netherlands	20.8	21.9	24.7	32.7	42.2	49.4	48.3
Portugal	na	25.3	27.7	32.4	39.1	50.5	60.1
Spain	na	27.5	29.5	34.3	43.6	59.6	71.6
Sweden	na	29.3	33.0	39.3	44.8	48.0	47.3
UK	na	26.3	26.9	31.6	39.6	45.6	46.9
Iceland	18.9	20.5	21.8	28.8	38.8	44.0	47.3
Japan	19.4	27.5	37.4	49.7	52.7	63.7	70.6
Switzerland	na	24.4	26.9	32.7	43.8	52.9	55.0
USA	21.3	21.0	21.7	28.4	36.2	38.0	38.7

Source: US Census Bureau – International Database; own calculations.

As shown in Table 2.4 the comparison of projected old-age dependency rates gives some interesting insights into the future development of the age structure in different countries. In the year 2000, the dependency rate varies around 25 retirees per 100 workers. Even rapidly ageing countries do not differ substantially from this average level. This confirms our previous claim that the process of ageing is not yet fully visible. In the following decades the variable increases significantly in all countries, even in Iceland and the United States. But while the rate more than doubles in most countries, it only increases by 80 per cent in the US, starting from a relatively low

basis. Hence, the US ends up with 38.7 retirees per 100 workers at the
end of the projection horizon, a number which several European countries
will already have reached by around 2020. Another remarkable fact is that
in Germany, Denmark, the Netherlands or Sweden the highest dependency
rates will occur around 2035 to 2040. This implies that the ageing process
is much further advanced in countries like Germany where the dependency
rate will stagnate after 2040 and eventually begin to fall when small cohorts
get closer to the end of their lives. In all other countries, the dependency
rate increases further and in some cases dramatically until 2050. Spain,
for example, will experience an increase by another 12 percentage points
between 2040 to 2050.

2.2   INTERNATIONAL LABOR MOBILITY

In the previous section, we discussed the problem of ageing societies. One
of the main findings is that over the next decades total population in most
countries will decrease because the number of deaths will exceed the
number of births by far. A second finding is that the number of old persons
relative to young persons will increase substantially and thus it will become
ever more difficult to support retirees. Countries therefore have to answer
the question whether to accept this development or to work out strategies
against it. A possible solution would be to enact policy measures to induce
childbearing and to support families. However, an enormous baby boom (in
the sense of women having far more than 2.1 children) would be necessary
to stabilize total population because today's cohorts in fertile age are very
small. Therefore, an active policy in support of families with children can
at most be a partial and long-term solution to the ageing problem. Hence,
there remains only one policy measure which can immediately contribute to
a solution of the ageing problem: an active immigration policy which allows
in particular young fertile persons into the country. If immigration policy is
well conducted, the result will be an improved old-age dependency rate and
a higher average fertility rate.

In the following, we will discuss whether we can expect immigration
to make a major contribution to the above-mentioned problems. As a
benchmark we will first consider past net immigration to the EU countries
which is displayed in Figure 2.2. The long-run average net immigration is
about 210 000 immigrants to Germany, but only 97 000 to France and 22
000 to the UK. Italy has even lost population: there were on average 6 000
emigrants per year. The EU-15's time series shows a movement very similar
to the German one which can therefore be seen as an important driving force
for the European development.[3] Only in 1962, after Algerian independence

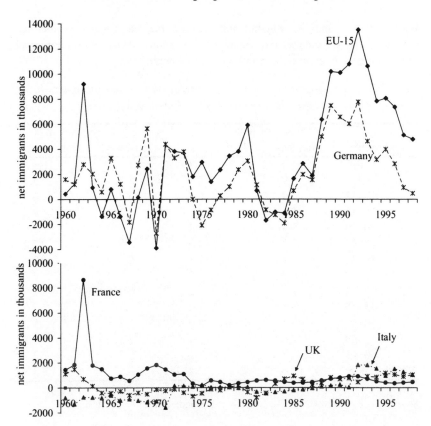

Source: US Census Bureau – International Database; own calculations.

Figure 2.2. Net immigration to selected European countries, 1960–1998

did France provide the dominant impact. Otherwise immigration in France, Italy and the UK shows a steady development at rather low levels. On the other hand, Germany displays an erratic development over time. This is due to frequent changes in immigration regulations and international politics (asylum seekers and refugees from eastern Europe, returned settlers from former German settlements etc.). Starting with the upswing in the mid-1950s which caused an increase in job vacancies, recruitment by German firms took place mostly in southern European countries such as Italy, Spain, Greece, Portugal, Yugoslavia and Turkey. This also explains the average loss of population in Italy shown in Figure 2.2.

Hence, at least some of the decline in the native populations of European countries may be offset by immigration. We can now discuss two important aspects regarding the effect of immigration on the domestic population.

First, we will analyze whether immigration has an impact on the age structure, and second, whether there will be a sufficiently large number of immigrants to overcome the problem of an ageing society.

Table 2.5.   Age structure within the groups of natives and foreigners living in Germany in 1998 (per cent of total group size)

Age group	Share of males in %		Share of females in %	
	Natives	Foreigners	Natives	Foreigner
0–4	4.9	7.2	4.3	8.5
5–9	5.9	4.9	5.2	5.7
10–14	5.9	5.4	5.2	6.2
15–19	5.6	8.6	4.9	9.3
20–24	5.4	8.4	4.8	9.4
25–29	7.2	12.5	6.5	12.2
30–34	9.1	12.1	8.1	10.4
35–39	8.7	9.0	7.8	7.9
40–44	7.6	7.2	6.9	7.6
45–49	6.9	7.0	6.4	7.5
50–54	5.7	6.0	5.4	5.3
55–59	7.6	5.1	7.3	3.8
60–64	6.4	3.2	6.3	2.3
65 and older	13.0	3.4	20.7	3.8

Source: Eurostat (2000, p. 88); Statistisches Bundesamt (1999, p. 60); own calculations.

Taking the most important European immigration country, Germany, as an example, we can investigate how immigration affects the age structure.[4] Table 2.5 splits the German population into two groups: natives and foreigners. For both males and females we find that the age distribution of foreigners is much 'younger' than the age structure of the German population, that is, the age distribution is skewed towards lower age groups. The differences are particularly striking among females. While only 24.4 (27.7) per cent of all German females (males) are aged 0–24, 39.1 (34.5) per cent of all foreign females living in Germany are in this age group. Among females aged 50 and older, the share is 39.7 (32.7) per cent for Germans and only 15.2 (17.7) per cent for foreigners. The reason for these differences can easily be seen from a comparison of the share of retirees (65 years and older) which is about 5.5 (3.8) times higher for native females than for foreign females. This is because the first large waves of guest workers are just about to retire and because many older foreigners choose to return to their home countries after retirement.

In fact, one can show that during the 1990s substantial net immigration of young foreigners aged 0–24 took place, although in some years there was total net emigration. Among all immigrants the group of children, students and young workers was always the largest. On the other hand, for those aged 50 and older, there was continuous emigration in the second half of the 1990s. Notice also that net immigration or emigration of this group has always been negligible. Hence, a typical immigrant is younger compared to the native German average and there is hardly any migration of elderly people.

Table 2.6. *Average annual net immigration 1995–2050 by scenario and country, absolute and per 1 million inhabitants*

	Constant total population	Constant age group 15–64	Constant ratio 65+/14–65
	Average annual number		
France	27 000	99 000	1 705 000
Germany	324 000	458 000	3 247 000
Italy	235 000	357 000	2 176 000
Japan	312 000	609 000	10 064 000
UK	48 000	114 000	1 087 000
USA	116 000	327 000	10 777 000
Europe	1 821 000	2 934 000	25 203 000
EU-15	863 000	1 447 000	12 736 000
	Per 1 million inhabitants		
France	500	1 854	30 430
Germany	4 244	6 009	44 825
Italy	4 414	6 531	39 818
Japan	2 705	5 103	82 634
UK	899	2 132	20 383
USA	465	1 310	43 201
Europe	2 650	4 460	37 511
EU-15	2 548	4 262	36 194

Source: United Nations (2000), pp. 24-25

These observations hold analogously in other countries. They show that immigration helps to stabilize the population size and improves the age structure in the target country. These are unambiguously positive effects but the question remains whether the number of immigrants is sufficiently large to offset the effect of ageing entirely or only partially. The United Nations (2000) has calculated the necessary 'replacement migration' which allows different measures of population to be stabilized until 2050. Table 2.6 shows the results of this calculation.

The first measure is the number of immigrants which will be necessary to stabilize total population. Taking the projected development of the total population and assuming that there is no further immigration, the year with the largest projected population is used as a reference point. Then, it is estimated how many immigrants will have to enter the country if the population is to remain constant at the maximum level of the reference year until 2050. For very fertile countries, such as France or the US, the population maximum will occur rather late (in 2025 and 2030, respectively), that is, the population in these countries is still increasing. Only a little immigration is needed to keep the population at the maximum level until 2050. The necessary annual immigration ranges between 27 000 for France and 116 000 for the US which is equivalent to 500 annual immigrants per one million French citizens in 2000 and only 465 annual immigrants per one million US citizens (see the lower part of Table 2.6). How do countries with low fertility rates and rapidly ageing societies compare to this? Germany needs 324 000 and Italy 235 000 immigrants per year to keep total population constant. In both cases the reference year with maximum population was in 1995. Remember that the long-run net immigration average for these countries is 210 000 and –6000, respectively. In terms of today's total population, necessary annual immigration is about 4200 and 4400 immigrants per one million inhabitants.

Keeping total population constant does not, however, imply that the process of population ageing in a society is halted. The age structure nevertheless changes and citizens get older on average, thus other measures may be more appropriate. One possibility is to keep the working-age population (15–64 years) constant, which has been done in the middle column of Table 2.6. The effect is an even larger level of necessary replacement migration. This is because the baby boomer cohorts eventually retire and too few children are born to compensate for this effect, which does not play a role in the constant total population scenario (there, the baby boomers do not disappear from the reference group until they die).

The problem with the constant working-age population scenario is that it does not account for increasing life expectancy. Therefore, in a final scenario the old-age dependency rate is kept constant at its 1995 level. The effect is dramatic. To be able to compensate for the consequences of low fertility rates, increasing life expectancy and retirement of the baby boomers, huge numbers of immigrants have to be allowed into the countries. Nevertheless, there are still substantial differences between the countries. Germany and Italy need an annual inflow of 3 427 000 and 2 176 000 persons, respectively, which is about 45 000 and 40 000 immigrants per one million inhabitants. In France, 1 705 000 immigrants per year or about 30

Table 2.7. *Total population in 1995 and 2050 and per cent of post-1995 immigrants and descendants in total population in 2050*

	1995	Constant total population	Constant age group 15–64	Constant ratio 65+/14–65
		Total population (in 1000)		
	1995	2050	2050	2050
France	58 020	61 121	67 130	187 193
Germany	81 661	81 661	92 022	299 272
Italy	57 338	57 338	66 395	193 518
Japan	125 472	127 457	150 697	817 965
U.K.	58 308	58 833	64 354	136 138
U.S.	267 020	297 970	315 644	1 065 174
Europe	727 912	727 912	809 399	2 346 459
EU-15	371 937	372 440	418 509	1 228 341
% of post-1995 immigrants and descendants in total population in 2050				
France		2.9	11.6	68.3
Germany		28.0	36.1	80.3
Italy		29.0	38.7	79.0
Japan		17.7	30.4	87.2
U.K.		5.5	13.6	59.2
U.S.		2.5	7.9	72.7
Europe		17.5	25.8	74.4
EU-15		16.5	25.7	74.7

Source: United Nations (2000), pp. 25 and 27.

000 per one million inhabitants are needed; thus, even France is hit severely by population ageing. Interestingly, the US will approach to rapidly ageing countries such as Germany under this scenario (43 000 annual immigrants per 1 million inhabitants).

Finally, Table 2.7 shows the total population in 2050 when immigration is used to replace shrinking native populations, given the scenarios discussed before. Under the last scenario, the population of the EU would have to more than triple compared to today's population. Total population will then be more than 1200 million persons of whom about 75 per cent are post-1995 immigrants and their descendants as can be seen from the lower part of the table. The situation is similar for single countries, although fertile countries like France 'only' double their total population while the Japanese population has to increase by 550 per cent.

These numbers show that immigration can only partially but not completely help to solve the problems of ageing societies. It would be quite unrealistic to imagine that 1200 million persons will live in the EU or that there will be about 850 million immigrants potentially on their way to Europe. Nevertheless, any level of immigration will positively contribute to the solution of the demographic challenge.

2.3 CHAPTER SUMMARY

The societies of most industrialized countries are ageing at a rapid speed. Many countries experienced a baby boom in the 1950s and 1960s, but in the decades that followed total fertility rates decreased substantially. As the baby boomer cohorts grow older but have few offspring themselves, the age structure of the societies changes. The age pyramid turns into a tree-shaped form with a broad crown of baby boomer cohorts but a narrow trunk of young cohorts.

This development, together with an increasing life expectancy, has important consequences. The old-age dependency rate which measures the ratio of old persons (mainly retirees) to persons óf working age will worsen significantly in the future, that is, there will be more and more old people per worker. In the next chapter we will argue that this will cause enormous problems for the public pension systems.

Is there any possible solution to the problem of ageing societies? We found that the only immediate easing of the situation might come from immigration as this raises total population and improves the age structure. But we also saw that if past immigration levels were to continue in the future this would not even suffice to keep total population constant. Much higher immigration levels would be necessary.

NOTES

1. The distinction between young and old workers will be used later in this book when we discuss public choice models of pensions and immigration.
2. The old-age dependency rate may also be measured as retirees per (one) worker.
3. An ordinary-least squares (OLS) regression of the German net immigration time series on the EU-15 time series shows that 62 per cent (adj. R^2) of the European development can be explained by the German one.
4. Using an aggregate of countries (such as the EU) instead of a single country causes the problem that any migration of EU citizens between member states has to be excluded.

3. Unfunded pension systems, ageing societies and immigration

In the previous chapter we investigated the process of ageing in industrialized countries and claimed that a falling old-age dependency rate constitutes a problem for societies because an increasing number of old people has to be supported by a relatively small number of young people. This problem may assume very different forms. For example, there may be too few (young) nurses for elderly people in need of care. These non-economic issues, however, will not be the focus of our discussion. This chapter will instead consider the pension system which is the institution that is most strongly affected by the process of ageing.

Therefore, we will start by giving an introduction to the theory of pension systems which will be the basis for all following discussions. In a first step, we will present two basic types of pension systems, fully-funded (FF) and pay-as-you-go (PAYG) systems. While FF systems depend on the capital market return, PAYG systems are closely related to population growth. A comparison of internal rates of return of both systems, for the FF system the market interest rate and for the PAYG system the reproduction rate, indicates a better performance of the first system. The prospect of an ageing society threatens even to enlarge the difference. However, we will argue that this view is too simple and an extensive discussion of the concepts of implicit taxes and implicit debt will explain why this is the case. We will even show that a Pareto-improving transition from an FF to a PAYG system is not possible, unless some distortions can be removed.

In the rest of this chapter, different types of pension systems will be introduced and compared based on the degree of inter- and intragenerational redistribution. This allows us to classify real-world pension systems. Finally, we will ask whether immigration is a possible countermeasure to overcome the problems of ageing.[1] We learned from Section 2.2 that immigrants are on average young and, thus, potential contributors to the pension system. But we will see that it is not so much the fact that immigrants are younger than natives that explains the positive effects of immigration on the pension system. We will instead show that immigration causes a positive externality via the pension system on the domestic population. This externality will be calculated and the value of an immigrant for the domestic population will be determined. However, positive externalities are a rather abstract concept. In public debate the relevant question is whether contribution rates and/or pension benefits change. We will briefly turn to this topic and show that the 'design' of the pension system determines who gains from immigration, the young or the old.

3.1 BASIC PRINCIPLES OF PENSION SYSTEMS

3.1.1 Definitions and Assumptions

Before we enter into the discussion of how the ageing of societies influences pension systems, we will begin by analyzing the basic principles of pension systems. Let us start with some definitions and assumptions that will be useful throughout the following chapters. We define N_t to be the total population born in period t where period t is – for simplicity – considered to be an entire generation of about 30 years' length. The population growth rate is given by

$$n_t \equiv \frac{N_t - N_{t-1}}{N_{t-1}}. \tag{3.1}$$

Wage income in period t is denoted as w_t and its growth rate is defined as

$$g_t \equiv \frac{w_t - w_{t-1}}{w_{t-1}}. \tag{3.2}$$

In later chapters, we will assume – without loss of generality – that $g_t = 0$. Furthermore, it will be assumed that in any period today's workers, that is, contributors to the pension system, will be tomorrow's beneficiaries, that is, retirees:

$$N_{t-1}^{workers} = N_t^{retirees} \quad \forall \quad t. \tag{3.3}$$

We will skip the superscript whenever this is possible without causing ambiguities. Assumption (3.3) is the very essence of an overlapping-generations (OLG) model. Each generation lives for exactly two periods, a working period and a retirement period, which are assumed to be of equal length. During the working period children are born who enter the labor force exactly when their parents retire. At any point t in time there are two (overlapping) generations, workers born in period t and retirees born in period $t - 1$. Notice that one can easily operate with more than two generations which overlap.[2]

3.1.2 Fully Funded vs. Pay-as-you-go Pension Systems

We start our discussion of pension systems by contrasting the two most basic types of pension systems, the FF and the PAYG system. Their comparison gives valuable insights into the functioning of the PAYG system, which will be the focus in the rest of this book.

In the FF system individuals pay contributions to their individual savings accounts which are usually administered by pension funds. The savings or funds are invested in the capital market. During retirement collected savings plus interest payments are available to finance old-age consumption. In marked contrast stands the PAYG system in which no (real) capital stock is built up. Therefore, this system is also called 'unfunded'. Instead, all contributions are immediately transferred to the then-retired generation. Redistributing directly from the contributors to the retirees without building up a capital stock is an extremely helpful method if no store of value is available. In that case, a person who can no longer earn his livelihood because of old age or disability will nevertheless be supported. The simplest form of a PAYG pension system is the family, where family members of working age support their parents and raise children and are then supported themselves in old age.

Let us make the following important assumption that will hold throughout all chapters. We assume that the pension system's budget is always balanced, that is, legally claimed pension benefits never exceed or fall short of contribution payments. For an unfunded pension system this implies that in any period no more than the total sum of contributions can be transferred to the retirees. In the case of the funded system we argue that the net present value of contributions and benefits is zero, that is, because of perfect foresight any retiree will have used up his entire savings by the time he dies.[3]

Fully funded pension systems
Contributions in period t will be invested in the capital market and will therefore earn interest on the capital stock. Let the capital market interest rate be r_{t+1}. In period $t + 1$, the entire contributions from period t plus the interest are paid out to the then-retired individuals. For any generation the present value of future benefits exactly equals today's contributions. Of course, this presupposes that the property of strict equivalence between individual contributions and benefits holds. Strict equivalence implies that no horizontal or intragenerational restribution takes place in the sense that, for example, contributions to the pension system are income-related while pensions are paid out as flat benefits.

If participation is voluntary, private savings and contributions to the

FF pension system are perfect substitutes. Notice that in order to receive benefits in period t retirees must have saved in period $t - 1$ via the pension system. The system works so as to reallocate resources intertemporally but it does not redistribute intergenerationally as no funds are directly transferred between workers and retirees in the same period. Today's benefits depend strongly on the recent performance of capital markets. There may be vast differences between benefits today and tomorrow because of the capital or stock market risk underlying funded pension schemes.

We can formalize the funded pension system in the following way. Let r_t be the market interest rate, τ_t^{FF} the contribution rate and p_t^{FF} the pension benefit in period t. Then we get

$$p_t^{FF} = (1 + r_t) \cdot \tau_{t-1}^{FF} \cdot w_{t-1}. \tag{3.4}$$

The pension benefit is past contributions plus interest. The internal return i_t of a pension system can (in general) be measured as the ratio of pension benefits over contributions. Thus, by applying (3.4) we get

$$1 + i_t^{FF} = \frac{p_t^{FF}}{\tau_{t-1}^{FF} w_{t-1}} = 1 + r_t \iff i_t^{FF} = r_t \tag{3.5}$$

for the fully funded pension system. The internal rate of return of the FF system is just the market interest rate.

Pay-as-you-go pension systems
The situation is different in PAYG pension schemes where all contributions are directly transferred from contributors to retirees. The future pension benefits of today's contributors depend on how much tomorrow's workers pay into the system. Let us introduce what we may call the 'fundamental budget equation' of the PAYG system. The sum of contributions in period t is just the contributions collected from each member of the generation of working age, that is, from N_t young workers. The sum of pension benefits is the per-capita pension benefit times the number of retirees, which is the generation born in $t - 1$. Again, τ_t is the contribution rate, p_t is the per-capita pension benefit and w_t is wage income, so we get

$$\tau_t \cdot w_t \cdot N_t = p_t \cdot N_{t-1}. \tag{3.6}$$

Notice that the introduction of a PAYG pension system will immediately generate payments to a first generation of retirees although they have not paid any contributions before. These pension benefits to the first generation of retirees are therefore called the 'introductory gift' of a PAYG system. This gift does not occur in an FF pension system. Hence, the PAYG system leads to an intergenerational reallocation of resources which is not the case in the FF system.[4] Using the definition of the population growth rate from (3.1), we can rewrite (3.6) as

$$p_t^{PAYG} = \tau_t \cdot w_t \cdot \frac{N_t}{N_{t-1}} = (1 + n_t) \cdot \tau_t \cdot w_t. \qquad (3.7)$$

In terms of the internal return we have to take into account that wages grow at rate g_t. If the contribution rate is unchanged in $t - 1$ and t, that is, $\tau_t = \tau_{t-1}$, we get

$$1 + i_t^{PAYG} = \frac{p_t^{PAYG}}{\tau_{t-1}w_{t-1}} = \frac{\tau_t(1 + n_t)(1 + g_t)w_{t-1}}{\tau_{t-1}w_{t-1}}$$

$$= (1 + n_t)(1 + g_t) \iff i_t^{PAYG} \approx n_t + g_t \qquad (3.8)$$

if n_t and g_t are small such that $n_t \cdot g_t$ is negligible. Therefore, the internal rate of return of the PAYG pension system is the growth rate of the total wage bill (total sum of wages) or approximately the sum of the population growth rate and the growth rate of wages. If we assume $g_t = 0$, the internal rate of return is just what Samuelson (1958) calls the 'biological' interest rate n_t, that is, the population growth rate. The ageing of societies will show up in this variable. If the population is shrinking, $n_t < 0$ and the internal rate of return is negative. As contributions are related to employment a decreasing number of jobs has a similar effect as a falling reproduction rate.

Notice that the internal rate of return for the first generation of retirees is infinitely high as not having paid any contributions shows up as $\tau_{t-1}w_{t-1} = 0$ in the denominator of (3.8). An increase in the contribution rate has a similar effect on the internal rate of return. This becomes immediately obvious if one imagines that the increase in the contribution rate could be used to set up a new PAYG system from which again an introductory gift can be received.

Sometimes, the budget equation of the PAYG system in (3.6) is written differently. Either lump-sum contributions are assumed: this implies that we have $\tau_t^{LS} \cdot N_t$ on the left-hand side of (3.6) where τ_t^{LS} is a lump-sum payment. Or it is assumed that benefits are related to the average wages of the population. Instead of $p_t \cdot N_{t-1}$ on the right-hand side of (3.6), we get $q_t \cdot w_t \cdot N_{t-1}$ where q_t is the replacement rate. The replacement rate is defined as the value of a pension as a proportion of a worker's wage during some base period (World Bank, 1994), here the average wage of the entire worklife, w_t. In both cases, there is no wage term in the budget equation. We get either

$$\tau_t^{LS} \cdot N_t = p_t \cdot N_{t-1} \quad \text{or} \quad \tau_t \cdot N_t = q_t \cdot N_{t-1}. \qquad (3.9)$$

Hence, under these pension regimes the internal rate of return of the PAYG system is the biological interest rate and depends only on the reproduction behavior of the population. We will turn back to these differences when we review the existing literature on pensions and international labor mobility.

Optimal life-cycle savings decision

Let us close the model by introducing utility-maximizing individuals who optimize their savings decisions over the life cycle. Let c_t be consumption in period t, z_{t+1} consumption in $t+1$ and s_t savings in t, then we get the following optimization problem:

$$\max_{c_t, z_{t+1}} U(c_t, z_{t+1}) \tag{3.10}$$

such that

$$c_t = (1 - \tau_t)w_t - s_t \tag{3.11}$$

$$z_{t+1} = p_{t+1}^i + (1 + r_{t+1})s_t \tag{3.12}$$

where U is a strictly monotone and quasi-concave ordinal utility function. Savings are used to transfer resources across periods. Although they cancel out later they are important to achieve the individual's intertemporally optimal consumption path.

Using (3.4) and (3.7), we can derive the intertemporal budget constraint of an individual by summarizing (3.11) and (3.12), depending on the underlying pension system (which enters the model via p_{t+1}^i, where i is either FF or PAYG). This gives (for $g_t = 0$):

$$\text{FF: } c_t + \frac{z_{t+1}}{1+r_{t+1}} = w_t \tag{3.13}$$

$$\text{PAYG: } c_t + \frac{z_{t+1}}{1+r_{t+1}} = w_t \left(1 - \tau_t \frac{r_{t+1} - n_{t+1}}{1+r_{t+1}}\right). \tag{3.14}$$

The FF pension system has no effect on the intertemporal savings decision because it is just equivalent to private savings. In the PAYG system an additional term, $\tau_t w_t \frac{r_{t+1} - n_{t+1}}{1+r_{t+1}}$, enters the intertemporal budget constraint. If we relate this term to contributions, $\tau_t w_t$, we get the ratio $\frac{r_{t+1} - n_{t+1}}{1+r_{t+1}}$ which indicates whether a generation can enjoy its entire wage income or whether some part is taxed away. This is the case whenever the term is positive, that is, if $n_{t+1} < r_{t+1}$.

3.1.3 Implicit Taxes and Implicit Debt

The previously derived tax term in the PAYG system is a consequence of the introductory gift to the first generation of retirees. In the following the concepts of implicit taxes and implicit debt will be used to explain this argument in more detail. We will argue that the difference of the returns between FF and PAYG systems can be explained by the existence of this tax. For Germany, for example, Sinn (2000) shows that the expected internal rate of return of the PAYG system has decreased from 2.8 to 1.5 per cent while the market interest rate for German 10-year government bonds has remained roughly constant at about 4 per cent through time. Hence, the market interest rate has exceeded the growth rate of the wage bill at any given time.

Explicit debt and transfers to the retirees

Let our discussion start with a simple intuitive argument in which we consider explicit (government) debt in order to finance a transfer to the old generation.[5] The concept of implicit debt works along the same lines. Assume that the government plans higher expenditures and will therefore increase government debt in period 0, Δ_0, by $d\Delta_0 = \Delta_0 - \Delta_{-1} > 0$. The new debt is not supposed to be paid off. However, in each period interest has to be paid which amounts to $r \cdot d\Delta_0$ for the newly issued debt. These payments take the form of taxes. If r does not change over time we can easily calculate the present value of future interest payments:

$$\sum_{t=0}^{\infty} \frac{r \cdot d\Delta_0}{(1+r)^t} = \frac{r \cdot d\Delta_0}{r} = d\Delta_0.$$

Hence, we find that the present value of future interest payments or taxes exactly equals the amount of new government debt. Assume now that we have two overlapping generations. The additional government expenditures are given to the old generation as a transfer payment. The young generation has to save money for old age consumption, which is equivalent to participating in a funded pension system. Hence, any working generation today and in the future has two responsibilities. First, individuals have to save via the FF pension system. Second, they have to pay taxes to cover the interest payments for the 'explicit' debt issued in period 0. If some future young generation plans to pay off the debt, it has to come up with additional funds (in addition to retirement savings and interest payments), that is, it has to give up consumption and will be worse off compared to any other generation. Clearly, there is no incentive to redeem the debt voluntarily. It will exist until the infinite future.

Implicit taxes and savings

In the previous example taxes had to be paid to cover the interest payments related to the explicit debt. In the case of a PAYG pension system we can argue in a similar way. However, we now talk about implicit taxes and implicit debt. The term 'implicit' is used here because taxes and debt are inherent in the pension system.

Implicit taxes T^{imp} occur if there is a difference between pension benefits and contributions, both in present value terms. In other words, if the present value of contributions exceeds the present value of benefits, some share of the contributions are in fact taxes. Only the residual is eventually returned to the contributor as a pension benefit. This residual may be called the 'implicit saving'.

Regardless of the type of pension system, future benefits are just today's contributions times the internal return factor, that is, $\tau_t w_t (1 + i_{t+1}^j)$, $j =$ FF, PAYG. Hence, we get

$$T_t^{imp} = \tau_t w_t - \frac{\tau_t w_t (1 + i_{t+1}^j)}{1 + r_{t+1}}. \tag{3.15}$$

For the FF pension system with $i_t^{FF} = r_t$ the implicit tax is zero because the discount rate and the internal rate of return are the same, namely, the market interest rate. Assuming only the biological interest rate as the internal rate of return of the PAYG system, its implicit tax turns out to be

$$T_t^{imp} = \tau_t w_t \left(\frac{r_{t+1} - n_{t+1}}{1 + r_{t+1}} \right), \tag{3.16}$$

which is just the tax term from the intertemporal budget constraint in (3.14). Hence, the existence of a PAYG system affects lifetime consumption whenever $r \neq n$. The implicit tax rate is given by dividing the implicit tax by total contributions:

$$t_t^{imp} = \frac{T_t^{imp}}{\tau_t w_t} = \frac{r_{t+1} - n_{t+1}}{1 + r_{t+1}}. \tag{3.17}$$

From (3.17) it follows that the implicit tax rate under a PAYG system is between zero and one, such that we can think of dividing total pension contributions $\tau_t w_t$ into two parts: the implicit tax T_t^{imp} and implicit savings S_t^{imp}:

$$\tau_t w_t = T_t^{imp} + S_t^{imp}. \tag{3.18}$$

Sinn (2000) gives an intuitive explanation for this division. He argues that one can think of partly using the contribution payment to buy in the capital market a pension claim equal to the future PAYG pension benefit. The return on this part of the contributions, the implicit saving, is the market interest rate. If contributions were higher than implicit savings, the residual part is the implicit tax. According to (3.17), $T_t^{imp} = t_t^{imp} \cdot \tau_t w_t$. Using (3.18) and (3.7), we get

$$S_t^{imp} = (1 - t_t^{imp}) \tau_t w_t = \frac{1 + n_{t+1}}{1 + r_{t+1}} \tau_t w_t = \frac{p_{t+1}}{1 + r_{t+1}}. \tag{3.19}$$

Implicit savings and the discounted pension benefit are equivalent. In other words, we can define implicit taxes either as the discounted difference between total contributions and benefits or as total contributions minus implicit savings.

In the following, we will discuss two important aspects related to the concept of implicit taxes. First, we will show that dynamic efficiency requires $n < r$ such that $t_t^{imp} > 0$. Second, we will briefly investigate the special cases of $t_t^{imp} = 0$ and $t_t^{imp} = 1$.

Dynamic efficiency

Empirically, in most countries the growth rate of the total wage bill has been below the market interest rate for most of the time. The implicit tax rate $t_t^{imp} = \frac{r_{t+1} - n_{t+1}}{1 + r_{t+1}}$ appears to be always positive. Let us return to the argument about the explicit debt at the beginning of this section in order to give some insights into why this result can be expected from theory.

So far, we have not explained which role the population growth rate n_t plays for our result. Consider the per-capita government debt which is given by $\Delta_t^{p.c.} = \Delta_t / N_t$ in each period. Hence, each individual's share in the interest or tax payment is $r \cdot \Delta_t^{p.c.}$. As the population grows at rate n_t there are additional tax payers in each period. If the per-capita debt is allowed to stay at its initial level, total government debt can be extended by $n_t \cdot \Delta_t$, such that $\Delta_t^{p.c.} = [(1 + n_t)\Delta_t] / [(1 + n_t)N_t] = \Delta_t / N_t$ is unchanged. For a constant per-capita debt we can now compare the possible increase in government debt with the total interest payments:

$$
\begin{aligned}
n_t \cdot \Delta_t - r \cdot \Delta_t^{p.c.} \cdot N_t &= n_t \cdot \Delta_t^{p.c.} \cdot N_t - r \cdot \Delta_t^{p.c.} \cdot N_t \\
&= (n_t - r) \cdot \Delta_t^{p.c.} \cdot N_t \gtreqless 0.
\end{aligned}
$$

If this equation is positive, per-capita debt is smaller compared to the previous period because there is less new debt issued than taxes collected from new-born individuals (at the same rate as before). Hence, if the population growth rate exceeds the market interest rate, interest payments per capita and thus implicit taxes can be lowered. This implies that the ratio of implicit savings and implicit taxes improves for the new-born generation, that is, its members have to pay relatively less to their parent generation.

This intuitive argument produces results which are equivalent to the results of the neoclassical or Solow–Swan growth model. A formal derivation of this model is presented in Appendix A. The model tells us that in an OLG economy with linearly homogeneous production technology there exists a 'golden-rule' growth path of the economy. In the steady state, this growth path maximizes consumption in each period and for each generation. The condition for this result is the equality of the marginal productivity of capital and the exogenous population growth rate, that is, $f_k(k^{GR}) = n$

where k^{GR} is the capital–labor ratio $\frac{K}{N}$ on the golden-rule growth path. As we usually assume $f_k(k) = r$ we get a situation in which the market interest rate and the population growth are – as before – the relevant variables.

If $f_k(k) = r < n$, the economy is in a 'dynamically inefficient' state, because more capital has been accumulated (over-accumulation) than on the golden-rule growth path $(f_k(k) < f_k(k^{GR}) \Leftrightarrow K > K^{GR})$. For a given population growth rate this implies that the capital–labor ratio changes although it should remain constant in the steady state. Decreasing investments in the capital stock would help to return to the golden-rule path. However, less investment implies that there is a larger share of output available for consumption and at least one generation can be made better off, that is, a Pareto improvement is possible.

For $f_k(k) = r > n$, additional investment is necessary to return to the golden-rule path but this requires a reduction in consumption which will make people worse off. Hence, we have 'dynamic efficiency' as no Pareto improvement is possible. If we assume that individuals will always exploit any possible Pareto improvements, a dynamically inefficient situation cannot be sustained in the long run. While for some time the population growth rate may exceed the market interest rate, we would expect dynamic efficiency to be the rule rather than the exception.

In a dynamically inefficient state the intergenerational reallocation of ressources is equivalent to an intergenerational redistribution from today's and future young generations to the then-retired generation. Because the PAYG system crowds out private savings (there is no need to save for old age), the resulting under-accumulation of capital will lead to fewer consumption possibilities for future generations compared to a situation without a PAYG system.

Let us now return to the discussion of the PAYG pension system. Analogously to the expression derived before the implicit tax rate $(r_{t+1} - n_{t+1})/(1 + r_{t+1})$ may be positive or negative, depending on whether the market interest rate or the population growth rate (or, for $g_t \neq 0$, the growth rate of the wage bill) is larger. Given our previous argument about dynamic efficiency, we would expect the implicit tax to be positive, just as the data suggest.

However, if in some years dynamic efficiency does not hold, we get a situation which is often called Aaron's (1966) 'social insurance paradox'. It states that an unfunded pension system may yield a higher return than a funded pension system, despite the fact that no (real) capital is accumulated. As long as the biological interest rate exceeds the market interest rate, the PAYG system performs better than the FF system in terms of the internal rate of return.

Inter- vs. intragenerational redistribution

From the previous discussion we learned that contributions can be split into implicit savings and implicit taxes and that the share of these variables is between zero and one. An interesting question is whether there are any characteristics of pension systems that explain why implicit tax rates are closer to zero or closer to one, possibly even taking on these extreme values. In fact, it is the degree of 'actuarial' or 'intragenerational fairness' that plays an important role. Actuarial fairness measures how close the link between contributions and benefits is (Lindbeck and Persson, 2003). This boils down to measuring the difference between the internal rate of return of a pension system and the market rate of return, that is, the market interest rate. In an FF pension system, $i^{FF} = r$ such that we can call the system (perfectly) actuarially fair. The implicit tax rate is zero ($t_t^{imp} = 0$).

Consider now a PAYG pension system without any link between contributions and benefits, for example, a system with earnings-related contributions but flat-rate benefits. Two aspects have to be considered. First, as discussed before in a PAYG system 'intergenerational' redistribution from the young to the old generation takes place. Second, by acquiring pension claims to the same level of benefits the rich have to contribute relatively more than the poor. Hence, within the same generation (claims to) resources are redistributed from the rich to the poor. This is a form of 'intragenerational' redistribution. From these two facts it follows that the entire contribution is equivalent to a tax which implies $t_t^{imp} = 1$. No implicit saving is generated.

This is, however, an extreme case. Often, one finds that contributions and benefits are linked in PAYG systems as well. These systems may even entirely exclude intragenerational redistribution if both contributions and benefits are related to the same benchmark, such as wage income. The implicit tax is the same for all members of the same generation. Here, the link is via the growth rate of the total wage bill which is then to be compared with the market interest rate. Because a specific return can be expected from individual contributions, implicit savings is positive and thus $0 < t_t^{imp} < 1$.

These results show that the implicit tax rate depends on the degree of inter– and intragenerational redistribution. When intergenerational redistribution takes place, the implicit tax cannot be zero. The implicit tax becomes the larger, the higher the level of intragenerational redistribution, that is, the looser the link between contributions and benefits.

Implicit debt

So far, we have shown that an implicit tax t_t^{imp} occurs in PAYG pension systems but not in FF systems. Unless the PAYG system is perfectly intragenerationally redistributive, we have $0 < t_t^{imp} < 1$ whenever the economy is in a dynamically efficient state. But we have not yet answered the question why the implicit tax occurs at all.

When a pension system is introduced for the first time, the first generation of retirees receives an introductory gift because the young generation starts to contribute to the pension system in order to acquire claims for future pensions. The collected contributions are transferred to the retirees even though they had not contributed to the pension system before. Their internal rate of return is infinite. The implicit tax is negative, that is, funds are transferred to the old generation. Later generations, on the other hand, have a rather low internal return on their contributions and the implicit tax is positive.

Proposition 1 (Sinn, 2000, pp. 394–395) *The transfer received by the first generation of retirees after the introduction of a PAYG pension system and the implicit taxes carried by all later generations are equal in present value terms.*

From this important proposition it follows that the existence of the introductory gift is the reason why implicit taxes exist. The introductory gift creates an implicit debt that has to be serviced by all future generations by paying implicit taxes. The proof of this result is delegated to Appendix A.

Since the implicit debt is related to implicit taxes, the difference between market interest rate and the internal rate of return is important. In the FF pension system no implicit debt occurs. For the PAYG system the implicit tax and the implicit debt are the larger, the larger the difference between the rates of return is. Furthermore, the level of intergenerational redistribution from the young to the old increases with this difference.

Regardless of the return difference the first generation of retirees will always gain from the introduction of a PAYG pension system. Later generations will gain only if the implicit tax is negative, that is, if they receive a transfer which is the case whenever the economy is in a dynamically inefficient state $(r < n)$. For $r = n$ they are indifferent while for $r > n$ they lose.

There have been some attempts to estimate the implicit debt for different countries. This is usually done by adding the expected future pension rights of those still working and yet unborn generations to the already accrued rights of today's living generations. This estimation may involve major difficulties and methodological problem as pointed out by Franco et al. (2004). Because of this the absolute numbers of estimates in Table 3.1 can hardly be compared. Hagemann and Nicoletti (1989) and Van den Noord and Herd (1993) estimate unfunded pension liabilities of all individuals living in a certain base year. The difference in the estimates depends mostly

Table 3.1. *Implicit debt in per cent of gross domestic product (GDP) for selected countries*

	HN89	VdNH93	Kuné93	CJ96	F01
Canada		121		68	189
France		200	106	114	225
Germany	355	149	179	111	242
Italy		182	184	76	123
Japan	217	173		107	285
UK		116	70	5	84
USA	158	91		26	150

Notes: HN89 = Hagemann and Nicoletti (1989), VdNH93 = Van den Noord and Herd (1993), Kuné93 = Kuné et al. (1993), CJ96 = Chand and Jaeger (1996), F01 = Frederiksen (2001).

Source: Franco et al. (2004, Tables 3 and 5); Frederiksen (2001, Table 3); own calculations.

on the assumptions about the discount rate. Kuné et al. (1993) use a similar approach but do not take into account the future flows of contributions to the pension system. This tends to overestimate pension liabilities. Chand and Jaeger (1996) add future generations, as does Frederiksen (2001). The principal finding in all studies is that the implicit debt exceeds explicit debt and even GDP by far in most countries. In the next section we will show that this is one reason why a transition from a PAYG to FF system is hardly possible.

3.1.4 The Efficiency of the Pay-as-you-go System

Today's public debate about pension systems and solutions to the ageing crisis sometimes puts forward the idea that existing PAYG systems should be replaced – at least partially – by FF systems. This is usually justified by the argument that PAYG systems must have some intrinsic inefficiency because of the lower internal rate of return compared to the FF system. Reducing the inefficiency would then allow a switch from the existing systems to FF systems in a Pareto-improving way. Considering the previous discussion about the introductory gift and implicit taxes this argument may be too simple. In this section, we will therefore discuss whether a Pareto improving transition is possible or not. If it is, the PAYG system is not efficient.

The implicit debt of an existing pension system has to be redeemed if a transition from an FF to a PAYG pension system is planned. The existing pension claims of the old generation have to be settled by the government by issuing explicit government debt while the young generations start to save for their retirement in the new FF system. While in the PAYG system contributions are higher because both implicit savings and taxes are covered, the FF system involves lower contribution payments (or, equivalently, has a higher return) as there is no implicit tax. If the members of the new FF system were to cover the settlement of the implicit debt through taxes caused by newly issued government debt, they would end up with the same total payments as in the PAYG system. Given the size of implicit debt shown in Table 3.1, an immediate transition is very unlikely due to the resulting extremely high tax burden.

The question is whether this also holds if the current young working generation has to cover only some part of repayment while the rest is shifted to future working generations via long-term government debt. The answer is given in the following proposition which will be proved in Appendix A.[6]

Proposition 2 (Sinn, 2000, p. 396) *The present value of the tax burden after a transition from an FF to a PAYG pension system does not differ from the implicit debt of the PAYG system. The transition will therefore not generate an efficiency gain as the burden of the introductory gift will exist under both scenarios.*

Even shifting the redemption of the debt into the future will not solve the problem that the debt – be it implicit or explicit – has to be fully repaid. While the proposition appears to be somewhat trivial there has nevertheless been an extensive academic debate on this topic. It is, in fact, possible to construct models that lead to Pareto improvements. However, the efficiency gains can often be achieved even without a transition to a FF system. They result from removing distortions which may also be removed by different means. There are different arguments which may be relevant in this context such as the distortion of the savings decision or the existence of risk premia in the stock market.[7] Our focus will be on the distortion of the labor–leisure choice as it picks up the idea of intragenerational redistribution again which will play an important role in later chapters.

The underlying idea of this approach is that contributions to a PAYG system which include the implicit tax usually take the form of payroll taxes. These taxes tend to distort the labor–leisure choice of workers. If this is the case, switching to non-distorting lump-sum taxes during the transition phase allows for welfare gains from reducing the distortion. Hence, a welfare-improving transition from a PAYG to an FF pension system seems possible (see, for example, Homburg and Richter, 1990; Homburg, 1990; Breyer and Straub, 1993) although the availability of lump-sum taxes is questionable. If one follows this line of arguments, the PAYG system is not Pareto efficient.

The welfare-improving effect, however, does not depend on the fact that the newly introduced pension system is fully funded. Moving from a flat-rate benefit ($t^{imp} = 1$) to a PAYG system with a tight link between contributions and benefits ($t^{imp} < 1$) may lead to a welfare gain as well. In the first system the implicit tax rate which is proportional to wage income is higher than in the second system. Hence, the distortion in the flat-rate benefit regime is stronger and a transition to the other system is a Pareto improvement. There is no longer an unambigious answer to the question whether the PAYG system in general is Pareto efficient. The reason for this result is that the payroll or income tax is used for redistributing income between heterogeneous individuals. If this form of intragenerational redistribution is to be abandoned, an efficiency gain may be possible (see, for example, Brunner, 1996). At the same time, however, distributive goals may have to be given up as well. This holds even more if the transition aims at introducing an FF system.[8] For policy makers this implies that efficiency gains and a reduction of intragenerational redistribution have to be weighed up.

Obviously, a PAYG system with intragenerational redistribution is not Pareto efficient because reducing redistribution leads to a welfare gain. However, one can show that a PAYG system without intragenerational redistribution is Pareto efficient as no welfare-improving transition to a FF system is possible. Fenge (1995) investigates a PAYG system in which an individual who makes κ per cent of the average contribution of all workers will receive exactly κ per cent of the average pension.[9] This system is intragenerationally fair because the implicit tax rate is the same for each individual. Let us realistically assume that no lump-sum taxes are available. The implicit debt of the existing PAYG system will be replaced by explicit government debt, which is to be serviced by an income tax as well. Since the government controls only one instrument, the net wage rate, in this scenario and because the distortionary income tax is needed to service the debt there is no other instrument left to improve generational welfare, for example, by lowering the tax burden of those generations burdened during the transition. Hence, the distortive implicit tax is simply replaced by an equally distortive income tax if the same distributive goal is to be reached.

These results show that efficiency gains are possible whenever intragenerational redistribution takes place within a pension system. These gains are achieved when the link between contributions and benefits is tightened and the distortion of the labor–leisure choice is reduced. If there is no intragenerational redistribution in the PAYG system, a welfare-improving transition to an FF system is not possible. This is because the implicit debt generated by the introductory gift has to be serviced in any case. In the PAYG system this happens via implicit taxes, in the FF system via explicit taxes on wage income. The distortion of the labor–leisure choice is the same in both cases.

3.2 INSTITUTIONAL DIFFERENCES OF EXISTING PENSION SYSTEMS

Pension systems may be differently designed, depending on the degree of inter- and intragenerational redistribution. We will now distinguish existing pension systems along the lines suggested by Lindbeck and Persson (2003).

The authors choose a three-dimensional classification. The first dimension is the distinction between defined-benefit and defined-contribution systems which we have not yet considered. We will therefore begin this section with an introduction to these concepts. The second and third dimension is funded vs. unfunded and actuarial vs. non-actuarial systems, that is, with or without intragenerational redistribution, both of which were topics in the previous section. We will return to these dimensions later in this section.

3.2.1 Defined Benefit vs. Defined Contributions

The basic idea of a defined-benefit system is to guarantee retired individuals a certain (minimum) standard of living. One appropriate means to achieve this goal is a flat-rate benefit. A similar approach is to link benefits at a fixed (replacement) rate to previous earnings. The replacement income guarantees a lower but constant standard of living relative to the one during working life. The consequence of this approach is that a balanced budget of the pension system may require an adjustment of the endogenous contribution rate if any of the exogenous parameters, such as the population growth rate, changes. The defined-contribution system is the reverse image to the previous system. Here, the contribution rate is constant over time while the pension benefit is determined endogenously.

While this distinction is not very meaningful for the intertemporally optimal savings decision in the FF system, it may play an important role in the PAYG system. With budget equation (3.6) we can show the two polar cases with either fixed contributions or benefits. We assume that fertility and wages are exogenously given. Furthermore, we state the following definition. As the old-age dependency rate is the ratio of retirees over members of the working generation we can denote it in terms of our basic model as

$$D_t := \frac{\text{retirees}}{\text{workers}} = \frac{N_{t-1}}{N_t} = \frac{1}{1+n_t}. \qquad (3.20)$$

Ageing can therefore be defined as a 'worsening' of the dependency rate which occurs if D_t increases, that is, if fewer workers have to support a given number of retirees.

The first type of pension system may also be called fixed-benefit regime. Here, the pension benefit is kept constant at level $\bar{p}$. Any change of the exogenous variables will therefore induce a change of the contribution rate τ_t which is endogenously determined:

$$\tau_t = \bar{p} \cdot \frac{1}{w_t} \cdot \frac{N_{t-1}}{N_t} = \bar{p} \cdot w_t^{-1} \cdot D_t. \qquad (3.21)$$

The second pension system is a fixed-contribution rate regime in which the contribution rate is fixed at $\bar{\tau}$ while the endogenous variable is p_t. Hence, we get

$$p_t = \bar{\tau} \cdot w_t \cdot \frac{N_t}{N_{t-1}} = \bar{\tau} \cdot w_t \cdot D_t^{-1}. \qquad (3.22)$$

Partial derivatives show the effects of changes in the exogenous variables, in particular, the effect of ageing. Taking w_t as given in (3.21) and (3.22), we find in the fixed-contribution rate regime that pension benefits are falling ($dp_t/dD_t < 0$). The explanation for this effect is simple: Because of a smaller number of contributors total contributions are reduced in the case of a fixed contribution rate. Hence, within the framework of the PAYG system there is less money to be redistributed to the old generation, that is, pension benefits are lower. In the fixed-pension benefit regime total pension payments do not change while the number of contributors decreases. Hence, each member of the working generation has to pay more contributions. The contribution rate has to increase ($d\tau_t/dD_t > 0$).

Real-world pension systems are not likely to resemble any one of the two polar regimes but lie somewhere in-between. This implies that ageing will lead to both falling pension benefits and increasing contribution rates. In the following discussion we will turn to a more detailed analysis of pension systems in the OECD countries.

3.2.2 Real-world Pension Systems

Based on Lindbeck and Persson's (2003) argument Werding (2003) presents a comparison of pension systems in various OECD countries. The results are based on a combination of all three pillars of the pension system according to the World Bank (1994, pp. 8–9) definition:

- public pay-as-you-go pension plans (first pillar);
- occupational plans (second pillar);
- personal saving and annuity plans (third pillar).

The discussion about pension systems usually centers around the first pillar as this is the most visible and controversial part of the pension system. Usually, it is a government-run and mandatory PAYG system with almost universal coverage. Most often it offers defined benefits based on payroll contributions and involves intragenerationally redistributive elements. The second-pillar occupational plans are privately administered pension plans offered by employers, sometimes facilitated by tax concessions by the government. They help to attract and retain workers. In many countries they used to be defined-benefit plans with only partial funding. However, today there is a clear tendency towards defined contributions and a high degree of funding.[10] The third pillar covers most forms of private savings based on fully funded defined-contribution plans. Participation is voluntary but many countries provide tax incentives or subsidies (see also Chapter 9).

In Figure 3.1 the evaluation of national pension systems, including all three pillars, is presented. The vertical axis of the box dinstinguishes pension systems by the degree of funding. Most continental European pension systems rely on pension systems which are mostly based on PAYG financing. The US and Great Britain are the most notable examples for countries with a high degree of funding. The horizontal axis orders countries by the degree of actuarial fairness. No country offers flat-rate pensions or is even close to doing so. This holds even for countries which have a 'Beveridgian' tradition such as Great Britain. A pension system is called Beveridgian if it offers only a very weak link between contributions and benefits which is the case for flat-rate benefits. The reason for this finding is that flat-rate benefits are usually intended to guarantee only a certain minimum standard of living such that only a small first pillar is needed. At the same time the non-redistributive second and third pillars play an important role. In sum, the degree of intragenerational fairness is rather high. In the German or French first pillar, by comparison, the degree of actuarial fairness is very high due to a tight link between individual contributions and benefits. A pension system with this property is called 'Bismarckian'. Finally, there exists a distinction between defined-benefit, defined-contribution and mixed systems. Most (continental European) countries have defined-benefit systems. Only two countries have so far switched towards defined contributions, Sweden and Italy.

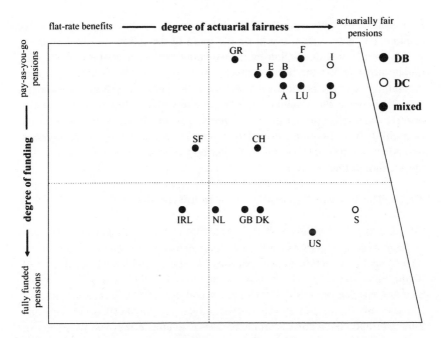

Notes: DB = defined-benefit system, DC = defined-contribution system; A = Austria, B = Belgium, CH = Switzerland, D = Germany, DK = Denmark, E = Spain, F = France, GB = United Kingdom, GR = Greece, I = Italy, IRL = Ireland, LUX = Luxembourg, NL = Netherlands, S = Sweden, SF = Finland, US = United States.

Source: Werding (2003), p. 15

Figure 3.1.   Characteristics of national pension systems – first, second and third pillar (2002)

3.3   HOW DOES IMMIGRATION AFFECT A PAY-AS-YOU-GO PENSION SYSTEM?

In the previous sections, we argued that ageing leads to a worsening of the dependency rate which may be compensated by either increasing the contribution rate or by reducing the replacement rate (or the pension benefit). This was the main idea of equations (3.21) and (3.22). However, we have ignored so far the possibility of influencing the dependency rate directly. This can be done by changing the effective retirement age which ceteris paribus changes the dependency rate. Increasing the retirement age reduces the number of retirees relative to the number of workers. An analogous effect can be achieved by increasing the number of young (working) persons, for example, by increasing the birth rate or by allowing immigrants into the country. The latter scenario will be the focus of the following discussion.

Let us start this discussion by investigating the direct welfare effects that immigrants have on the host country's pension system. We will assume that the immigrants will become contributors to the pension system immediately after they enter the country. It will be shown that this will generate a positive externality on the domestic population which is similar to the birth of a child. It is, however, even larger than for a child because immigrants immediately start contributing after entering the country and have on average more children than natives.

3.3.1   The Positive Externality from Immigration

Consider the following empirical observation: countries such as Germany or Italy with strong PAYG pillars in their pension systems often also have rapidly ageing societies. Other countries like the US with a higher degree of funding have fewer problems. Can we therefore conclude that there is a link between the existence of PAYG systems and ageing? Empirical studies, for instance, by Cigno and Rosati (1996), Cigno et al. (2000) or Ehrlich and Zhong (1998), have found strong empirical evidence that the existence of PAYG pension systems discourages fertility. How can this be explained if at the same time the performance of PAYG systems depends strongly on the population growth rate?

An explanation provides the 'social-security hypothesis' which states that the existence of PAYG pension systems in fact contributes to the decline of fertility rates. Based on Becker's seminal work on fertility (see, for example, Becker, 1960) several authors have embedded an endogenous fertility approach in the analysis of pension systems.[11] The main argument for the lower number of births is the existence of positive externalities which children generate in PAYG systems. An analogous positive externality is generated by immigrants as well as we will learn soon.

Bearing children is an investment decision as children will eventually support their parents in old age when they are no longer able to earn their livelihood. Without a pension system this support takes the form of intra-family transfers such that there is a direct link between the investment in children and the return in old age. With a PAYG pension system the transfer works differently. The children start paying contributions to the pension system when they enter the labor force while their parents receive these contributions as pension benefits. However, in PAYG pension systems the rule is usually that those who contributed to the pension system during their working life will receive pension benefits later on, regardless of whether they raised children or not. A family bearing a child will therefore carry the entire investment cost alone but has to share the pension benefits (which are just their children's contributions) with those retirees who do not have children. Hence, they receive only a fraction of the return on their investment.

This implies that investing in children generates a positive externality on those who participate in the system without having children. It should be clear immediately that the incentive to invest in children is reduced if the expected return is lowered, given the cost of investment. One could argue in the opposite direction as well: for an individual there is a strong incentive to save on the cost of investment by not having children, knowing that there will nevertheless be a positive pension benefit in old age. Then, the return from the PAYG system is infinitely high. Notice, however, that the expected pension is only one among several reasons to decide for or against children.

The previous description of the effects of the positive externality was implicitly based on a three-generations model with children, workers and retirees. Here, the working generation has two obligations. First, it has to support parents in old age, and second, it has to raise children as only this will guarantee support during retirement. However, most models do not explicitly consider children as a generation. Instead children are assumed to be a consumption good. In this case the existence of a positive externality on childless persons is simply ignored by those who are willing to have children. When deciding on the optimal number of children they do not internalize the positive effects on others via the pension system. As a consequence the number of children will again be too small compared to the Pareto optimum. While the result is the same, the implications for economic or family policy differ. In the three-generations scenario, childless persons behave like free riders who save on one of their obligations. Therefore, it may be reasonable to impose an extra burden on them. Sinn (2001) suggests a hybrid system in which those who do not invest in human capital (children) should instead invest in real capital. For the two-generations model it seems more natural to introduce Pigovian subsidies for families. Childless individuals are not considered to be free riders here.

For immigrants, the argument is analogous. As soon as immigrants enter a country, accept a job and start to contribute to the pension system they generate a positive externality on the members of the host country's pension system. This externality is caused by the fact that additional resources for the parent generation are made available by the immigrants although the immigrants' parents are not members of the pension system. Hence, one could argue that an introductory gift is made by the immigrants to their host country's native population. Therefore, Sinn (2001) calls this externality an 'entrance fee' to be paid by the immigrants which may be justified, for example, by congestion costs caused by the immigrants' use of impure public goods.

There is a further positive effect that comes from the fact that immigrants have on average more children than natives. These children will eventually contribute more to the pension system than would be necessary to support their parents, assuming that the latter will receive an average pension. This implies an intragenerational redistribution from immigrant families to native families. A similar effect occurs – even if net immigration is zero – if immigrants induce qualitative improvements in the composition of the pension system's membership. This is the case if immigrants have, for example, a higher average skill level compared to domestic workers which means that they will contribute relatively more to the pension system than natives,[12] if they have a lower unemployment rate than natives or if they offer labor that is a complement to domestic labor which helps to lower unemployment. Obviously, the positive effect is reduced if the opposite holds, that is, if immigrants are unskilled, have very few children and are very likely to become unemployed.

3.3.2   The Value of an Immigrant

It is possible to calculate how much the domestic population actually gains from immigration. In order to do so it is useful to start the argument again by considering a new-born child first and later extend the analysis to immigrants.

Obviously, a new-born makes a direct net contribution in present value terms of

$$X_t = \tau_t^{LS} - \frac{p_{t+1}}{1 + r_{t+1}}, \tag{3.23}$$

to the pension system where τ_t^{LS} is the total (lifetime) contribution to the pension system[13] and

$$p_{t+1} = n_t^T \cdot w_t \cdot \tau_t^{LS} \tag{3.24}$$

is the pension benefit of a member of generation t where n^T is the average number of children per member of this generation. Combining (3.23) and (3.24), we get a familiar expression:

$$X_t = \tau_t^{LS} \left(1 - \frac{n_{t+1}^T \cdot w_{t+1}}{1 + r_{t+1}} \right) \tag{3.25}$$

which states that the net contribution of a member of generation t to the pension system is positive if the rate of return on the capital market exceeds the internal rate of return of the PAYG pension system. If we replace τ_t^{LS} by $w_t\tau_t$ in (3.23) and take the pension benefit $p_{t+1} = (1 + n_t)\tau_t w_t$ from (3.7), we would end up with $\tau_t w_t \frac{r_{t+1} - n_{t+1}}{1 + r_{t+1}}$ which is the expression for the implicit tax. Hence, the net contribution of a child to the pension system is connected to the implicit debt because an additional child reduces the implicit debt. Servicing the implicit debt becomes easier for the recent members of the system.

However, equation (3.25) does not take into consideration that new members of the pension system, that is, new-born children, have children themselves. Each new-born child may found a dynasty of potential contributors to the pension system that will never cease to exist. Taking this into account the following proposition will state the effect of a new-born child on the pension system (the proof can be found in Appendix A).

Proposition 3 (Sinn, 2001, p. 86) *If an additional child is born in period 0, the present value V_0 of the total direct net contributions of all descendants of this child is $V_0 = \tau_0^{LS}$. Hence, the net present value of all future payments of the dynasty founded by a new-born child equals exactly the gross contribution of this child to the pension system.*

If the child born in period 0 were allowed to set up its own PAYG pension system with only its own descendants, this child would not need to pay contributions. Instead, it would simply raise its children, who will later come up with the necessary pension payments by paying contributions (or intra-family transfers). Under these circumstances the founder of the dynasty would receive an introductory gift. However, children are usually born into an existing pension system and will therefore be required to pay contributions which will be received by all retirees, not just by their own parents. Hence, the entire gross contribution of an additional child benefits the rest of the society and therefore has to be viewed as a positive externality. Or to put it differently, the new dynasty creates a gain to the society because children contribute to the pension system which helps to lower contributions or to raise benefits. Between any two following generations of the dynasty the usual intergenerational transfers will occur, that is, each generation will pay for their parents and receive from their children.[14] It is the underlying idea of Proposition 3 that these transfers 'cancel out' exactly. On an infinite horizon the repayment of this introductory gift will be transferred into the infinite future, just as in the case of the implicit debt.

Having calculated the positive externality from an additional child, we can turn to the effect that an immigrant has on the society. We argued previously that bearing a child and allowing an immigrant into the country lead to analogous implications for the pension system. Consider a temporary immigrant who returns to his home country in retirement and who will not have a family in the host country. This immigrant will generate a positive externality equal to the one of a child given in (3.23). However, compared to a child he will most likely start to contribute immediately because he will usually enter the country after his childhood. In present value terms the value of an immigrant will be higher than for a child as contributions are discounted over a shorter period.

In the case of permanent immigration the entire gross contribution will again benefit the rest of the society. Sinn (2001) suggests, however, stating the value of an immigrant to the pension system's members more precisely by taking into account that fertility rates and earnings of immigrants may differ from those of the natives. Let the immigrants' average income be a multiple $a < 1$ and the number of immigrant children a multiple $b > 1$ of domestic children. Then the value of an immigrant may be written as

$$V_0 = \tau_0^{LS} + \tau_0^{LS}(a - 1)\left(1 - \frac{n_1^T w_1}{1 + r_1}\right) + (b - 1)\frac{\tau_1^{LS}}{1 + r_1}, \qquad (3.26)$$

where τ_0^{LS} and τ_1^{LS} are typical contributions of members of the pension system in the first and second generations after immigration. Given $a < 1$ and $b > 1$, the second term turns negative and the third term positive, that is, the value of an immigrant is reduced by his below-average income while it is increased due to the larger number of children.[15] We will return to this argument in Section 4.2 where we investigate the effects of differing fertility rates and skill distributions between natives and immigrants. Notice that almost all of these results here and in the following section rest on the important assumption that the number of descendants of immigrants is on average higher than that of the domestic population although there are no robust empirical estimates about the adjustment of fertility rates and about self-selection with regard to the relative fertility of immigrants.[16]

The previous discussion on externalities also sheds some light on what may be called the 'age-structure effect' and its role for the pension system. Usually the age distribution in a country is expected to improve due to immigration because most immigrants belong to cohorts at the lower end of the age distribution, that is, they are relatively younger compared to the native population. This makes the entire population after immigration 'younger' compared to before immigration. It is a popular argument that this has a particularly positive effect on the pension system but from a more general perspective this is not the case.

Consider a country with a pension system that has a tight link between contributions and pension benefits such as Germany or France. If rather old immigrants (compared to average native workers) enter the country, they will pay contributions only for a short time which constitutes some part of the positive externality because contribution rates can fall or benefits can increase a little. But notice that these persons will receive only small pensions because of the short contribution period. Their children, however, will pay the same full contributions as the native children although this is more than what is needed to support their parents. Hence, there is another part of the externality paid for by the immigrants' children via intragenerational redistribution. While young immigrants will come up with the externality or entrance fee alone, old immigrants will share it with their children. In sum, the externality remains the same.

3.3.3 The Effects of Immigration on the Pension System's Budget Equation

In the previous sections, we investigated the positive externality of immigration on the pension system and determined its size. Now we will turn to the direct effects of immigration on the PAYG pension system's fundamental budget equation.[17] This helps us to understand who will gain from immigration, the retirees or the workers or both. Furthermore, we will consider the effect of immigration on wage income which is an important parameter in the pension system as well and which has not been taken into account until now.

Instead of using the simple budget equation from Section 3.1.2, we will use an extended version of the equation which allows for comparisons of different models dealing with unfunded pension systems and labor mobility. Our starting point is the fact that with migration the size of the labor force changes. We assume the labor force, which inelastically supplies one unit of labor per person, to equal the number of contributors to the pension system. Hence, we may write $N_t = \tilde{N}_t + M_t$ where $\tilde{N}_t$ is the number of domestic workers (before migration) and M_t is the number of migrants which are assumed to be young.

The fundamental budget equation for the commonly used two-generations model is given by

$$\sum_{i=1}^{K} \tau_t^i \cdot w_t^i(N_t^i) \cdot N_t^i = \sum_{i=1}^{K} q_t^i \cdot W_t^i \cdot N_{t-1}^i \qquad (3.27)$$

where the index $i = 1, \ldots, K$ describes the number of different types of individuals, for example, high-skilled and low-skilled workers. On the left-hand side of equation (3.27) the contribution rate τ_t to the pension system is a proportional payroll tax rate. The tax base is $w_t^i(N_t^i) \cdot N_t^i$ where w_t^i is the equilibrium wage determined in competitive domestic labor markets. It equals labor income for the inelastic individual labor supply of one unit per period. Since migration increases total labor supply we expect immigrants to change the marginal productivity of labor and to lower wages, that is, $dw_t(N_t)/dM_t < 0$.[18]

On the right-hand side of the budget equation the replacement rate q_t describes which share of some income measure W_t^i a retired individual receives as a pension. Most models assume $q_t = 1$ for simplicity but real-world pension systems usually have lower shares. The income measure W_t^i may take on quite different forms depending on the design of the pension system. Recall the concept of intragenerational redistribution or the distinction between Bismarckian and Beveridgian pension systems from Section 3.2. Bismarckian pension systems do not involve intragenerational redistribution because benefits are calculated entirely on the basis of (uprated) past individual earnings, that is, $W_t^i = \tilde{w}_t^i = \varsigma w_{t-1}^i$ where $\tilde{w}_t^i$ are uprated individual earnings and $\varsigma > 0$ is a factor measuring by how much the uprated wage exceeds the past wage. Usually, the uprating is done by indexing wage income based on productivity growth or inflation. Beveridgian pension systems, on the other hand, lead to flat-rate benefits which are often based on the recent average wage, that is, $W_t^i = \overline{w}_t$ (this implies indexation by definition). Real-world pension systems base pensions on a weighted average of individual earnings and average earnings, i.e. $W_t^i = \alpha \tilde{w}_t^i + (1 - \alpha)\overline{w}_t$ (see Casamatta et al., 2000a, 2000b) where $\alpha \in [0, 1]$ is the so-called 'Bismarckian factor' which measures how much of the individual's pension benefit stems from an 'individual account' and how much is redistributed intragenerationally.

For further reference, we define $p_t \equiv q_t \cdot W_t^i$ to be the per-capita pension benefit and $P_t \equiv q_t \cdot W_t^i \cdot N_{t-1}$ the total pension benefit. In the latter definition, N_{t-1} is the number of retirees. It equals $\tilde{N}_{t-1}$, the number of 'native' workers born in the previous period. This does not necessarily imply that no migration took place in the past. Even if it did, say by migration of young workers to the home country, domestic workers and immigrants can no longer be distinguished after one period. This is because most models assume that immigrants immediately adopt the fertility pattern of the domestic population when they enter the country (perfect assimilation hypothesis). This assumption implies that immigrants raise enough children to be supported by them in old age. The domestic population remains unaffected.

Again, an important underlying assumption is that immigrants belong to the young generation. This seemingly strong assumption can be defended on two grounds. The first argument is that in most countries immigrants are in fact on average younger than the native population. Most of them are potential members of the labor force and therefore contributors to the pension system. If one splits the population into only two groups, workers and retirees, the assumption of migration of the young fits the facts well.

There is, however, another argument which is based on the pension regulations that prevail for international labor migrants, particularly within the EU. The relevant regulations by the European Council state that migrating retirees hold claims only against the national pension system which they have contributed to, regardless of their place of residence (see

Section 8.1 for a more detailed description of European pension regulations). Moving to another country and entering its pension system does not change the pension claims acquired before; it is just that the source of the final benefit will be not just one but two or more countries. Immigration of the group of retirees has no direct impact on the budget equation of the pension system in the target country since there are no legal claims against this country's pension system. Hence, there is no explicit need to account for migration of the elderly in our model of the PAYG system.

Migration of older (and possibly richer) persons may nevertheless have an impact. In the holiday resorts in southern Europe, for example, the revenue from VAT may increase due to migration of the elderly while it decreases in the source countries where the pension system is possibly subsidized from general tax revenues. The tax burden of the remaining young generation then has to be raised, which in turn may create migration incentives for the young. Their migration should finally affect the pension system directly.

In Section 3.2, the concept of the dependency rate was introduced, describing the ratio of the number of persons dependent on transfers (here: retirees) divided by the number of contributors (here: labor force), that is, $D_t = N_{t-1}/N_t = 1/(1 + n_t)$. Introducing migration into this framework, we get

$$D_t(M_t) = \frac{N_{t-1}}{N_t + M_t}$$

with $dD_t(M_t)/dM_t < 0$ for positive immigration ($M_t > 0$). The dependency rate improves because due to immigration the labor force becomes larger compared to the group of retirees. If, however, $M_t < 0$, the dependency rate worsens in the sense of having relatively more retirees.

This result can easily be introduced into the pension system's budget equation. Assuming the simplest case in terms of (3.27), that is, $W_t^i = w_t$, $K = 1$ and $q_t = 1$, we get

$$\tau_t \cdot N_t = p_t \cdot N_{t-1} \iff p_t = \tau_t \cdot \frac{N_t}{N_{t-1}} = \tau_t \cdot D_t^{-1},$$

an expression which we already know from (3.22). If we assume that immigration takes place ($M_t > 0$) and affects the dependency rate, that is, $D_t = D_t(M_t)$, then we have

$$p_t = \overline{\tau} \cdot D_t^{-1}(M_t) \quad \text{with} \quad \frac{dp_t}{dM_t} > 0 \qquad (3.28)$$

for the fixed-contribution rate pension system and

$$\tau_t = \overline{p} \cdot D_t(M_t) \quad \text{with} \quad \frac{d\tau_t}{dM_t} < 0 \qquad (3.29)$$

for the fixed-benefit regime. Hence, with immigration, either the pension benefit increases or the contribution rate decreases or there is a combination of both effects. In any case, immigration has a positive effect on the pension system in the sense that domestic contributors or domestic retirees or both gain from it immediately. This is the direct consequence of the existence of the positive externality.

It is important to realize that immigration is not unambiguously positive in a richer framework which includes wages as well. Consider a budget equation with flat benefits but wage-related contributions in the form of a payroll tax. From (3.27) it follows that

$$\tau_t \cdot w_t(N_t + M_t) \cdot (N_t + M_t) = p_t \cdot N_{t-1}$$

with – in the case of a fixed-contribution rate regime – the following derivative with respect to immigration:

$$\frac{dp_t}{dM_t} = \overline{\tau} \cdot D_t^{-1} \cdot \left(\frac{dw_t}{dM_t} - w_t \frac{dD_t}{dM_t} D_t^{-1} \right). \tag{3.30}$$

The second term in the bracket is positive $(-dD_t(M_t)/dM_t > 0)$ and describes the effect of an increasing number of contributors via the dependency rate. The impact on wages (dw_t/dM_t) can easily be derived from the previously mentioned marginal productivity argument. Let us be somewhat more precise in our argument by considering different types of labor here. If, for example, the input factor labor is homogeneous then the increasing number of workers leads either to a lower factor reward or to higher unemployment, if there are labor market rigidities. If, on the other hand, the factor labor is non-homogeneous then the wage effect depends on whether immigrants and domestic workers are substitutes or complements. If they are substitutes, immigration should have a negative income effect on the domestic population. Here, we assume homogeneous labor, so the wage effect is clearly negative $(dw_t/dM_t < 0)$ and we get two offsetting effects of immigration, which have to be balanced in the immigration optimum. Notice that as long as there is at least a small positive dependency rate effect there will always be a positive number of immigrants that should optimally be allowed into the country. The negative wage effect may also be offset by an indirect labor demand effect which is induced by the immigrants' demand for goods.

Most empirical studies show small effects of immigration on domestic wages: an increase in the share of foreigners in domestic population by 10 per cent will cause a wage drop of only 1 per cent (see the survey study by Friedberg and Hunt, 1995). Assuming heterogeneous labor, the impact will be small as well (see, for example, Bauer, 1998).

3.4 CHAPTER SUMMARY

Fully funded and pay-as-you-go systems are the most basic types of pension systems. The FF system is characterized by a lack of inter– and intragenerational redistribution, that is, no resources are shifted between generations (from the young to the old) or within the same generation (from the rich to the poor). The internal rate of return is simply the market interest rate and pension savings and private savings may be seen as equivalent. Within a nation's pension system, FF systems can most often be found in the second and third pillars, which are usually not public. The reason is that governments pursue redistributive goals in the pension systems as well. These goals can more easily be achieved in a PAYG pension system. Therefore, the *public* first pillar of the pension system is PAYG financed.

A PAYG system redistributes between generations as the entire contributions of the working generation are immediately transferred to the retirees. When a PAYG system is implemented the first generation of retirees receives an introductory gift as they did not contribute before. This gift creates an implicit debt which has to be serviced by all following generations. As a consequence some part of the individual's contributions to the pension system has to be considered as an implicit tax while only the residual part is implicit saving.

The existence of the implicit debt forecloses the possibility of a Pareto-efficient transition from a PAYG to an FF system because the debt will remain, except if the retirees' claims are ignored (which is unlikely). Even if the internal rate of return of the FF system appears to be higher than the PAYG system's biological return, that is, the reproduction rate, taxes need to be levied to cover the old generation's claims after the transition. The only possibility for an efficiency-enhancing transition is to remove distortions, for example, in the labor–leisure choice, which are created by contributions proportional to wage income. This, however, may conflict with a society's preference for redistribution.

While real-world pension systems are diverse, they may all face an ageing problem because they all include at least some fertility-dependent, PAYG-financed parts. In the western world and particularly in Europe rising contribution rates and falling pension benefits can be expected in the future. This is the consequence of the low population growth rate and a low labor-force participation. Raising fertility rates is, however, a difficult task and even if it is successfully accomplished, it takes about 20 to 25 years before the larger cohorts will enter the labor force.

A more promising approach to increase (immediately) the population or labor force appears to be immigration. The effect of increasing the number of contributors via immigration may take different forms: falling contribution rates, increasing pension benefits or both. The explanation is a positive externality that immigrants generate for the domestic population and which reduces the implicit debt of an existing PAYG system. If the perfect assimilation hypothesis holds, that is, if immigrants become indistinguishable from natives as soon as they enter the country, the value of an immigrant is the same as that of a new-born child. It is just the gross contribution of the immigrant to the pension system. Under fortunate circumstances, the positive effect is even higher, for example, if immigrants have on average more children than natives. There is always the positive effect of having additional contributions from new members of the pension system which benefit the domestic members of the system. These contributions are similar to the first generation's introductory gift as the redemption is shifted to the infinite future. For this reason the immigrants' contributions have to be considered as an entrance fee which may be substantial but is probably not sufficient to stabilize the pension system entirely. On the other hand, immigration allows other necessary reforms to be less severe compared to a situation with closed borders. The next chapter will therefore deal with the question whether or not natives will allow immigrants to enter the country.

NOTES

1. The discussion in this chapter and the following ones has been outlined in Krieger (2001) and Krieger (2002).
2. In the following we will use the terms 'entering the labor force in t' and 'being born in t' equivalently within the context of the OLG model. This assumes implicitly that children are not considered as a generation. Instead we follow Samuelson (1958) by assuming that they are part of their parents' consumption.
3. Bequests should be interpreted as a part of old-age consumption here.
4. The only problem that may arise in an FF system is that it can cause an intertemporal reallocation of resources within each generation in the sense that the resulting consumption pattern does not accord with individual preferences. This would, for example, be the case if contributors were forced to save more than they would do voluntarily, given a strong preference for consumption today. However, there is no transfer of resources to other generations.
5. A similar argument has been made in Wellisch (1999, pp. 7–9).
6. Note that these findings are derived from a partial analytic approach.
7. See, for example, Breyer (2000) and Sinn (2000).
8. Notice, however, that in an FF system individuals' pension benefits may as well be unrelated to individual savings. In that case, intragenerational redistribution is not abandoned by the transition. Any assertion regarding Pareto efficiency is then very difficult and depends on the specific design of the pension system.

9. This basic feature can, for example, be found in the French or German pension systems.

10. However in France, there still exists an occupational pension system based on PAYG financing.

11. See, in particular, von Auer and Büttner (2004) for an extensive discussion of the topic of endogenous fertility and externalities in pension systems. For an introduction to the issues of endogenous fertility models see, for example, Werding (1997) and Fenge and Meier (2003).

12. If there is a strict equivalence between contributions and benefits, this problem will not arise. However, all real-world pension systems redistribute intragenerationally.

13. Here, we simply assume that the contribution takes the form of a lump-sum payment, independent of the wage income.

14. If dynasties can be founded, they can also be ended. In that case, there is a last member of the dynasty who has to be supported by the rest of the society. If the population is constant or increasing, however, there will always be enough newly founded dynasties, that is, children, to cover the expenses induced by the ending dynasty.

15. Both the value of a child and the value of an immigrant have been estimated for Germany by Sinn (2001). In the 1990s average immigrant women in Germany had 35 per cent more children than average German women while immigrants' average earnings were slightly less at about 97 per cent. Both numbers are approaching the level of the domestic population within one generation or even faster. Based on 1997 cross-section data and assuming a labor-income growth rate of 1.5 per cent, a capital market interest rate of 4 per cent and a contribution rate of 20 per cent, the present value of the lifetime contributions of a new-born child amounts to about €90 000 (or €140 000 for an individual aged 20). The estimate of the value of an immigrant is €175 000.

16. Berman and Rzakhanov (2000) consider migration to a higher income region as a human capital investment which explains higher fertility levels. Altruistic (immigrant) parents bear migration costs while their children share the returns. This implies that immigrants may be self-selected on fertility.

17. This section is based on Krieger (2001).

18. We assume implicitly that immigrants do not bring any capital into the country such that capital intensity remains unchanged and that they adopt the same savings behavior after immigration as natives.

4. The political economy of pension policy and immigration

In the western world demographic change is a rather slow and predictable process which will go on for several decades. For societies this is both good and bad news. The good news is that a society can prepare for the change and that there is usually no necessity for sudden harsh reforms. But the slow process is a problem as well because many people do not recognize the need for reform in the beginning and even if they do recognize it, they may decide for different reasons to postpone reforms. Already in the 1970s scientists and some politicians in fast ageing countries like Germany or Italy discussed the consequences of low birth rates for future retirees and contributors to the pension systems. However, these discussions had no consequences and potentially helpful reforms at this early point were not carried out. In fact, even in the late 1990s it was still possible to win important elections by opposing urgently needed pension reforms, for example, in Germany. In other countries, there is even today no political consensus for reforms because governments fear to lose elections when important groups of voters such as the retirees are hurt by the reforms.

This chapter will deal with precisely this type of decision problem. How will a democratic society decide on pension issues when different groups in society have very different preferences with respect to the parameters of the pension system? Will socially optimal parameter values be chosen? What happens if – instead of directly influencing the pension system's parameters – other variables are changed which affect the PAYG system indirectly? This allows us to return to the case of immigration, which implies a changing size of the labor force. We will ask how voters decide on immigration policy if they take into account that there will be consequences for their own future pension benefits or today's contribution payments.

Our discussion will start by introducing the well-known model by Browning (1975). This median-voter model asks how a democratic society will vote on the level of contribution rates. The outcome of the model is that the rates will always be suboptimally high. Based on the Browning model we will develop models of voting decisions on immigration and public pensions in Chapters 5 and 6.

It is appropriate to defer these models to later chapters because it is useful to first introduce a basic majority-voting model on immigration given a pension system. Following Razin and Sadka (1999), the model shows that unskilled immigration should unambiguously be supported by the domestic population because it will not harm any group in society. Based on rather strict assumptions there will not be any negative effects, only a positive externality on pension benefits. Hence, the model serves as a reference point which requires, however, a thorough discussion of the underlying assumptions. A first extension of the model will be the relaxation of the 'perfect assimilation hypothesis'. Given this, the outcome is no longer unambiguous. If, for example, immigrants' children do not achieve the skill level of domestic children, there may be opposition to immigration. The same holds for negative effects on natives' wage income.

The remainder of the chapter presents a review of the recent literature on the political economy of public pensions and immigration. Furthermore, there will be a brief introduction of the generational accounting method, which is a different approach to evaluating the effect of immigration.

4.1   VOTING ON THE PARAMETERS OF THE PENSION SYSTEM

Browning (1975) was one of the first to take an explicit public-choice view of the pension system. His model deals with voting decisions on pension issues when individuals of different age are allowed to vote and when their preferred choices depend on their age. As Browning's model is based on the median-voter theorem, it is useful to briefly restate this theorem first.

4.1.1   The Median-voter Theorem

A formal proof of the median-voter theorem can be found in most textbooks on public choice theory such as Mueller (2002) or Persson and Tabellini (2000). The central idea of the median-voter theorem is a voting decision to be made on a single political issue. This issue may, for example, be the level of a tax rate or of redistribution or – as we will later argue – the number of immigrants allowed into the country. These issues need to be defined along a single-dimensional vector of alternatives: tax rates can take any value between 0 and 100 per cent and the number of immigrants is defined on the set of all non-negative integers. Each voter is assumed to have exactly one 'ideal point' among the given alternatives which gives him the maximum utility. Any other alternative will induce a lower level of utility for this voter. The voter's preferences therefore have the property of 'single-peakedness'.

Individual preferences on political issues differ. Some people prefer little redistribution, others like higher levels of redistribution better. Along the vector of alternatives there will be one alternative corresponding to the voter on the median position, that is, there will be precisely one half of the voters preferring less redistribution and the other half preferring more. From this follows the median-voter theorem:

Theorem 4 (Median-voter theorem) *Under the previously stated assumptions the voter at the median position cannot lose the election under the majority rule.*

Hence, it is the median voter who will always decide the vote. Any party platforms in a representative two-party system will therefore always focus on the median voter. The explanation for this result is that under the majority rule the vote of the median voter is needed to win an election because only then will a party gain 50 per cent plus one vote. If the median voter decides for an alternative proposal, the opposition will gain the majority. Due to his single-peaked preferences the median voter will incur a utility loss if he moves away from his ideal point. In fact, parties will compete for the median voter by approaching his ideal point. The dominant strategy is to propose a platform that is identical to the median voter's preferred position. Hence, the median voter's choice will determine the final voting outcome.

The median-voter theorem is obviously a very simplified representation of the voting process. It ignores several problems such as cycling voting decisions, the existence of more than two parties or multidimensional issues, the possibility of logrolling and so on. These problems are extensively discussed in the textbooks by Mueller (2002) and Persson and Tabellini (2000). The theorem has, however, a major advantage. It allows to introduce a political decision-making process in complex models without making the models intractable. In some cases, election campaigns even boil down to one dominating issue such as a major social reform. Then, median-voter models for representative democracies are not too far from reality because voters choose among different reform proposals which hurt people to different extents.

4.1.2   Browning's Model

Political decision-making deals with future laws and rules but rarely with past events which cannot be undone. This somewhat trivial statement has important consequences for pension policy. When, for example, a decision is to be made on a transition from a PAYG to an FF system, one has to accept that an implicit debt exists and cannot be ignored even if today many people would prefer an FF system if they had the chance to newly introduce a pension system (Sinn, 2001). When changes in the parameters of the pension system are voted on a similar situation arises. A young person may think differently about the optimal contribution rate than an old person because for an old person own past contributions are 'sunk'. Changes regarding future policy, on the other hand, are clearly relevant. Hence, if the government plans to reform the pension system, voters will evaluate any reform proposals based on the effects on their future income. If a loss is expected from the pension reform, the reform will be opposed, regardless of whether the pension rules may have been (overly) favorable in the past. Clearly, the effects on future income depend on the age of the voters and the source of income. This is most obvious for retirees, who receive only transfer income and no longer pay contributions during the rest of their lives. For them, there is no reason to oppose high contribution rates.

This is the main idea of Browning's (1975) model, which was later formalized by Sjoblom (1985). It considers a voting decision on contribution rates to a PAYG pension system and asks how forward-looking and selfish individuals evaluate a potential change in the contribution rate, that is, how they vote on this topic. In the following we will introduce this basic closed-economy model[1] before we discuss the open-economy extensions for the case of international labor mobility.

The model assumes three generations: young workers, old workers and retirees. There is a steady-state development through which the exogenous parameters develop accordingly. The individual utility function is strictly concave, strictly monotone and additively separable. In a one-time vote a contribution rate will be determined that will hold today and in the future. There is an underlying PAYG pension system of the fixed-contribution rate type. The number of retirees is normalized to one and the population growth rate is given by n. Hence, in period t there are $1 + n$ old workers and $(1 + n)^2$ young workers. This implies that the pension benefit p is given by

$$p = \tau \cdot w \cdot (1 + n) + \tau \cdot w \cdot (1 + n)^2 = \tau \cdot w \cdot (1 + n)(2 + n). \quad (4.1)$$

Taking period t as the base year the utility of the young generation depends on consumption in all three periods of life:

$$U^y = U(c_t^y) + U(c_{t+1}^o) + U(z_{t+2}) \quad (4.2)$$

where c^y is consumption during the period of being a young worker, c^o is an old worker's consumption and z is consumption during retirement. For a young worker born in period t, this consumption takes place in the periods t, $t + 1$ and $t + 2$, respectively. For old workers the forward-looking nature of the optimization problem comes into play. If past events are no longer taken into account, the individual decision is based only on the future income stream. Hence, the utility function is given by

$$U^o = U(c_t^o) + U(z_{t+1}). \tag{4.3}$$

Analogously, we get for retirees:

$$U^r = U(z_t). \tag{4.4}$$

In each period the individual budget constraint must hold. For a young worker we have:

$$c_t^y = (1 - \tau)w - s_t^y \tag{4.5}$$

$$c_{t+1}^o = (1 - \tau)w - s_{t+1}^o \tag{4.6}$$

$$z_{t+2} = p + (1 + r)^2 s_t^y + (1 + r)s_{t+1}^o \tag{4.7}$$

$$= \tau w(1 + n)(2 + n) + (1 + r)^2 s_t^y + (1 + r)s_{t+1}^o$$

where p is given by (4.1) and s^y, s^o are savings rates. For old workers and retirees analogous constraints can be determined. Based on utility functions and individual budget constraints the Kuhn-Tucker method[2] can be employed to determine the optimal contribution rates from an individual's perspective. We will delegate the formal derivation of the final voting outcome to Appendix B and give instead an intuitive explanation for the voting outcome that will be stated in the following proposition.

Proposition 5 (Voting outcome of the Browning model) *When three differently aged groups in society (young workers, old workers, retirees) vote on the contribution rate of a PAYG pension system with fixed contribution rates and a balanced budget, the preferred contribution rates of the three groups are given by*

$$\tau^* < \tau^{**} \leq 1 \tag{4.8}$$

where τ^* is the contribution rate chosen by young workers, τ^{**} by old workers and 1 by retirees.

Let us first consider the selfish retirees who choose a contribution rate of 100 per cent. They do not care about high contribution rates as they do not contribute at all. However, due to the specific structure of the PAYG system they gain from higher contribution rates because any additional contibutions are transferred directly to them. The situation is slightly different for individuals who are close to retirement such as old workers. They will lose from high contribution rates as long as they still work. This, however, is only for a short time. Then they can enjoy higher pension benefits which follow from the increase in contribution rates. They will therefore weigh up the costs of higher contributions and higher benefits. This will determine their optimal choice of τ. Clearly, they will not support a contribution rate that is as high as the retirees' choice because they still have to pay some contributions.

Finally, young workers have to be considered. They will gain from higher pension benefits as well. However, they will have to pay for it during their entire working life. This group will therefore internalize all future payments to and all future benefits from the pension system. By weighing these effects, young workers will come up with the lowest preferred contribution rate of all groups because they are hurt most by the payments of contributions. Due to the internalization of all contributions and receipts the young workers' choice corresponds to the social optimum if the benchmark is a utilitarian optimum defined as the maximum of the discounted sum of the welfare of all currently alive and future generations. This is easy to see: an infinite number of future generations has precisely the same optimization problem as today's young generation whose optimal choice is τ^*. Consider any $\tau \neq \tau^*$, then an infinite number of individuals will not be in its utility maximum. Even if some living generation such as the old workers is now in its utility maximum, this finite utility gain will not outweigh the infinite utility loss by the yet unborn generations (see, for example, Persson and Tabellini, 2000, p. 129, for a similar argument).

Notice that the assumptions of the median-voter theorem do hold here. We have a single-dimensional issue (contribution rate) and single-peaked preferences. If we assume that neither young workers nor retirees have a majority of votes,[3] the median voter will be among the old workers. The voting outcome will therefore be $\tau^{**} > \tau^* = \tau^{SO}$ where τ^{SO} is the socially optimal contribution rate. The voting process in a democracy will therefore lead to a situation which is not socially optimal; the contribution rate will be too high. The reason for this result is that unborn generations cannot vote on an issue which will nevertheless have a strong impact on them. If the unborn generations could vote the social optimum τ^{SO} would be chosen.

The only solution to this problem would be to let only the young generation decide on issues that may have effects on future generations as well. However, even this may not suffice because fiscal policy may not be intertemporally sustainable. While it is not possible within the framework of the model, in the real world there exist possibilities to shift some of the burden towards future generations, for example, by increasing the government debt despite the young generation's internalization of lifetime contributions and benefits. The generational-accounting literature (for example, Auerbach et al., 1991 and 1992) deals with this problem. We will briefly turn to this approach in Section 4.4 but in general we will simply assume that the young generation is representative for all future generations and will therefore determine the social optimum.

Important extensions of the Browning model have been made by Hu (1982) who introduced uncertainty of benefit receipts, Boadway and Wildasin (1989) who considered an explicit capital market, or Veall (1986) who assumes altruism between generations. Sjoblom (1985) introduced a generational contract which prevents the young generation from quitting the pension system in case of the existence of an implicit tax.

The voting results of the Browning model and its successors will become less clear-cut in a richer theoretical framework, in particular if capital accumulation is added. In a closed economy this should generate general equilibrium effects because we expect a larger PAYG pension system to reduce savings which then induces further effects. Cooley and Soares (1999) find that these general equilibrium effects may in some cases play a dominant role in determining preferences over the PAYG pension system.

4.1.3 Median Age and the Pension System – Some Empirical Evidence

The previous section highlights the importance of the median voter's age for decisions on the parameters of age-dependent systems like the pension system. Let us now take a closer look at the median age as this will tell us which voting outcome can be expected and whether reforms will be possible.

An economy in which retirees have the majority of votes may be called a 'gerontocracy' or 'gerontocratic regime'. The dependency rate D_t, that is, the ratio of retirees to workers, is greater than 1 because $N_{t-1} > N_t$. The population growth rate will be negative: $-1 < n_t < 0$. The internal rate of return of the PAYG pension system, that is, $i_t^{PAYG} \approx n_t + g_t$, may become negative as well if population shrinks by more than wages grow. For this situation Browning's (1975) model predicts that no reform is possible that takes away any of the burden for the young generation. The question that immediately arises is whether rapidly ageing countries like Germany or Italy are going to become gerontocracies in the future. Recent population projections show that even in their most severe variants (with a strong increase in life expectancy, little immigration and a low retirement age) these countries are not expected to end up as gerontocracies, although they may become close to being so (for example, Statistisches Bundesamt, 2003, p. 44).

However, we argued before that not-yet but soon-to-be retired persons may vote like gerontocrats as well. Being close to retirement they are not very much hurt by contribution rate increases but gain substantially from higher benefits. This has to be taken into account. Übelmesser (2004a) therefore compares the median age of the electorate and the indifference age in order to see for how many more years reforms that harm retirees will be possible. In her simulation model the median age in France, Germany and Italy is considered, which will increase by another seven, eight and ten years, respectively, until 2030. According to the Browning model older generations will become more and more influential under this scenario.

The indifference age is defined in such a way that a cohort of this age is not affected by a pension reform. This cohort is therefore indifferent when reform is voted on. Older cohorts lose while younger cohorts win. Hence, as long as the indifference age exceeds the median age the median voter will gain from the pension reform and the reform will be possible. If the situation turns around, it is too late for reforms. Übelmesser (2004a) considers a stylized pension reform for given real-world pension systems in which the contribution rate is set one percentage point below what would have resulted without a reform. In order to balance the budget not only the young but also retirees have to carry some of the expected burden of ageing in all three countries. The indifference age anticipates the future development of the pension system but usually with some time lag. Hence, in recent years the indifference age usually falls short of the median age but will exceed it in later years. Until that year pension reforms are possible. In Italy this will happen by 2006 while France and Germany have a little more time. In the first half of the next decade the indifference age will for the first time exceed median age. The political implication should be obvious: if age-dependent political decisions such as pension reforms do not take place very soon, these decisions will be dominated by older generations which may have a bias away from the social optimum.[4]

While the previous discussion presented future perspectives it is instructive to investigate whether the predictions of the Browning (1975) model are supported by empirical evidence from the past. Several studies have tested whether the population's demographic composition has an impact on the size of public pensions. Usually, a cross-country approach is employed to see how different measures of age structure, such as median age or the old-age dependency rate, affect measures of the size of public pensions such as the share of pension expenditures in GDP.

Breyer and Craig (1997) investigate the effect of median voter age on the size of the pension system, measured as pension benefits as a fraction of GNP, for a cross-section of OECD countries. They find a strong and positive effect of median-voter age on the size of the system. An increase of median voter age by one year will add half a percentage point to the GNP share of pension benefits. Using instead benefits per retiree as the dependent variable the effect of an increasing median age is still positive but insignificant. Also using OECD data for the years 1960–81, Lindert (1996) shows that raising the relative size of the group of retirees to the group of those aged 40 to 64 years led to an increase in both total pensions and even total government spending. Tabellini (2000) combines the effects of intergenerational and intragenerational redistribution (see also Persson and Tabellini, 2000, chapter 6, for a similar model). He finds that the size of the pension system is larger, the larger the share of retirees in the population and the greater the inequality of pre-tax income. Finally, Strömberg (1999) tested a model based on the median-voter age against a social-planner alternative in which the first model was supported.

While most studies find support for Browning's hypothesis, Razin et al. (2002) recently challenged this view. They find a negative correlation between the dependency rate and different measures of the size of the welfare state (tax rate on labor income, generosity of social transfers) for 13 industrialized countries. This finding is explained by a bundling of benefits to the young and to the old.[5] The social contract requires up-front benefit payments to the young to make them honor the contract. The size of the tax-transfer system is determined endogenously. Given an ageing society in political equilibrium, two effects have to be balanced: the demand for benefits increases with the greater number of retirees but at the same time it reduces the willingness of the young population to accept higher taxes and transfers since current workers are the net losers of the welfare state. If the second effect dominates the first one, an increasing dependency rate may lead to lower transfers.

4.2 RAZIN AND SADKA'S MODEL OF THE IMPACT OF IMMIGRATION ON NATIONAL PENSION SYSTEMS

From Section 3.3 we learned that immigration may have an impact on the dependency rate which leads to changes in contribution rates or pension benefits. This can be explained by the positive externality generated by immigrants to the host country's pension system. Hence, whether a society votes on contribution rates directly or indirectly via the number of immigrants allowed into the country does not make a difference from a theoretical point of view. In both cases voters can opt for their preferred pension system and its parameter values.

In a simple framework Razin and Sadka (1999)[6] show how different overlapping generations evaluate immigration policy and its effects on the pension system. In the following, we will present a generalized version of this model which will be used as a reference point for richer frameworks in later chapters.

While in Section 3.3 the effect of immigration was explained by looking at homogeneous agents, that is, average natives and average immigrants, RS assume that within these groups there may be heterogeneous individuals with possibly different preferences regarding immigration policy. Not only does this appear to be a more realistic description of the reality, it also allows us to introduce intragenerational redistribution into the model.[7] RS start by introducing the decision by differently skilled individuals on whether to invest in human capital or not. As a consequence, the population self-selects on becoming skilled or unskilled. Immigrants, on the other hand, are assumed to be always unskilled. The question that arises is whether under these circumstances natives still support immigration. In RS's basic set-up no generation will be harmed by immigration but we will see that this is not necessarily true in an extended framework.

Skill differences play an important role in the discussion on immigration. There is a consensus in most industrialized countries that immigration should generally be regulated to avoid a large inflow of low-earning, low-skilled workers. It is feared that unrestricted immigration presents a challenge to national social security systems as people expect low-skilled immigrants to be net beneficiaries of the welfare state.[8] Also, a depression of wages in the low-skilled labor market segment is feared. Hence, there is some resistance to this type of immigration in the host countries.[9] High-skilled workers on the other hand are warmly welcomed by most countries.

In the following, we will introduce RS' model in a modified form (developed in Krieger, 2004) which differs from the original model in three respects. First, we will not consider the education decision explicitly. This is possible because the education part and the migration-pension part of the original model are perfectly distinct. Second, we will relax the perfect assimilation hypothesis. Third, we ask explicitly which generations support unskilled immigration and which do not. This is a first step towards the political-economy models that will be the focus of the next chapters.

4.2.1 Basic Assumptions of Razin and Sadka's Model

Razin and Sadka's (1999) model aims at finding the optimal level of unskilled immigration into a country with a PAYG pension system. They use a two-generations infinite-horizon OLG model with a given pension policy and two heterogeneous groups of workers which contribute to the pension system: skilled and unskilled workers, indexed by H and L.[10] Contribution rates are fixed, total contributions are equal to total pension benefit P_t which is distributed equally among the retirees. In terms of the fundamental budget equation (3.27) with $i = H, L$ and $K = 2$ we can write:

$$\tau \left(w_t^H \cdot H_t + w_t^L \left(L_t \right) \cdot L_t \right) = P_t \quad \forall \, t \tag{4.9}$$

where L_t is the sum of domestic and foreign unskilled workers.

The model, however, rests on rather strong assumptions. First, it assumes a small open economy with access to the international capital market and no fixed factors in production. Assuming a linearly homogeneous production function $f(K, N)$ with the usual properties and perfect international capital mobility leads not only to an exogenous (world market) interest rate on the factor capital ($f_K = r^{fix}$) but also to exogenously given wages, $f_N = w^{fix}$. Hence, the pension benefit is a function of unskilled immigration M^L only while all other parameters are given:

$$P_t = P_t(M_t^L; \bar{\tau}, w^{fix}). \qquad (4.10)$$

Immigration increases the labor force and thus the number of contributors which leads to an increasing pension benefit P_t. Retirees gain while workers remain indifferent for reasons that will be discussed below. Clearly, if one relaxes the fixed factor price assumption and allows for a negative wage reaction due to a falling marginal productivity of labor in the course of immigration, the outcome may look different.

For the moment it will be assumed that wages remain unchanged and exogenously given, analogously to RS's original model. This allows us to turn to the perfect assimilation hypothesis, which consists of two important assumptions that will be relaxed in the following. The first assumption is that the reproduction rates of natives and immigrants are equalized as soon as the immigrants enter the country. Immigrants adopt the natives' fertility rate. Furthermore, we relax the assumption that the ability (in the sense of acquired 'destination-country specific' human capital) of the immigrants' offspring is distributed identically to that of the natives. Therefore, we will allow for (i) differing fertility rates between natives and immigrants and (ii) different skill distributions of the natives' and the immigrants' offspring.

We find that for realistic parameter values, that is, immigrants having a higher fertility rate than natives and the skill distribution being skewed in favor of the natives, there are two offsetting effects on the expected pension benefit of today's working generation. Depending on the parameter values either the positive fertility effect or the negative skill effect will dominate and cause the workers either to accept or to reject young unskilled immigration. Hence, even if interest rates and wages are constant (as in RS) two effects result from immigration: a positive one on the domestic retirees due to higher total contributions and an ambiguous one on domestic workers and future generations which depends on the two before-mentioned effects. If in total a positive redistributive effect towards the domestic population occurs, one can consider this to be Sinn's (2001) entrance fee for the immigrants.

4.2.2   Labor Supply

In this version of RS's model the education decision of workers is not explicitly modeled. Instead, we assume that there are two groups of homogeneous workers of a given size in the beginning. The population is normalized to unity. Hence, instead of using absolute numbers of workers and immigrants as in budget equation (4.9) we use shares of the workforce. Let h_t be the share of skilled workers and let l_t be the share of unskilled workers. So, we have $h_t + l_t = 1$. There are m_t immigrants allowed into the country in period t who are assumed to be unskilled.

The effective labor supply in t is given by

$$N_t = h_t + \varphi l_t + \varphi m_t = (1 - \varphi)h_t + (1 + m_t)\varphi, \qquad (4.11)$$

where we assume $\varphi < 1$ which implies that unskilled workers provide only φ units of effective labor per unit of working time and where l_t is substituted by $1 - h_t$.

In contrast to RS we assume that fertility rates between natives and immigrants may differ. We denote the natives' reproduction rate as n_t and the immigrants' rate as $\tilde{n}_t$, so RS assume: $n_t = \tilde{n}_t$. Furthermore, we assume that a share α with $\alpha \in [0, h_t]$ of the immigrants' offspring will become skilled in period $t + 1$. The parameter α is exogenously given and may differ between societies. This implies that the share of unskilled children of immigrants ranges between the level for the native unskilled population, which is $1 - h_t$, and unity.[11] Or to put it the other way round: we assume that in the long run it is not possible for immigrants to perform better than the natives (in the sense of becoming skilled workers). This may be due to the fact that both groups will attend the same school system.

In principle, a contrasting view is possible. If it is assumed that immigrants are a positive, highly skilled selection of the source country's population, one may argue that the average immigrant's skill level is even higher than the average native's one. If the immigrants' children inherit their parents' skill level, they should on average perform better than their native counterparts. This is, however, an empirical question. Studies of past immigration show that it takes a long time until immigrants can close the earnings gap between them and the natives.[12] Obviously, they are not able to transfer their skills immediately to the source country. This is potentially a bad prerequisite for their children's school performance. Therefore, it seems justified to restrict the domain of α to $[0, h_t]$ since the assumption of a positive selection seems – at least on average – not too plausible.

The effective labor supply in $t + 1$ turns out to be

$$
\begin{aligned}
N_{t+1} &= h_{t+1} + \varphi l_{t+1} \\
&= h_t(1 + n_t) + \alpha m_t(1 + \tilde{n}_t) \\
&\quad + \varphi[l_t(1 + n_t) + (1 - \alpha)m_t(1 + \tilde{n}_t)] \\
&= (1 + n_t)[(1 - \varphi)h_t + \varphi] + (1 + \tilde{n}_t)m_t[(1 - \varphi)\alpha + \varphi].
\end{aligned}
\qquad (4.12)
$$

We can easily derive RS's result by assuming $n_t = \tilde{n}_t$ and $\alpha = h_t$. Then, equation (4.13) collapses to $N_{t+1} = (1 + n_t)(1 + m_t)[h_t + \varphi l_t]$.

4.2.3 The Pension System

Analogously to RS we assume that in each period t workers pay contributions to the pension system which are transferred to the retirees as individual benefits p_t. Contributions take the form of a payroll tax where τ_t is the tax rate per unit of income. Hence, in period t the budget equation of the PAYG system is given by

$$\tau_t w_t \left[h_t + \varphi(l_t + m_t) \right] = p_t \left(h_{t-1} + l_{t-1} \right) \tag{4.13}$$

where the bracketed terms are the relevant labor supplies in each period. Making use of (4.11) and the fact that $(h_t + l_t) = (1 + n_{t-1})(h_{t-1} + l_{t-1})$, we can solve (4.13) for p_t:

$$p_t = (1 + n_{t-1})\tau_t w_t \left[(1 - \varphi)h_t + (1 + m_t)\varphi \right]. \tag{4.14}$$

Taking the derivative with respect to immigration m_t shows that an increasing number of immigrants raises the pension benefit $(\partial p_t / \partial m_t = (1 + n_{t-1})\tau_t w_t \varphi > 0)$. This is because for a given contribution rate immigration increases total contributions which benefits the constant number of retirees in period t.

Turning now to period $t + 1$ we can derive a new budget equation for the pension system. To do so, we have to take into account the labor supply from equation (4.13):

$$\tau_{t+1} w_{t+1} \left\{ (1 + n_t) \left[(1 - \varphi)h_t + \varphi \right] + (1 + \tilde{n}_t)m_t \left[(1 - \varphi)\alpha + \varphi \right] \right\}$$
$$= p_{t+1} \left(h_t + l_t + m_t \right) \quad (4.15)$$

Notice that $h_t + l_t = 1$ on the right-hand side. Hence, solving for p_{t+1} leaves us with

$$p_{t+1} = \tau_{t+1} w_{t+1}$$
$$\times \frac{(1 + n_t) \left[(1 - \varphi)h_t + \varphi \right] + (1 + \tilde{n}_t)m_t \left[(1 - \varphi)\alpha + \varphi \right]}{1 + m_t}. \tag{4.16}$$

Again, RS's original result can be established by assuming $n_t = \tilde{n}_t$ and $\alpha = h_t$. Then the pension benefit is $p_{t+1} = \tau_{t+1} w_{t+1}(1 + n_t)[h_t + \varphi l_t]$. Notice that in this case the pension benefit in $t + 1$ and all following periods is independent of immigration in t. Assuming no wage effect in t, RS's result implies that native workers are indifferent with respect to immigration.

This is the fundamental result of RS's model: while retirees gain from immigration, workers are indifferent such that even unskilled immigration generates an unambiguous gain to the society.

Taking the derivative of (4.16) with respect to n_t, $\tilde{n}_t$, h_t, φ and α gives the expected positive signs. If either one of the two reproduction rates increases, there will be more contributors and the individual pension benefits increase. If the share of skilled workers in the total population increases or if the productivity φ of unskilled workers is raised (for example, due to an improved school system), the effective labor supply will be higher and therefore total contributions will be higher. Finally, if the parameter α becomes higher (for example, due to special training for immigrants), a larger share of the immigrant's offspring becomes skilled. Again, productivity improves.

Let us now investigate whether the overall impact of immigration on the pension benefit in period $t + 1$ is positive. The first-order condition can be written as

$$\frac{\partial p_{t+1}}{\partial m_t} = \frac{\tau_{t+1}w_{t+1}}{(1+m_t)^2}\{(1+\tilde{n}_t)(1+m_t)\left[(1-\varphi)\alpha+\varphi\right]$$
$$- \left[(1+n_t)\left[(1-\varphi)h_t+\varphi\right]-(1+\tilde{n}_t)m_t\left[(1-\varphi)\alpha+\varphi\right]\right]\}. \quad (4.17)$$

Simplifying this expression we can state the following proposition.

Proposition 6 (Krieger, 2004, p. 180) *There is a positive impact of immigration on the future pension benefit in the modified RS model, that is, $\partial p_{t+1}/\partial m_t > 0$, if the following condition holds:*

$$\frac{(1+\tilde{n}_t)}{(1+n_t)} > \frac{(1-q)h_t+\varphi}{(1-q)\alpha+\varphi}. \quad (4.18)$$

We can look at some special cases to see the implications of equation (4.18). First, we can replicate RS's fundamental result by using their basic assumptions.

Lemma 7 (Razin and Sadka, 1999, p. 147) *For $n_t = \tilde{n}_t$ and $\alpha = h_t$, immigration has no impact on pension benefits in period $t + 1$ because both sides of (4.18) equal 1. Immigration in period t leaves all generations retiring in $t + 1$ or later indifferent while the first generation of retirees gains from additional contributions. Unskilled immigration leads to a Pareto improvement.*

We now relax the assumption that fertility rates have to be the same. It is reasonable, at least for unskilled immigrants, to assume $n_t < \tilde{n}_t$.[13] Taking the RS case as a starting point the left-hand side of (4.18) increases and exceeds the right-hand side. Hence, not only do the retirees of the immigration period t (as in RS) gain from immigration but also the young and future generations.[14]

One can also keep the equality of fertility rates and allow for differences in the skill distribution of both groups' offspring. The right-hand side of (4.18) is 1 if the upper limit of the domain of α is attained, that is, if $\alpha = h_t$. If $0 \le \alpha < h_t$, the right-hand side becomes greater than 1. For $n_t = \tilde{n}_t$, any $\alpha < h_t$ causes a negative impact of immigration on the pension benefit. The reason for this result is that due to immigration the share of unskilled workers increases in period $t + 1$ compared to that in period t. The effective labor supply falls and native workers have to carry some of the burden of the immigrants.[15] This is because an average immigrant's child contributes less to the pension system than an average native child. But at the same time, the pension benefit is the same for natives and immigrants. Hence, some redistribution takes place between natives and immigrants.

Obviously, there are two counteracting effects: on the one hand, immigration may have a positive effect on pension benefits in future periods due to relatively higher fertility rates. On the other hand, immigration that is followed by a relatively poor performance of immigrants' children in attaining destination-country-specific human capital leads to falling pension benefits in $t + 1$. Notice the analogy to equation (3.26) for the value of an immigrant. In this equation, Sinn (2001) assumes a lower income for immigrants ($a < 1$) which possibly results from a lower skill level and a higher reproduction rate of immigrants ($b > 1$) compared to natives.

4.2.4 Voting Outcome

The voting outcome in period t can easily be derived. Let us first turn to the retirees who maximize their pension benefit p_t (according to equation (4.14)) with respect to the level of immigration. We have already seen that immigration increases the pension benefit, so the retirees will be in favor of boundless immigration. If we assume a regime in which population ageing is so strong that the retirees have a majority of votes, unrestricted immigration will be the voting outcome. If this is not the case (which is a more likely scenario), we have to turn to the group of workers active in period t. The decision of the working generation constitutes the final voting outcome if we assume that the working generation is greater than the retired generation. As the model assumes that the marginal products of input factors do not change, today's wages remain constant in the face of immigration. Only the (discounted) future pension benefit plays a role in their optimization problem. Under the assumptions of the RS model workers are indifferent with regard to immigration. However, considering differing reproduction rates and skill distributions we find that their voting behavior depends on the parameter values for $\tilde{n}$ and α. If the positive effect of immigrants' relatively higher fertility more than offsets the negative effect of the immigrants' offspring's relatively low skill level, allowing immigrants into the country will be the optimal choice. If, however, the negative effect dominates zero immigration will be voted for. Hence, even if one does not consider any negative impact of immigration on gross wages, it may be possible – unlike in RS where no generation will lose from immigration – that zero immigration is the voting outcome.

4.2.5 Relaxing the Fixed Factor-price Assumption

The fixed factor-price assumption is rather restrictive. Storesletten (2000, p. 315) finds that the general-equilibrium effects of immigration to the US may be substantial. The simulation analysis in Razin and Sadka (2000, pp. 475–6) shows that if one allows for a falling marginal productivity of unskilled labor due to unskilled immigration, young and future generations are hurt. We will briefly present some of their findings.

Again, contribution rates are assumed to be fixed. Starting in a steady state with no immigration, that is, $m = 0$ in period $t = -1$, a given immigration shock of size m occurs in $t = 0$. In the infinite future ($t \to \infty$) the economy will return to the steady state as the immigration shock slowly loses its impact. In a model with a constant-returns-to-scale production function this can be seen from the path of the capital–labor ratio k which is given by[16]

$$k_0 = K_0 / N_0 \tag{4.19}$$

for period 0 where K_0 is the aggregate capital stock in period 0 and N_0 is taken from (4.11), replacing subscript t by 0. In the next period, we have

$$k_1 = \frac{1}{N_1} \left(\frac{\delta}{1+\delta} w_0 (1-\tau) N_0 + \frac{p_1(1+m)}{(1+\delta)(1+r)} \right) \tag{4.20}$$

where δ is the intertemporal discount factor and N_1 is taken from (4.13), replacing subscript $t + 1$ by 1 and accepting the perfect assimilation hypothesis. Clearly, k_1 depends on immigration m. Starting with period 2, we get

$$k_t = \frac{\delta w_{t-1}(1-\tau)}{(1+\delta)(1+n)} + \frac{(1+n)\tau w_t}{(1+\delta)(1+r)} \quad \forall \ t > 2, \tag{4.21}$$

which does not depend on immigration any longer. Therefore, the immigration shock from period t and its impact in later periods will fade away over time.

Given a Cobb-Douglas production function, Razin and Sadka's simulation analysis shows that when immigrants arrive in period 0 the capital–labor ratio falls and the pension benefit p_0 increases as there are additional contributors. Besides the gain from higher pensions the retirees also benefit from a higher rate of return on their capital because k_0 falls (since $r_t = f'(k_t) - 1$).

In the following periods the capital–labor ratio increases until it returns to its steady-state level. Hence, the gain from the higher rate of return becomes smaller. Because the positive effect of additional contributors disappears in period 1 the pension benefit will fall below its steady-state level since there is only the negative wage effect. Slowly (with monotonically rising capital–labor ratio) the wage effect on the pension benefit will vanish such that it finally reaches the steady-state level again.

While the retirees in the immigration period gain, all other groups (from the highest skilled to the unskilled) in all other periods lose from immigration. The larger the immigration shock, the higher the losses that can be expected. The reasons for this result is that while immigrants are net contributors to the pension system their total discounted net contribution does not suffice to support the gain of the retirees in the immigration period. Hence, although immigrants generate a positive externality on retirees, the burden of the welfare loss borne by all subsequent generations which is caused by falling wages more than offsets the gains.

Furthermore, RS show that a higher elasticity of substitution (compared to Cobb-Douglas) may cause gains for other groups in society as well. This comes from the fact that workers with a very high skill level own relatively large shares of the capital stock, so for them the gain from a higher return on capital may more than offset the loss induced by the pension system.

Falling marginal productivity of labor is also the driving force in other studies on the fiscal consequences of unskilled immigration such as Canova and Ravn (1998). They find that the previously existing level of redistribution to the unskilled can no longer be sustained under these circumstances. But even if wages drop, the findings of our discussion show that a welfare gain may nevertheless occur: when there is a strong positive effect on future pension benefits through immigrants' very high fertility rates or a high skill level, then even a negative impact of immigration on wages may be compensated.[17] This is in line with Storesletten (2000), who finds in a calibrated general-equilibrium model that the fiscal problems associated with the ageing of the baby boom generation in the US may be solved by immigration alone if the age and skill distribution as well as the number of immigrants are chosen properly by an active and selective immigration policy. This implies an increase of annual immigration from 0.44 to 0.62 per cent of the population, provided that the new immigrants are high-skilled and between 40 and 44 years old.

4.2.6 The Case of Immigrants being Net Beneficiaries of the Pension System

While the previous discussion shows that in richer frameworks the positive effects of unskilled immigration may – even where immigrants are net contributors – no longer be sustainable, RS's basic model has an interesting extension which we will briefly outline here. It can be shown that there is a gain from immigration to existing and future generations even if immigrants are net beneficiaries of the pension system.

Let $NB = p/(1 + r) - \tau w \varphi$ be the net benefit to an unskilled immigrant.[18] For p, plug in RS's version of the pension benefit, that is, $p = \tau w (1 + n)(h + \varphi l)$. After some transformations we get

$$NB \gtreqless 0 \iff \frac{1 - \varphi}{\varphi} \cdot h \gtreqless \frac{r - n}{1 + n}. \qquad (4.22)$$

Clearly, $NB > 0$ if $n > r$. However, this is not a dynamically efficient state. Hence, for $r > n$ immigrants may be net contributors if the right-hand side exceeds the left-hand side of the equation. For the unskilled immigrant to become a net beneficiary of the pension system either the share of skilled workers has to be sufficiently large or the productivity measure φ of the unskilled has to be sufficiently small.

Consider now a situation in which the world ceases after period 1 because neither native nor immigrant workers have children. While $p_0 > 0$ we get $p_1 = 0$ as there are no more contributors. Retirees in period 1 live off their savings from period 0. This is a zero-sum game because immigrants are net contributors to the pension system ($NB = -\tau w \varphi < 0$) and their contributions are transferred to the retirees in period 0. Native-born workers in period 0 are unaffected by immigration. This, however, no longer holds if immigrants become net beneficiaries (for example, due to some form of compensation taking place). Then, the native-born workers in period 0 have to come up with these expenses as the retirees' gain will remain unchanged.

Within the working generation we still have a zero-sum game in which compensation is possible, so this generation does not reject immigration.[19] Hence, the fundamental results by RS hold. This is also the case in an infinite-horizon framework but a burden caused by immigration can be added to the already existing implicit debt and shifted into the infinite future.

4.3 NOTES ON RELATED LITERATURE

In the following, we will review some recent public choice literature on immigration and public pensions.[20] First, models that directly respond to

and extend Razin and Sadka (1999) will be presented. Then, the focus will
be on models which introduce immigration directly into Browning's model.

4.3.1   Extensions of Razin and Sadka's Model

The rather simple framework of Razin and Sadka's (1999) model has
provoked some extensions of the model, besides the one presented in the
previous section. Leers et al. (2004) investigate short-run and long-run
migration effects in ageing countries. Like RS they argue that in the long
run favorable immigration flows will occur. However, during the transition
process towards the long-run state periods of 'emigration' may take place in
which the dependency rate worsens.

   The authors assume that after a demographic shock to the native
population which reduces the number of workers (via a lower reproduction
rate) two opposing effects occur from the perspective of the mobile segment
of population. First, wages increase due to a higher marginal productivity
of labor which should lead to immigration of mobile workers from abroad.
Second, the political power of the elderly increases, which allows them
to increase contribution rates in a simple pension system as given by
(3.29). In the short run, the second effect may dominate the first one. In
the long run, immigration and an improving dependency rate will assist
a to return to the steady state, characterized by a welfare gain from
immigration. To exclude corner solutions in which all mobile workers leave
the country, the political-power effect has to be quantitatively weaker than
the dependency-rate effect on wages.

   Kemnitz (2003) introduces non-competitive labor markets into the RS
framework. Trade unions set wages of unskilled workers in order to
maximize their members' utility. Wages turn out to be above the competitive
level. This generates unemployment. The total welfare effect of unskilled
immigration for the natives in this model is positive as it allows them to shift
some of the costs of redistribution to the immigrants. The fixed-contribution
rate regime has different effects on the welfare of the native population
depending on the level of immigration. If the number of immigrants is
low, marginal gains of immigration occur from increasing contributions and
income is shifted to the natives via increasing marginal productivities of
skilled labor. This happens although there is a counter-effect from increasing
unemployment of the unskilled. If immigration is large scale, however, there
is a still positive but reduced effect because the increasing labor market
distortions offset some of the gains. There are fewer contributions and the
marginal productivity of the skilled is relatively lower. Hence, in this case,
immigration is beneficial despite the existence of the pension system.

4.3.2 Voting Models on Immigration and Pension Policy

The median-voter model by Browning (1975) allows for a direct vote on the parameters of the pension system. However, the pension system as well as other redistributive measures can be influenced indirectly as well by steering the number of immigrants. With the deepening of European integration and through the discussion of the ageing problem of many societies, the issue of intergenerational redistribution in open economies, including political-economy aspects, has gained more attention recently.[21]

The models usually set the Browning framework in a small open economy setting. In the following, we will introduce the most important models of this type. These models take the pension systems as exogenously given and investigate which immigration policy is optimally chosen in an open economy framework with intergenerational redistribution. A typical example is the model by Scholten and Thum (1996) in which the decision parameter is immigration policy, not the pension system's contribution rate. Immigration will have different effects on each of the three living generations since the amount of immigration will not only have an impact on current and expected pensions payments but also on wages. Haupt and Peters (1998) extend the model by introducing a distinction between the different pension policy regimes of the fixed-pension benefit (more precisely: fixed-replacement rate) and the fixed-contribution rate type from Section 3.2. Furthermore, Haupt and Peters allow for rational voters who anticipate the effect on future generations' voting behavior today instead of assuming individuals to be myopic as in Scholten and Thum (1996).

Both models fit very well into an extended version of the pension system's budget equation (3.27) which allows for more than two generations. The generalized version of the budget equation can be written as

$$\sum_{j=1}^{J}\sum_{i=1}^{K} \tau_{t+j}^{i} \cdot w_{t+j}^{i}\left(N_{t+j}^{i}\right) \cdot N_{t+j}^{i} = \sum_{i=1}^{K} p_{t+J}^{i} \cdot N_{t}^{i} \qquad (4.23)$$

where J is the number of working generations. Hence, $J = 2$ describes a three-generations model.

In both models, there are two working generations of the same type ($K = 1$) contributing $\tau_t w_t (N_t + N_{t-1})$ to the pension system and one retired generation receiving a benefit of $q_t w_t N_{t-2}$ since $p_t = q_t w_t$ is assumed where q_t is the replacement rate. Both contributions and benefits are calculated with respect to the current wage w_t. When immigrants are young, the generation born in period t increases ($N_t = \tilde{N}_t + M_t$). Using the concept of the dependency rate D_t, we get

$$\tau_t = q_t \cdot \frac{N_{t-2}}{N_t + N_{t-1}} = q_t \cdot D_t(M_t). \qquad (4.24)$$

Following Haupt and Peters (1998), under the fixed-replacement rate regime the replacement rate is exogenously given at some level $q_t = \bar{q}$. We may simply write

$$\tau_t = \bar{q} \cdot D_t(M_t). \tag{4.25}$$

The contribution rate adjusts endogenously to changes of the exogenous variables $(\bar{q}, D_t(M_t))$. Here, instead of fixing the benefits, only the replacement rate is taken as given. Hence, we have a fixed replacement-rate regime with $p_t = \bar{q} \cdot w_t$ where $\bar{q} < 1$. The model by Scholten and Thum (1996) is based on this regime. The opposite case is the fixed-contribution rate regime in which a constant exogenous contribution rate $\tau_t = \bar{\tau}$ is assumed. Here, the replacement rate adjusts endogenously:

$$q_t = \bar{\tau} \cdot D_t^{-1}(M_t). \tag{4.26}$$

Under both regimes the dependency rate is influenced negatively by immigration $(\partial D_t / \partial M_t < 0)$, that is, there is a positive effect of immigration on the age structure which corresponds to the positive fiscal externality (or entrance fee) that a new member of the pension system creates to the rest of the society. By assumption, immigration also reduces gross wages at least temporarily, that is, $\partial w_t / \partial M_t < 0$.

In the fixed replacement-rate regime, retirees will be worse off as their pension benefit is a fixed share of the gross wage $(p_t = \bar{q} \cdot w_t)$ which falls as a result of increasing labor supply. The active generations face shrinking gross wages as well but at the same time the contribution rate falls according to (4.25), which more than offsets the wage reduction. A young worker gains twice from this effect (in period t and $t + 1$) while a member of the middle-aged generation does so only once. Therefore, the young generation is in favor of a more liberal immigration policy than the middle-aged generation. From a welfare point of view the young generation's choice is closest to the social optimum as the young are the only living generation internalizing all costs and benefits of immigration to pension systems. The argument is the same as holds in Browning's (1975) model in Section 4.1.2. But again the median voter is a member of the middle-aged generation.[22] Compared to the social optimum the median-voter generation chooses a sub-optimally low level of immigration.

The median voter generation is myopic if it ignores the voting behavior of future generations in its own decisions. Myopic median voters choose an immigration policy in which the marginal reduction of net wages equals the marginal reduction of the contribution rate due to a more favorable dependency rate. Compared to this outcome a rational median voter favors a more liberal immigration policy than the myopic one. The intuition for this result is that a more liberal immigration policy today will reduce the tax burden in two periods due to the improved dependency rate, that is, this period's and next period's median voters will be better off. Therefore, in the following period there is less need for immigration and a more restrictive immigration policy can be chosen. This improves the expected pension benefit of today's median voter since future gross wages will decrease less. Anticipating the effects resulting from future voting decisions, today's median voter behaves more liberally and allows more immigrants into the country since this will have a positive effect on his future pension benefit.

The fixed contribution-rate regime is more complex. If the immigration elasticity of wages is assumed to be in a reasonable range ($-1 < \eta < 0$), the old generation will advocate unrestricted immigration. The increase in pension benefits due to an improved replacement rate more than offsets the decrease in pension benefits from falling gross wages. In contrast, the young generation faces only decreasing gross wages but has no offsetting gains from immigration.

Again, the members of the middle-aged generation decide how many immigrants are allowed in. The utility from their rest-of-life incomes does not depend on previous decisions on immigration policy, hence myopic and rational policy coincide in this case because there is no impact of today's policy on future decisions. The result is a corner solution which depends on the parameter values: either the negative effect of lower income in the remaining working period (no immigration at all) or the positive effect of higher benefits in the retirement period (maximum possible immigration) dominates. Usually, a zero-immigration policy is considered optimal if the share of pensions in lifetime income is negligible.

In sum, the results strongly depend on how the pension system is set up. If one compares both policy regimes, one finds that a change from one regime to the other will turn the incentives of the generations upside down. The main lesson to be learned from these models is that in order to evaluate immigration policy along the lines of pension policy, it is decisive to know whether the pension system is of the DB (defined-benefit) or the DC (defined-contribution) type. Recall from Figure 3.1 that – except for Sweden and Italy – most pension systems in industrialized countries are DB systems, while some are mixed. Hence, in most cases a policy of keeping the replacement rate constant is conducted.

From this it follows that the young generation is not only hit most severely by the effects of ageing on the pension system but also that young workers may gain most from immigration. The younger the workers, the longer they can shift parts of their contribution payments to immigrants. This is even more true as the potential negative wage effects are rather small (recall Section 3.3.3) such that the net effect can be expected to be positive. Under these conditions the acceptance of older workers and retirees will depend on the specific pension formula. If wage effects are negligible and replacement rates are fixed, retirees and older workers are basically indifferent with regard to immigration issues.

4.4   GENERATIONAL ACCOUNTS AND VOTERS' PREFERENCES FOR IMMIGRATION

Rest-of-life net benefits which are decisive in the previous models are also used in the concept of generational accounts.[23] While the ultimate goal of the generational accounting method is to evaluate sustainability of fiscal policy at an aggregate level, the impact of immigration on different cohorts of natives can be measured as well.

Given some base year, age profiles (generational accounts) of the present value of rest-of-life tax payments and benefits for each living cohort can be estimated by extrapolation of today's parameters. Usually, a generational account indicates for the first decades of life that the present value of future tax payments exceeds the present value of pension benefits (but notice that pension benefits are discounted over a much longer period). At about age 45 to 50 the discounted pension benefits start to exceed the remaining tax payments. The generational account indicates a net benefit until the end of life. Pension reformers have to take this finding into account. Reforms which harm the elderly may not be supported by the median voter cohort if this cohort has already passed the 'break-even age'. These results show once more the problems of closed-economy pension reforms. It is rather unlikely that socially optimal outcomes will be achieved.

The generational accounting framework has also been used to estimate the effect of immigrants' additional contribution payments on natives' generational accounts (see, for example, Bonin et al. (2000).[24] In the first years of young immigrants' lives government spending attributed to this group exceeds its rest-of-life net tax payments. Later, immigrants start to become net contributors. Eventually net contributions to the public sector turn negative again, similar to the natives' break-even age. Often the immigrants' net contributions exceed on average those of the domestic population. The main reason is that pension claims of immigrants are rather low because of short contribution times and lower labor earnings.

From the perspective of domestic citizens it is therefore particularly attractive to have immigration of individuals who arc net contributors to the public sector.[25] For Germany, Bonin et al. (2000) show that immigrants should be aged 12 to 45 in order to have a positive net effect. In this case the intertemporal fiscal net gain per household turns out to be substantial (see also Bonin 2001, 2002). The results for Germany are in contrast to the findings for the US. Auerbach and Oreopoulos (1999) suggest that the impact of immigration on the fiscal imbalance could be very small. Notice also that deviating from the perfect assimilation hypothesis reduces these gains. Bonin (2002) finds, for example, that a long integration phase reduces the fiscal net gain from immigration substantially.

4.5   CHAPTER SUMMARY

Preferences of voters are sometimes correlated with the voters' age. This is particularly true for voting decisions on the parameters of the pension system. The reason is that past decisions are considered to be sunk. Retirees paid contributions in the past but they are not directly affected by today's contribution rates any more as they no longer have a wage income. Hence, increasing contribution payments does not harm them; instead they even benefit because there is more money to be redistributed. The higher the contribution rate, the better off retirees are. On the other hand, persons who enter the labor force for the first time still have all contribution and benefit payments ahead. Although increasing contribution rates are favorable to them in old age, they will at the same time hurt them during working life. The young workers' preferred contribution rate therefore weighs these two effects optimally.

The older a persons gets, the less important are future contribution payments relative to future benefits. This is the essence of Browning's (1975) model. Of all age groups, a young person will choose the lowest contribution rate, which also determines the social optimum because it internalizes all future contributions and benefits. The voting outcome, however, differs from this result because the median voter is close to retirement and chooses therefore a relatively higher contribution rate.

An analogous argument has been made for a scenario in which voters have to decide on immigration policy. Immigrants generate a positive externality on domestic members of a country's pension system. Thus, by voting on the number of immigrants one indirectly votes on the parameters of the pension system as well. But the gain from immigration will not necessarily accrue to all groups in society and certainly not to all groups to a similar extent. Additionally, one also has to take into account negative wage reactions, which may hurt different groups differently. When the positive externality comes as a reduction in contribution rates, the gains from immigration mainly accrue to the young while retirees may even lose if their benefits are related to wage income. Again, voting outcome and social optimum differ because the middle-aged median voter does not internalize all positive and negative effects from immigration.

These results are different from Razin and Sadka's (1999) model in which no negative effects occur. The immigrants' contributions raise the pension benefit while working and future generations are not affected at all. Relaxing the perfect assimilation hypothesis may lead to negative effects that hurt the working generation alone when there is redistribution from natives' children to immigrants' children. If citizens can vote on the level of immigration, young voters may reject immigration. This result becomes even more pronounced if the negative effect on wage income is added. Even if the overall welfare effect of immigration is positive due to the positive externality, voters may nevertheless reject immigration if the gains are concentrated on a minority. Razin and Sadka's unambiguously positive effect can no longer be sustained in richer frameworks.

In the following chapter, we will extend the model by Scholten and Thum (1996). Given that a decision has to be made on immigration policy, we will ask what happens if voters differ not only by age but also by their skill levels.

NOTES

1. The description of the model follows Breyer (1990).
2. The Kuhn-Tucker method has to be applied because the choice variables, that is, the contribution rates, need to be non-negative.
3. This would be the case if the population growth rate (see Breyer, 1990, p. 143) is either ≤ -38 per cent (majority of retirees) or $\geq +62$ per cent (majority of the young).
4. This holds even if altruism is not excluded because there are fewer and fewer persons altruism can be directed to. Hence, it becomes more natural to behave non-altruistically.
5. For example, in some countries payroll social security taxes are used to finance both old-age transfers and unemployment benefits or health care.
6. In the following, we will refer as RS to this article and to Razin and Sadka (2000), which contains an extended version of the model.
7. This, however, will be done only in the following chapters.
8. There is an ongoing debate on this topic. It is argued that immigrants are immediately subject to taxation but will not be eligible for all welfare programs. See, for example, Borjas (1995) and LaLonde and Topel (1997) for general facts on immigration.
9. Razin and Sadka (1996) show this effect in a model with two factors of production: skilled and unskilled labor. The immigration of unskilled workers leads to falling wages for the unskilled workers and increasing wages for the skilled. A simple redistribution system with a subsidy financed by a lump-sum tax on skilled workers is assumed. Since in a democracy migrants cannot be excluded from (at least some) of the entitlement programs, migration changes the income redistribution frontier in a systematic way. This leads to a welfare

loss and resistance of the domestic workforce towards immigration.

10. The original model assumes that there is a continuum of differently skilled workers. Below a certain cut-off level, workers do not invest in human capital (which is costly) and remain unskilled. Above that level, workers invest according to their individual skill level.

11. We can interpret this assumption in the following way: it takes some (costless) 'integration effort' on the part of the natives to have the immigrants' offspring attain the same skill distribution as the natives' offspring, for example, by communicating with the immigrants' children in order to help them improve their language skills etc. If no integration effort takes place, the immigrants' offspring remain unskilled. Otherwise, at least some percentage of the immigrants' children will become skilled, that is, they will be able to compete with skilled natives for jobs.

12. For Germany, Schmidt (1992) finds that the average immigrant to Germany earns initially about 12 per cent less than the average German. It takes him about 17 years to close this gap. Dustmann (1993) and Licht and Steiner (1994) estimate moderate assimilation effects while Pischke's (1992) result seems to reject assimilation almost entirely.

13. Storesletten (2000) finds that the average total fertility rate for medium- and low-skilled immigrants to the US is 7 per cent and 50 per cent, respectively, higher than for natives. For high-skilled immigrants, however, it is 16 per cent lower. Sinn (2001) states that during the 1990s, the average immigrant woman had 35 per cent more children than the average German woman.

14. Within the RS framework one could also argue in the following way: if migration is perpetually taking place, then migration with the same fertility rate for migrants as for the native population is equivalent to a one-shot migration with migrants having higher fertility rates, and leads to a gain for future generations.

15. In addition to this effect the skill level of natives in $t + 1$ may as well fall due to unskilled immigration. This may be the case, for example, if schoolteachers need to put a great effort into improving the language skills of immigrant children, thereby slowing down the pace of instruction. Then, the effective labor supply will fall even further.

16. See Appendix B for a derivation of equations (4.19) through (4.21).

17. Here, a sufficiently low immigration elasticity with respect to gross wages needs to be assumed.

18. Notice that in equation (3.23) we defined the direct net contribution of a new member of the pension system to be $X_t = \tau_t^{LS} - p_{t+1}/(1 + r_{t+1})$ which is approximately the negative of NB.

19. Razin and Sadka (2001) take up the basic model again, however in a static framework, and investigate the attractiveness of a developed welfare state with both high taxes and high transfers to immigrants. They find that an increase in redistribution attracts immigration, especially of unskilled workers. But here unskilled immigrants are net beneficiaries of the welfare system and share some of the benefits at the expense of the native-born unskilled. Hence, redistribution becomes more costly to the latter. More immigration then leads

       to native-born people supporting lower tax rates.

20.   This section is based on Krieger (2001).

21.   Until today, most of the research is still done on static redistribution in open economies. Lejour and Verbon (1996), for example, analyze decentralized social insurance policies with mobile capital. Similar are Persson and Tabellini (1992) and Gabszewicz and van Ypersele (1996). Verbon (1990) considers a mobile labor force and intragenerational redistribution. Cremer and Pestieau (1998) consider tax competition of countries that can choose to have more or less Bismarckian systems.

22.   Because of perfect foresight this generation's decision accords with the plans made at a young age.

23.   This concept was first proposed by Auerbach et al. (1991, 1992). For a brief introduction to the generational accounting method, see for example, Jägers and Raffelhüschen (1999) and Raffelhüschen (1999).

24.   Because immigrants cause additional government spending their tax payments have to be adjusted accordingly.

25.   Recall also Storesletten's (2000) result, discussed in Section 4.2.5, which shows that the ageing problem of the US baby boomers can be entirely overcome by appropriately choosing immigrants.

5. A general voting model on immigration and pensions

The previous two chapters had two main goals. First, they gave a general introduction to issues like unfunded pension systems, migration and the median-voter theorem that will be dealt with in this and the next chapter. Second, a brief review of related models of the public choice literature on pension systems and immigration was presented. We will now introduce a model that combines different strands of the literature and attempts to give a broader picture of the voting decision on immigration. The model is sufficiently simple to show further effects and impact factors such as social distance and – once more – skill differences between natives and immigrants, labor market distortions or return migration. The goal is to show how these impact factors shape the voting outcome.

5.1 THE BASELINE MODEL

5.1.1 A Brief Introduction to the Model and its Relation to the Existing Literature

Recalling Figure 3.1, we know that the majority of countries have pension systems of the defined-benefit type. Even Sweden and Italy had DB systems until very recently. This is different from Razin and Sadka's (1999) model where contribution rates are fixed and retirees are the main (or only) beneficiaries of immigration. Models assuming fixed benefits such as Scholten and Thum (1996) therefore fit the observations from real-world pension systems much better. For another reason, Scholten and Thum's (1996) model is closer to reality: it takes account of potentially negative wage effects due to immigration. In the public debate the fear of falling wage incomes or increasing unemployment plays an important role.

On the other hand, Scholten and Thum's (1996) as well as Haupt and Peters' (1998) models do not consider the fact that workers may be heterogeneous as in Razin and Sadka (1999, 2000). The simulation results in

Razin and Sadka (2000) indicate that (unskilled) immigration hurts unskilled native workers more than high-skilled native workers. For a median-voter framework this implies that there may be more distinct voter groups than just the old, the young and sometimes the middle-aged. The model that will be presented in the following will take care of all these aspects. There will be a voting decision by heterogeneous workers and retirees on unskilled immigration which takes into account the effects of immigration on a fixed-benefit PAYG system and on wage income.

We will then extend the baseline model by some real-world observations which we expect to have an impact on the optimally chosen immigration level. We first assume that social norms and customs are distorted by an increasing number of immigrants (as in Hillman, 2002). The increasing 'social distance' causes the median voter to choose an even lower level of immigration. However, the positive impact of immigrants on the pension system remains undisputed. Falling contribution rates will always lead to an interior solution with at least some immigration. Then, we will consider labor market rigidities which cause unemployment and which may therefore be another reason to be rather reluctant to allow for immigration.

A fact which is usually neglected in the literature on migration and public pensions is the problem of return migration (see Dustmann, 1996). Immigrants often move to a country only for a certain time period and return afterwards to their home country. During their stay they acquire pension claims which can eventually be transferred to their home country. In a PAYG system the next generation has to pay for these claims even if there are no more children of the former immigrants living in the country. If this can be foreseen by today's (young) voters and if they are not able to shift the entire burden of return migration to the next generation, this will make them less favorable towards immigration. Finally, we question again the perfect assimilation hypothesis from Section 4.2. It implies that immigrant and native children have the same skill distribution. We will show that, while we can in principle expect unskilled immigrants to have at least some unskilled children, the share of skilled immigrant offspring will increase compared to their parents' generation. This will cause two counteracting effects on the domestic voters' pension benefit: there are more skilled workers paying higher contributions but their wages fall.

5.1.2 Basic Assumptions

Consider the following overlapping-generations framework. In each period t the population consists of retirees and workers where workers are either skilled, H_t, or unskilled, L_t. The total labor force is N_t and retirees are simply workers born in period $t - 1$, that is, $N_{t-1} \equiv H_{t-1} + L_{t-1}$. We assume unskilled immigration where immigrants adopt the natives' fertility pattern immediately after immigration, that is, natives and immigrants will have the same number of children in the period following immigration. Furthermore, we assume that the skill distribution among the natives' and the immigrants' offspring is identical, that is, the ratio of skilled and unskilled workers is the same for both groups. Hence, the perfect assimilation hypothesis is assumed to hold and will only be relaxed in Section 5.5.

The three groups (skilled and unskilled workers, retirees) vote on immigration policy in a median-voter setting. The total labor force in t is

$$N_t \equiv H_t + L_t + M_t$$

where M_t are unskilled immigrants allowed into the country after a vote. Immigration policy can be described by the immigration ratio which is the ratio of total labor force and native labor force:

$$\gamma_t = \frac{H_t + L_t + M_t}{H_t + L_t} = 1 + \mu_t, \tag{5.1}$$

where $\mu_t = M_t/(H_t + L_t)$. Choosing a positive μ_t implies that immigrants are allowed into the country. For further reference note that $M_t = (H_t + L_t)(\gamma_t - 1)$.

The population growth rate is given by the ratio of the labor force today and in the previous period. Hence, we have

$$n_t = \frac{H_t + L_t}{H_{t-1} + L_{t-1}} - 1.$$

Among today's retirees there may be some former immigrants. They are not explicitly noted because in terms of the pension they are considered as being equal to natives after one period. We can also define the dependency rate as the ratio of retirees to total labor force, that is,[1]

$$D_t(\gamma_t) = \frac{N_{t-1}}{N_t} = \frac{H_{t-1} + L_{t-1}}{H_t + L_t + M_t} = \frac{1}{(1 + n_t)\gamma_t}. \tag{5.2}$$

Let us further assume that $Y = F(H, L)$ is a linearly homogeneous production function with the usual properties:

$$F_H > 0, \ F_L > 0, \ F_{HH} < 0, \ F_{LL} < 0, \ F_{HL} > 0.$$

In flexible labor markets wages depend on immigration as the total number of unskilled workers increases with each immigrant. The output after immigration may be written as $Y = F(H, L + M)$. In terms of the immigration ratio we get the following expressions for the wages of skilled and unskilled workers:

$$w_t^H(\gamma_t) \quad \text{with} \quad \partial w_t^H / \partial \gamma_t \ > \ 0 \quad \text{and}$$
$$w_t^L(\gamma_t) \quad \text{with} \quad \partial w_t^L / \partial \gamma_t \ < \ 0.$$

5.1.3   The Pension System

After immigration has taken place, the PAYG pension system's budget equation is given by

$$\tau_t(w_t^H H_t + w_t^L(L_t + M_t)) = q_t \omega_t(H_{t-1} + L_{t-1}) \qquad (5.3)$$

where τ_t is the contribution rate, q_t is the replacement rate and ω_t is the average wage given by $\omega_t = \theta w_t^H + (1-\theta)w_t^L$ with $\theta = H_t/(H_t + L_t + M_t)$. Here, each retiree receives the same basic pension which is related to the average wage. The latter depends on immigration as well $(\omega_t(\gamma_t))$, thus $\partial \omega_t(\gamma_t)/\partial \gamma_t = \left(H_t(w_t^L - w_t^H)\right)/(H_t + L_t + M_t)^2 < 0$ if $w_t^L < w_t^H$.

Following Scholten and Thum (1996), we assume a fixed-replacement rate regime with $q_t = \bar{q}$. Therefore, contribution rates have to adjust endogenously to changes of the underlying parameters such as fertility rates, life expectancy or the number of immigrants. From (5.2), (5.3) and the definition of ω_t follows

$$\tau_t = \frac{\bar{q}}{(1+n_t)\gamma_t} = \bar{q}D_t(\gamma_t). \qquad (5.4)$$

5.1.4   Voting Outcome

We can now investigate the outcome of a vote on the immigration ratio where $\gamma_t > 1$ indicates a positive preferred level of immigration while zero immigration is chosen if $\gamma_t = 1$. Consider first the group of retirees where each retiree will receive a pension of $\bar{q}\omega_t(\gamma_t)$.[2] Since $\bar{q}$ is constant and $\partial \omega_t(\gamma_t)/\partial \gamma_t < 0$, retirees will unambiguously lose from immigration and vote for $\gamma_t = 1$. Under a pension system in which only the contribution rate can change the retirees will not gain from the fact that there are more contributors to the system. Instead they will lose because unskilled immigrants will drive down average wages.

Before we investigate the voting behavior of skilled and unskilled workers, recall the assumption that immigrants have the same number of children as natives and that immigrants' offspring have the same skill distribution as the natives' offspring. If no further immigration takes place in the future, then the ratio of skilled and unskilled workers remains unchanged in period $t+1$. Hence, the average wage will not change and we get $\omega_t = \omega_{t+1}$. Clearly, if one takes future pension benefits into account when voting on immigration additional immigrants will not only drive down today's average wage but also the future average wage $(\partial \omega_{t+1}(\gamma_t)/\partial \gamma_t < 0)$.

Since immigration will always cause a gain to the domestic population which stems from the positive externality generated by the increasing number of contributors, it is likely that further immigration will occur in the succeeding periods. Still assuming unskilled immigration, ω_{t+1} will decrease further due to $\gamma_{t+1} > 1$. The negative pension effect anticipated by today's workers becomes even more pronounced. Qualitatively, however, there is no difference, so in order to simplify the analysis we will follow Scholten and Thum (1996) by assuming that voters are myopic. Hence, γ_{t+1} is taken as given and not considered in the optimization problem of the young generation, that is, we assume $\partial \omega_{t+1}/\partial \gamma_{t+1} = 0$.

Unlike in Haupt and Peters (1998) there is no strategic interaction between the median voters of two succeeding periods here. The reason is that in a two-generations model each new generation finds itself in a predetermined situation to start with. This includes prevailing wage levels which may already have internalized some previous immigration. Whether immigration took place before or not is irrelevant for the new-born generation. Therefore, decisions of a median voter do not have an impact on the following median voter, that is, there is no scope for strategic decisions.[3]

Given this, skilled and unskilled workers favor the immigration policy γ_t which maximizes today's net income plus the future pension benefit:

$$V^i(\gamma_t) = w_t^i(\gamma_t)\left[1 - \overline{q}D_t(\gamma_t)\right] + \overline{q}\omega_{t+1}(\gamma_t), \quad i = H, L. \quad (5.5)$$

The first-order condition of the workers $(i = H, L)$ turns out to be

$$V_{\gamma_t}^i = \frac{\partial w_t^i}{\partial \gamma_t}\left[1 - \overline{q}D_t(\gamma_t)\right] + \frac{w_t^i \overline{q}D_t(\gamma_t)}{\gamma_t} + \overline{q}\frac{\partial \omega_{t+1}(\gamma_t)}{\partial \gamma_t} = 0 \quad (5.6)$$

where we used the fact that $\partial D_t(\gamma_t)/\partial \gamma_t = -D_t(\gamma_t)/\gamma_t$ according to (5.2). The first term of (5.6) describes the direct wage effect of unskilled immigration on domestic workers. It is positive for skilled workers and negative for unskilled workers since $\partial w_t^H/\partial \gamma_t > 0$ and $\partial w_t^L/\partial \gamma_t < 0$. The second term is positive (and larger for skilled workers) because the dependency rate (5.2) falls with an increasing number of incoming workers. This implies that contribution rates can be lowered which increases net income. The third term is negative and identical for both groups, H and L. Therefore, immigration has more positive effects for skilled workers than for unskilled workers, who have to face an additional negative wage effect in addition to the negative pension effect. Only the decrease in contribution rates benefits the unskilled. Applying the median-voter theorem we can thus conclude that skilled workers favor a larger immigration ratio than unskilled workers which makes the unskilled workers the median-voter group since retirees prefer zero immigration (we exclude the possibility that one of the three groups in society has a majority of votes).

We can now determine the optimal immigration ratio chosen by the median voter. For an explicit solution, we define the elasticities of wages with respect to unskilled immigration in period t as follows:

$$\eta^i \equiv \frac{\partial w_{t+1}^i}{\partial \gamma_t} \cdot \frac{\gamma_t}{w_{t+1}^i}$$

where η^L is the elasticity of the unskilled worker's wage, η^H is the elasticity of the skilled workers' wage and η is the elasticity of the average wage ω (both in period t and $t+1$). We will assume the immigration elasticities to be constant over time. Let λ be the ratio of the average wage and the unskilled worker's wage: $\lambda \equiv \omega_t/w_t^L = 1 - \theta(w_t^L - w_t^H)/w_t^L > 1$.

Recalling that $D_t(\gamma_t) = 1/[(1+n_t)\gamma_t]$ and that $\omega_{t+1} = \theta w_t^H + (1-\theta)w_t^L$ with $\theta = H_t/(H_t + L_t + M_t)$ and using constant immigration elasticities, we can rewrite $V_{\gamma_t}^L$ from (5.6) as

$$\eta^L \left[1 - \frac{\overline{q}}{(1+n_t)\gamma_t} \right] + \frac{\overline{q}}{(1+n_t)\gamma_t} + q\eta\lambda = 0.$$

Solving for γ_t gives the median voter's preferred immigration level which is stated in the following proposition.

Proposition 8 *Given the previously stated assumptions and given strictly negative elasticities η^L and η, the median voter chooses the immigration ratio*

$$\gamma_t^{Med} = \frac{\overline{q}(\eta^L - 1)}{(1+n_t)(\eta^L + q\eta\lambda)} > 0. \tag{5.7}$$

For elasticities being sufficiently small negative numbers, low fertility rates and λ not excessively high, γ_t^{Med} is greater than 1 such that a positive number of immigrants is chosen by the median voter.

The last part of the proposition follows immediately. Immigration elasticities are usually small negative numbers (see Friedberg and Hunt, 1995), so the numerator would be slightly larger than $\overline{q}$ in absolute terms while the denominator is smaller than $\overline{q}$ if we assume the fertility rate to be close to zero. Then, the entire term will be greater than 1.

However, our result is sensitive to parameter changes. An increase in λ which measures the income dispersion leads to a decrease in the preferred number of immigrants. Unskilled natives are afraid that immigration will worsen their income position even further. This is a widespread fear in many countries although immigration elasticities are actually low. Therefore, it seems that people may overestimate this effect.

The signs of the derivatives of the immigration ratio with respect to both immigration elasticities, η^L and η, are positive. Since the elasticities are negative, this implies that a smaller negative wage reaction to unskilled immigration allows for a higher equilibrium level of immigration to be preferred by the median voter. Furthermore, the derivatives of γ_t^{Med} with respect to the reproduction rate and the replacement rate have the expected signs. The more native offspring there are, the fewer immigrants are needed. Higher pension benefits per retiree require additional contributors who may be immigrants.

5.1.5 The Welfare Optimum

Suppose, instead of a majority rule, a government caring about the welfare of all living and yet unborn future generations. Then, we can simply consider a representative generation to describe the normative benchmark case of a utilitarian optimum which we denote by γ^{SO}. This implies that we maximize steady-state utility of an arbitrary generation by considering lifetime income of both skilled and unskilled workers:[4]

$$\max_{\gamma} W^{Gov}(\gamma)$$
$$= \left[L \cdot w^L(\gamma) + H \cdot w^H(\gamma) \right] \left[1 - \bar{q}D(\gamma) \right] + (L + H)\bar{q}\omega(\gamma) \quad (5.8)$$

The first-order condition which determines the socially optimal immigration policy γ^{SO} can now be compared to the median voter outcome. We get

$$L \left(\frac{\partial w_t^L}{\partial \gamma_t} [1 - \bar{q}D_t(\gamma_t)] + \frac{w_t^L \bar{q}D_t(\gamma_t)}{\gamma_t} + \bar{q}\frac{\partial \omega_{t+1}(\gamma_t)}{\partial \gamma_t} \right)$$
$$+ H \left(\frac{\partial w_t^H}{\partial \gamma_t} [1 - \bar{q}D_t(\gamma_t)] + \frac{w_t^H \bar{q}D_t(\gamma_t)}{\gamma_t} + \bar{q}\frac{\partial \omega_{t+1}(\gamma_t)}{\partial \gamma_t} \right) = 0 \quad (5.9)$$

Since we are interested in the difference between the social optimum and the median voter's optimal choice, it suffices to investigate the condition at the point where γ is optimally chosen by the median voter. This is the case when the first bracketed term in (5.9) becomes zero and thus fulfils optimality condition (5.6) for L. The terms that remain thereafter describe the deviation of the planner's solution from the median voter's choice and correspond to the optimality condition of the skilled workers. Immigration is expanded beyond the median-voter outcome as long as the benefits from higher wages and from lower contribution rates exceed the cost of a lower pension income received by skilled workers. We already know that skilled workers prefer a higher immigration ratio than unskilled workers. Hence, the democratically adopted immigration policy given by the median voter's choice, γ^{Med}, is too small compared to the social optimum: $\gamma^{Med} < \gamma^{SO}$.

This result can be explained by the fact that the welfare of a representative generation is the average welfare of all its members, hence, optimal immigration policy should be averaged over these members' preferred levels.

This approach is justified because it cannot be foreseen whether a yet unborn person will become a skilled or an unskilled worker in the future.

5.2   SOCIAL DISTANCE

If one follows the public and political debate on immigration in most countries, there are arguments which are clearly non-economic. Several reasons are put forward why immigration should not take place or should at least be strictly limited. Empirical evidence shows that non-economic explanations for attitudes towards immigration or immigrants may dominate economic explanations (see, for example, Dustmann and Preston, 2002; Krueger and Pischke, 1997; Mayda, 2003).

Hillman (2002) suggests a possible explanation for these findings. He argues that there may be a sense of identity among citizens of a particular country which 'can be an impediment to immigration if people feel that their identity is diminished by the presence of foreigners' (Hillman, 2002, p. 216). If social norms and customs of immigrants are different from the ones of the domestic population, that is, if a 'social distance' between immigrants and natives exists, natives may be reluctant to support immigration policy as strongly as before.

We can now apply Hillman's approach to our baseline model. Suppose that the domestic citizen i maximizes his utility according to the following utility function:

$$U^i = V^i(\gamma) + W(B(\gamma)) \qquad (5.10)$$

where V^i denotes the income during i's remaining lifetime and $B(\cdot)$ is a measure of the benefit from (homogeneous) social norms and customs, as suggested by Hillman (2002). $W(\cdot)$ is a well-behaved concave utility function which is identical for all groups in society. $B(\gamma)$ is a continuous function of the immigration ratio, that is, the relation between the number of immigrants and the total national population defined in (5.1). With an increasing number of immigrants social norms become more and more distorted from a native's perspective, so we assume $\partial B/\partial \gamma < 0$. The derivative of W with respect to B is positive ($\partial W/\partial B > 0$), which implies that the more homogeneous are social norms, the higher is the utility.

Let us first consider the group of retirees which maximizes $U^R = V_t^R(\gamma_t) + W(B_t(\gamma_t))$. For simplicity we assume a first-time vote on immigration, thus B_t does not depend on γ_{t-1}. During retirement the retirees' income V^R simply equals the pension benefit $\bar{q}\omega_t(\gamma_t)$. Hence, the first-order condition of the retirees becomes

$$\frac{\partial U^R}{\partial \gamma_t} = \bar{q}(\gamma_t)\frac{\partial \omega_t}{\partial \gamma_t} + \frac{\partial W}{\partial B_t}\frac{\partial B_t}{\partial \gamma_t} = 0. \qquad (5.11)$$

Due to the fixed replacement-rate regime there are only negative terms in the first-order condition, the previously derived negative average-wage effect and a negative effect from distorted social norms. Therefore, as in the baseline model, retirees will choose to have no immigration at all.

Let us now consider the working generation which maximizes

$$U^i = V^i_t(\gamma_t) + W\left(B_t(\gamma_t), B_{t+1}(\beta\gamma_t)\right), \quad i = L, R, \quad (5.12)$$

where B_{t+1} is the level of social norms prevailing in period $t+1$. It depends on today's immigration as well because people still feel a disutility from distorted social norms after one period. However, people get somewhat accustomed to the changing social norms after a while, so past immigration from period t will change B_{t+1} only by a fraction $\beta \leq 1$. If we assume that the effect on social norms is the same in both periods t and $t+1$, we can simply write $W\left(B((1+\beta)\gamma_t)\right)$.

Again, we can show that the median voter is in the group of unskilled workers because the main distinction between a skilled and an unskilled worker is the wage effect which leads to a higher preferred immigration ratio for skilled workers whose increasing scarcity is reflected by a positive wage effect. To find the median-voter outcome we consider the lifetime income of the unskilled which is given by

$$V^L(\gamma_t) = w^L_t(\gamma_t)\left[1 - \bar{q}D_t(\gamma_t)\right] + \bar{q}\omega_{t+1}(\gamma_t).$$

The first-order condition for an optimal immigration ratio is

$$\frac{\partial U^L}{\partial \gamma_t} = \left[\frac{\partial w^L_t}{\partial \gamma_t}(1 - \bar{q}D_t(\gamma_t)) - \frac{w^L_t \bar{q}D_t(\gamma_t)}{\gamma_t} + \bar{q}\frac{\partial \omega_{t+1}}{\partial \gamma_t}\right]$$
$$+ (1+\beta)\frac{\partial W}{\partial B}\frac{\partial B}{\partial \gamma_t} = 0. \quad (5.13)$$

We can easily see that the bracketed term in (5.13) is just the optimality condition from the baseline model. But we now have two additional effects. First, there is the same negative effect from distorted social norms that retirees have to face. All groups in society are hit by this distortion to the same degree. Second, there is an additional negative effect which becomes relevant as in the next period there is a stock of immigrants living in the country. Hence, there is a further distortion of social norms although it is less pronounced. While there is still scope for immigration due to a positive counter-effect from falling contribution rates (and, for the skilled, from wages), the preference for immigration is unambiguously reduced compared to the baseline model.[5]

5.3 LABOR MARKET RIGIDITIES

So far, we have assumed flexible labor markets such that immigration can change the marginal productivities of skilled and unskilled labor. Many countries, however, exhibit to a smaller or larger degree rigidities in the labor markets. Keeping this in mind, it is understandable that a major concern of domestic workers is the increase in unemployment due to immigration. We will investigate in the following what impact on the voting outcome we can expect if there are some rigidities which create unemployment.

Let us consider a simple framework in which unskilled immigration has no impact at all on unskilled workers' wages.[6] Hence, the labor market is rigid in the sense that the unskilled worker's wage is inflexible, that is, $w_t^L = \overline{w}_t^L = const$. Given $\overline{w}_t^L$, a corresponding labor demand can be derived, assuming that there is no unemployment before immigration. Any additional unskilled worker entering the labor market can therefore only either substitute for another worker holding a job or become unemployed. Hence, the total number of immigrants allowed into the country equals the number of unemployed persons but not all immigrants will necessarily become unemployed. Let $\pi = L_t/(L_t + M_t)$ be the probability of becoming employed. Due to the substitution of unskilled workers, the ratio of skilled and unskilled workers remains unchanged such that the skilled worker's wage will not be influenced by unskilled immigration. This implies that the average wage in period t remains unchanged compared to the pre-migration situation. If perfect assimilation holds in the sense that there is a share of $M/(H + L + M)$ unemployed persons in period $t + 1$ as well, then the average wage will not be influenced by immigration at any time.

Unemployed persons receive an unemployment benefit u which is financed by contributions c. Let us assume an unemployment insurance scheme in which only unskilled workers are members because the scheme is relevant only to them.[7] The insurance system's budget equation is assumed to be balanced:

$$c \cdot w_t^L \cdot L_t = u \cdot M_t. \tag{5.14}$$

Let us briefly investigate whether the unskilled worker is still the median voter here. If the average wage in t does not change and q is fixed, retirees will be indifferent with respect to immigration and will therefore choose not to vote or to 'toss a coin', that is, on average half of them will vote in favor of and the other half against immigration. Hence, the larger group in society will have the majority of votes. As we assumed $L_t > H_t$, the group of unskilled workers will decide the vote.

For the optimization problem we now have to consider the expected income of the native unskilled workers as they may or may not become unemployed after immigration has taken place:

$$V^L(\gamma_t) = \pi \cdot \overline{w}_t^L [1 - \overline{q}D_t(\gamma_t) - c] + (1 - \pi)u + \overline{q}\omega_{t+1}. \quad (5.15)$$

Making use of $u = c \cdot w_t^L \cdot L_t / M_t$, $\pi = L_t/(L_t + M_t)$, $D_t(\gamma_t) = 1/((1+n_t)\gamma_t)$ and $M_t = (H_t + L_t)(\gamma_t - 1)$, we can take the derivative with respect to γ_t which gives

$$V_{\gamma_t}^L = \frac{\partial \pi}{\partial \gamma_t} \overline{w}_t^L [1 - \overline{q}D_t(\gamma_t)] + \pi \frac{\overline{w}_t^L \overline{q} D_t(\gamma_t)}{\gamma_t} = 0, \quad (5.16)$$

where $\partial \pi / \partial \gamma_t < 0$, that is, the more immigrants there are, the smaller is the probability of becoming employed. Therefore, the first effect can be interpreted as the negative impact of immigration on the probability of earning an employee's full income. The second term is the familiar positive effect that immigration has on the contribution rate to the pension system. Notice that this effect is only partially taken into account. The reason is that contributions are only paid on income, not on unemployment benefits.

By comparing our result with the baseline model we find that the negative wage effect in period t disappears, only to be replaced by the negative unemployment effect. The positive contribution rate effect is reduced. The only significant change is the disappearence of the negative pension term. In order to get more information on this effect, let us assume that unemployment is persistent in the sense that at least some children of unemployed persons become unemployed themselves. In the pension system every citizen receives a basic pension, regardless of whether he was employed or unemployed during his working life. In the extreme, each unemployed person has exactly n unemployed children (this is just the perfect assimilation assumption). This implies that there are $H + L + M$ retirees in period $t + 1$ but only $H + L$ contributors to the pension system as there are M unemployed persons. The contribution rate to the pension system in that period has to rise in order to keep the pension system balanced. Some of the burden of unemployment is shifted to the next generation.

5.4 RETURN MIGRATION

A problem which is usually not considered in economic models of pensions and migration is return migration. However, return migration is an empirical fact and certainly not negligible (see Dustmann, 1996).[8] In this section, we will assume that any immigrant who enters the country will leave the country after one period and return to his home country to enjoy his retirement.

This is clearly a strong and somewhat unrealistic assumption but we will use this simplification to analyze the most extreme case of return migration that may occur. Two further assumptions will be made. First, by returning to their home country the former immigrants will take their children with them. An explanation for this may be that the children's residence permit is connected to their parents' stay in the host country. Another reason may be that parents are concerned about their children adopting a lifestyle perceived not to be in line with traditional views and cultural heritage (see Dustman, 2003). Second, return migrants keep their claims against the host country's pension system, that is, any pension benefits they receive are paid for by the former host country. This assumption is in line with EU regulations and common in international labor migration.

The consequences of these assumptions can best be seen from the budget equation of the host country's pension system. In period t, this equation is given by $\tau_t = q/[(1 + n_t)\gamma_t]$. In period $t + 1$, the group of retirees consists of all contributors to the pension system in period t, that is, $H_t + L_t + M_t$, since all of them acquired claims to pension benefits. However, due to return migration the number of contributors in $t + 1$ is reduced as the immigrants' offspring leave the country with their parents. This implies a major problem for the PAYG system as its functioning presupposes that each entrant to the social contract will not only support his parents but will also have children who will support him in old age. This is no longer the case here, thus the returning migrants' pensions have to be financed by the natives' offspring. We can now write down the equation for the contribution rate which prevails under these circumstances (assume $n_t = n_{t+1}$):

$$\tau_{t+1} = q\frac{H_t + L_t + M_t}{(1 + n_t)(H_t + L_t)} = q\frac{\gamma_t}{(1 + n_t)}. \qquad (5.17)$$

The derivative of τ_{t+1} with respect to immigration in period t is positive ($\partial\tau_{t+1}/\partial\gamma_t > 0$), which is no surprise under a pure fixed-replacement rate regime. The entire burden of return migration is to be carried by the next generation and no altruism of the retirees is assumed. The median voter in period t has no reason to care about the problems resulting from return migration. On the contrary, he will allow even more immigrants into the country. Recall the median voter's optimality condition:

$$\frac{\partial w_t^L}{\partial\gamma_t}[1 - qD_t(\gamma_t)] + \frac{w_t^L qD_t(\gamma_t)}{\gamma_t} + q\frac{\partial\omega_{t+1}(\gamma_t)}{\partial\gamma_t} = 0. \qquad (5.18)$$

The negative third term resulted from the assumption that the ratio of the factors of production, that is, skilled and unskilled labor, does not change from t to $t + 1$. Allowing immigrants into the country in period t will therefore have an impact on both ω_t and ω_{t+1} compared to the situation without immigration. With return migration, however, we also return to the skilled/unskilled labor ratio that prevailed before immigration took place in t. Hence, in the optimization problem of the median voter γ_t no longer affects ω_{t+1}. The third term vanishes and, since it was negative, more immigrants will be allowed into the country.

This can easily be seen if we solve the resulting first-order condition

$$\frac{\partial w_t^L}{\partial \gamma_t}\left[1 - \frac{q}{(1+n_t)\gamma_t}\right] + \frac{qw_t^L}{(1+n_t)\gamma_t^2} = 0 \tag{5.19}$$

for γ_t which gives

$$\gamma_t^{RM} = \frac{q(\eta^L - 1)}{(1+n_t)\eta^L} > 0 \tag{5.20}$$

which differs from γ_t^{Med} only by the term $q\eta\lambda$ which no longer shows up in the denominator. Hence, there is one negative effect missing in the return migration scenario and we can conclude that $\gamma_t^{Med} < \gamma_t^{RM}$.

One of the consequences of the fact that the contribution rate in $t+1$ increases is that a reaction of the young generation in $t+1$ to this increase becomes more likely. Possible reactions are to allow even more immigrants into the country in order to lower the contribution rate (which might cause a problem of social distance) or to exit the pension system by either substituting labor with leisure or by emigrating.

It might be the case, though, that it is impossible to raise the next period's contribution rate by the necessary extent because of institutional constraints. In that case, changes in the way the pension system operates are likely to be conducted such that the replacement rate is lowered to balance the pension system again. We may interpret this as a renegotiation of the generational contract in which some of the burden is shifted from the young generation born in $t+1$ to the retirees born in t.

This implies that the effects of immigration in period t still prevail. They will therefore be considered by the generation born in period t. The pension benefit in $t+1$, however, will consist of two parts. First, there is the fixed-replacement rate part which is still independent of immigration. This part of the burden caused by return migration is solely carried by the generation born in $t+1$. We will denote this constant term as P. The second part of the benefit is the share of the burden to be carried by the generation born in t. Here, it is easiest to think of the calculation of the benefit in terms of a fixed-contribution rate regime. Hence, regarding the total pension benefit we assume that there is a share ν, $0 \leq \nu \leq 1$, which follows a fixed-contribution rate calculation, and a share $1 - \nu$ based on a fixed-replacement rate calcuation. Voters are assumed to correctly anticipate ν.

The endogenous replacement rate of the fixed-contribution rate regime follows from rewriting (5.17) as

$$q_{t+1} = \tau \frac{(1+n)}{\gamma_t}. \tag{5.21}$$

The unskilled workers' optimization problem now becomes

$$\max_{\gamma_t} V^L(\gamma_t) = w_t^L(\gamma_t)\left[1 - qD_t(\gamma_t)\right] + \nu \cdot q_{t+1}(\gamma_t)\omega_{t+1} + (1-\nu)P \tag{5.22}$$

where the average wage does not depend on immigration due to the occurrence of return migration. The first-order condition turns out to be

$$V_{\gamma_t}^L = \frac{\partial w_t^L}{\partial \gamma_t}\left[1 - qD_t(\gamma_t)\right] + \frac{w_t^L qD_t(\gamma_t)}{\gamma_t} + \nu \frac{\partial q_{t+1}(\gamma_t)}{\partial \gamma_t}\omega_{t+1} = 0 \tag{5.23}$$

which differs from the baseline model by not having the negative average wage effect on the pension benefit. Instead, there is a negative effect on the replacement rate because of $\partial q_{t+1}/\partial \gamma_t = -\tau(1+n_t)/\gamma_t^2$. A priori, we cannot state which impact the substitution of two negative effects has on the optimal immigration level. Compared to the previous model with return migration there is clearly a reduction in the preferred immigration ratio as an additional negative effect has to be taken account of.

Solving (5.23) for γ_t leads to

$$\gamma_t^{RM2} = \frac{q(\eta^L - 1) + \nu\tau(1+n_t)^2\overline{\lambda}}{(1+n_t)\eta^L} > 0 \tag{5.24}$$

where $\overline{\lambda} = \omega_{t+1}/w_t^L$. This is smaller than γ_t^{RM} due to the positive term $\tau(1+n_t)^2\lambda$ which makes the numerator less negative. A comparison with γ_t^{Med} depends critically on the value of ν. If the renegotiation of the generational contract imposes a sufficiently large burden on the retirees in $t+1$, the positive effect of the disappearance of the average wage effect on pensions is more than offset. Then, γ_t^{RM2} is smaller than the median-voter outcome of the baseline model.

5.5   THE IMPACT OF THE SKILL DISTRIBUTION OF IMMIGRANTS' CHILDREN

So far, we assumed – according to the perfect assimilation hypothesis – that the skill distribution of natives' and immigrants' offspring remains unchanged from period t to $t+1$. Taking a closer look at this assumption we see that it implies that members of all groups in society must have children with the same skill level as themselves. Therefore, unskilled immigrants will always have unskilled offspring which does not seem to be a very realistic assumption. Often, highly educated immigrants enter the country and accept low-skilled jobs. One reason for this is that certificates and qualification levels are not acknowledged or not comparable in the target country or that because of initial difficulties in adapting to the new environment employers prefer native workers. However, it is highly unlikely that the offspring of these workers will only be unskilled. Another explanation is that unskilled immigrants want to offer their children a brighter future in a foreign country which induces the offspring to take their chances very seriously.

Let us make the following simplifying assumptions. Native workers' offspring will still have the same skill distribution as their parents, although there is a general tendency to higher degrees among them as well. The share β of the unskilled immigrants' offspring will become skilled while $1 - \beta$ remain unskilled, assuming $0 \leq \beta \leq 1$. These assumptions have an important consequence: the share of skilled workers changes in $t + 1$ and thus the ratio of skilled and unskilled workers changes. The wages of skilled and unskilled workers and the average wage will change as well due to immigration.

Again, we are not interested in the retirees' preferences as retirees face the same situation as in the baseline model which means that they prefer zero immigration. The optimization problem of the young generation is identical to the baseline model (5.5) but the average wage term $w_{t+1}(\gamma_t)$ is more complex now:

$$\omega_{t+1}(\gamma_t) = \tilde{\theta}(\gamma_t)w_{t+1}^H(\gamma_t) + (1 - \tilde{\alpha}(\gamma_t))w_{t+1}^L(\gamma_t) \qquad (5.25)$$

with

$$\tilde{\theta}(\gamma_t) = \frac{H_{t+1}}{H_{t+1} + L_{t+1}} = \frac{(1 + n_{t+1})(H_t + \beta M_t)}{(1 + n_{t+1})(H_t + L_t + M_t)} \qquad (5.26)$$

which is the share of skilled workers in the total population in period $t + 1$. The unskilled median voter's optimal immigration ratio is given by

$$V_{\gamma_t}^L = \frac{\partial w_t^L}{\partial \gamma_t}[1 - qD_t(\gamma_t)] + \frac{w_t^L qD_t(\gamma_t)}{\gamma_t} + q$$
$$\times \left\{ \frac{\partial \tilde{\theta}(\gamma_t)}{\partial \gamma_t}[w_{t+1}^H(\gamma_t) - w_{t+1}^L(\gamma_t)] + \tilde{\theta}(\gamma_t)\left[\frac{\partial w_{t+1}^H(\gamma_t)}{\partial \gamma_t} - \frac{\partial w_{t+1}^L(\gamma_t)}{\partial \gamma_t}\right]\right\}.$$
$$(5.27)$$

The first two terms are the familiar negative wage effect from unskilled immigration and the positive contribution rate effect. The bracketed term combines two second-period effects. The first part is the effect of today's unskilled immigration on the future skill distribution; the second part determines how the new skill distribution in $t + 1$ affects wages. For $\beta = H_t/(H_t + L_t)$ the bracketed term is zero because $\partial\widetilde{\theta}(\gamma_t)/\partial\gamma_t = 0$ and $\partial w_{t+1}^H(\gamma_t)/\partial\gamma_t = \partial w_{t+1}^L(\gamma_t)/\partial\gamma_t = 0$ as the ratio of skilled and unskilled workers does not change over time. The optimal immigration ratio that we can derive from this equation is $\gamma_t^S = \gamma_t^{RM} > \gamma_t^{Med}$ because here the future pension term vanishes as well.

Things are less obvious when we have a situation in which β deviates from $H_t/(H_t + L_t)$. Suppose β is greater than the share of skilled workers. Now, additional immigration will increase the share of skilled workers in period $t + 1$ compared to the pre-migration situation. This has two effects: first, $\widetilde{\theta}(\gamma_t)$ will increase $(\partial\widetilde{\theta}(\gamma_t)/\partial\gamma_t > 0)$ and the first term in the bracket will be positive as long as $w_{t+1}^H(\gamma_t) - w_{t+1}^L(\gamma_t) > 0$ which we will assume in the following. Second, a relatively higher share of skilled workers will have a negative effect on skilled workers' wages. The more immigrants there are, the closer to β the share of skilled workers will be (and the further away from $H_t/(H_t + L_t)$). Hence, the derivative $\partial w_{t+1}^H(\gamma_t)/\partial\gamma_t$ will be negative while $\partial w_{t+1}^L(\gamma_t)/\partial\gamma_t$ will be positive such that the second term in the bracket will be negative. For $\beta < H_t/(H_t + L_t)$, the argument is analogous but with reversed sign.

The intuition for these results is simple: as the number of unskilled workers increases after immigration, the share of skilled workers in both periods is reduced. In the next generation the share of skilled workers increases somewhat because a fraction of the immigrants' offspring is skilled. For a sufficiently large β the share of skilled workers will increase strongly. The positive implication of this is that there are more workers with high contributions to the pension system (first term in the bracket) but at the same time the wages of these contributors fall (second term), which again lowers the contributions collected. The total effect depends on the parameter values as they determine which effect dominates.

5.6   CHAPTER SUMMARY

Immigration has positive effects on the domestic pension system. Therefore, it is often argued that a more liberal immigration policy should be introduced for ageing societies. But despite the positive effect imposed by immigrants via a reduction in contribution rates, public opinion about immigration is mainly negative. In the year 2000, for example, it was even difficult to sell in Germany the idea of introducing 20 000 greencards for urgently needed, highly skilled IT specialists.

The previously introduced median-voter model gives some possible explanations for these findings and discusses the impact of additional factors on the voting outcome. Furthermore, it extends the existing literature on this issue, particularly Razin and Sadka (1999) and Scholten and Thum (1996), to a more realistic setting. In our model's basic version the fear that unskilled foreign workers may compete with or even substitute domestic workers and thus reduce gross wages will lead to less acceptance of immigration although empirically the impact on wages is rather small. As the unskilled median voter ignores any further positive effects of immigration on other groups in society, the preferred level of unskilled immigration is too small compared to the social optimum.

But the negative wage effect is only one of several potential factors influencing the median voter outcome that should be taken into consideration. Some factors are economic, such as the effects of return migration, unemployment or a changing skill distribution. We find that these factors may drive down the preferred immigration level even further. However, this may depend on the parameter values and on the question of who has to bear the burden. Return migration, for example, has no additional impact on the median voter if the median voter is able to let the following generation pay pension benefits to the former temporary immigrants. The possibility of shifting the burden to the next generation induces the median voter to choose an even higher immigration level as before. But even then, he ignores the fact that fellow members of his generation would gain from further immigration. However, as soon as the young generation has to carry some of the burden from return migration it will become more and more reluctant to support immigration.

The risk of becoming unemployed has a negative impact on the voting outcome. The existence of unemployment insurance does not help to restore the outcome of flexible labor markets. The reason is that the positive counter-effect from falling contribution rates benefits only those who are employed while the unemployed usually do not pay contributions (which could fall). On the other hand, a more favorable skill distribution among immigrants' children than among the immigrants themselves may reduce the negative effects somewhat.

Other factors are non-economic and seem to be particularly important in political debates. The distortion of social norms and customs through immigration can be shown to drive down the preferred immigration level significantly below the socially already too low level of the benchmark model. But it is also important to recognize that immigrants also impose non-economic gains such as an interesting diversity of cultures.

Even if economists usually emphasize the positive effects of immigration on the PAYG pension system via a positive externality, there are negative counter-effects to be taken into consideration. These may reduce the positive effects substantially. The situation is even worse in a democratic society if the median voter is negatively affected by immigration. In this case, socially optimal levels of immigration may not be achieved. This holds for the basic model as well as for extensions of the model.

NOTES

1. We assume that the dependency rate is usually smaller than 1 when immigration takes place. So, even if the population is ageing, this can still be compensated by a sufficiently high immigration ratio.

2. Notice that we do not have a defined-benefit system in the strict sense of having a lump-sum benefit (see Section 3.1.2). Fixing replacement rate q still allows varying pension benefits in the case of changing wages. Nevertheless, this is a realistic scenario. Usually, defined-benefit systems assume a 'basic pension' which covers (at least) subsistence level. In most countries, this level is defined as half of the average household income, that is, half of the average wage in our model. Therefore, $\bar{q}\omega_t(\gamma_t)$ appears to be a good approximation of the pension benefit in a defined-benefit system.

3. This is different in a three-generations model in which the middle generation is the median voter (recall Section 4.3). Decisions made by this group have an impact on the young generation which will be the next period's median voter. Nevertheless, the use of a two-generations model is possible here (in contrast to from the models in Section 4.3). The problem that the young generation wants to abolish the pension system because of an existing implicit tax does not apply here. A sub-group of the young generation benefits from intragenerational redistribution. Similar results can be found in Azariadis and Lambertini (2003), Conde-Ruiz and Galasso (2003) and Tabellini (2000). See also the surveys by Breyer (1994) and Galasso and Profeta (2002).

4. Notice that this – commonly used – welfare criterion applies to steady-state comparisons. During the transition to a new steady state the old generation may be hurt by immigration. In that case, all generations but one may be better off such that, for example, the Pareto criterion fails. At the same time, a Pareto-improving compensation of the old generation is not possible as we recall from Section 3.1.4.

5. The effects get even more pronounced if we consider a situation in which the next period's median voter is expected to vote in favor of at least some immigration (we excluded this expectation by the assumption of a myopic median voter). The young generation in period t would then certainly internalize this in its optimization problem as – in addition to the already existing stock of immigrants from period t – there will be further immigration and social norms become even more distorted. Clearly, these effects presuppose that some immigration took place in period t. As a consequence of this expectation, the young voters in period t will choose an

even lower level of immigration.

6. This assumption has also been made in Razin and Sadka (1995). See Kemnitz (2003) for a model with an explicit trade union setting. Neither model, however, is concerned with political-economy aspects.

7. Kemnitz (2003) shows that a system which also includes skilled workers leads to qualitatively identical results.

8. For example, between 1993 and 2000 the number of foreigners leaving Germany ranged around 600 000 persons per year; in 1997 and 1998 there were even more emigrants leaving Germany than immigrants entering Germany.

6. Voting on immigration when pension systems differ

In the previous chapter, we pointed out that immigration has a positive effect on the pension system and its members but that it also has other effects which may strengthen or weaken the gain from immigration. Depending on which groups in society are affected and to what extent, the voting outcome may be more or less favorable regarding immigration. However, the impact factors that were investigated in the previous chapter were not directly related to the pension system. Instead, they were mainly concerned with the individual behavior of voters (social distance, fear of unemployment) or immigrants (return migration, skill level of immigrants' offspring). Only changes in the marginal productivity of labor had an immediate effect on the pension system.

For this reason, it is interesting to investigate the voting behavior of the domestic population for different types of pension systems. Given an otherwise identical set-up, we ask whether a different design of the national pension system will lead to a different voting outcome. Will the median voter in a country with a Beveridgian pension system choose a higher, a lower or the same level of immigration as a median voter in a Bismarckian country? Who will be in favor of unskilled immigration in a country with a fixed-contribution rate pension system compared to a country with a fixed-replacement rate regime? Will the voting outcome be socially optimal? Answers to these questions will be given by the model (developed in Krieger, 2003) that will be discussed in the remainder of this chapter.

6.1 THE BASIC FRAMEWORK OF THE MODEL

6.1.1 A Brief Introduction to the Model and its Relation to the Existing Literature

Analogously to Chapter 5 we will formalize and extend the idea of immigration having different effects on different groups in society. For the same three groups in society as before (skilled and unskilled workers, retirees), we consider preferences with regard to the immigration of unskilled foreigners. The members of each group will choose the optimal level of immigration by maximizing the expected rest-of-life income, taking into account the effect of immigration on wages and pensions.

So far, the literature has not paid too much attention to the question of how pension systems should be modeled in migration-pension frameworks. This is a problem because models on immigration policy and public pensions take the pension system as exogenously given. If one changes the underlying assumption about the pension system, preferences with regard to immigration may change substantially. Here, the median-voter approach is used to give a reasonable first approximation to describing the central sources of disagreement among the different groups in society which stem solely from the differences in the underlying pension systems.

This aspect of modeling has been emphasized by Haupt and Peters (1998),[1] who show that in a pension system which fixes the contribution rate immigration benefits the retirees because total contributions and thus pension benefits increase. In a fixed-replacement rate regime, on the other hand, immigration is advantageous to the working generations because a constant total sum of pension benefits is financed by an increasing number of contributors. Hence, the contribution rate can be lowered. Most other models assume just one of the two scenarios described before. Razin and Sadka (2000), for example, assume only fixed-contribution rates while Scholten and Thum (1996) consider a fixed-replacement rate regime.

Because of the importance of the way the pension system is modeled we will follow the distinction made by Haupt and Peters (1998). We explicitly distinguish between pension systems which are either characterized by fixed contribution rates and endogenously determined replacement rates or those with fixed replacement rates and endogenous contribution rates. It should be noted once more that this distinction describes only polar cases. Most pension systems are not purely of one or the other type but have relatively less variation in either one of the two parameters. As in Chapter 5 our model differs in an important respect from Haupt and Peters (1998). Their model assumes just one skill group but three generations, namely young workers, middle-aged workers and retirees. Our model has two distinct skill groups and two generations.

In addition to the distinction between fixed-contribution rate and fixed-replacement rate systems we will classify pension systems along the lines of the Beveridgian and Bismarckian types. These concepts were introduced in Section 3.2 and can also be found, for example, in Bonoli (1997), Cremer and Pestieau (1998) and Werding (2003). Both types of pension systems are characterized by earnings-related contributions. In the

Beveridgian system, however, there is a flat benefit in old age which is independent of previous earnings. The system is both intergenerationally and intragenerationally redistributive. Workers with high incomes contribute relatively more to the flat benefit than workers with low incomes. In our stylized Bismarckian system the individual pension benefit is related to individual earnings during working age. While one would expect this system not to be redistributive, we will show that this may nevertheless be the case. The literature has not yet turned to the question whether the existence of Beveridgian and Bismarckian pension systems has different impacts on immigration policy. We will therefore investigate how the existence of either one of the two different pension systems changes the voting outcome.

Hence, in total four different scenarios have to be investigated. There is the Beveridgian pension system with either fixed contribution rate or fixed replacement rate and there is the Bismarckian pension system with the same two possible features. In the following, we will present all four different pension systems and determine their median-voter outcomes. This allows us to compare the effect of distinct types of pension systems on the voting decisions of domestic citizens with respect to unskilled immigration.

6.1.2   Modelling the Economy

Consider a small open economy which has access to the international capital market where the exogenous interest rate is given by r_t. In contrast to the general linearly homogeneous production function in Chapter 5, here the production function of the representative firm is a Cobb-Douglas aggregate of skilled and unskilled labor, H_t and L_t:

$$Y_t = H_t^\alpha \cdot L_t^{1-\alpha}. \tag{6.1}$$

Individual labor supply is given and normalized to one. Labor markets are competitive for both factors of production. Labor is paid its marginal product, w_t^H for the H_t skilled workers and w_t^L for the L_t unskilled workers. The average wage is given by ω_t as in Section 5.1.3 with $d\omega_t/d\overline{M}_t^L < 0$ since $w_t^L < w_t^H$ by assumption and with $\overline{M}_t^L$ being young unskilled immigrants. The median wage is $w_{m,t} = w_t^L < \omega_t$ as we assume $H_t < L_t$.

The number of immigrants is assumed to be non-negative. This assumption implies that there will either be positive or zero immigration but no emigration. Furthermore, we will assume immigration to take place only once in period t. Once a policy is approved it remains for at least two periods until all generations who voted on this issue have ceased.

In each period t there live two generations, workers and retirees. Population grows at rate n_t. This rate holds for all groups in society independent of people's skills or origin. Hence, we have $H_t = (1 + n_t)H_{t-1}$ and $L_t = (1 + n_t)L_{t-1}$, respectively. Specifically, immigrants adopt the growth pattern of the domestic population immediately after entering the country. The perfect assimilation hypothesis is assumed to hold.

Based on the post-migration production function

$$Y_t = H_t^\alpha \cdot \left(L_t + \overline{M}_t^L\right)^{1-\alpha}, \tag{6.2}$$

let us note explicitly some relevant derivatives for further reference:

$$\frac{dw_t^H}{dM_t^L} = \alpha \left(1 - \alpha\right) H_{t-1}^{\alpha-1} \cdot \left(L_{t-1} + M_t^L\right)^{-\alpha} > 0, \tag{6.3}$$

$$\frac{dw_t^L}{dM_t^L} = -\alpha \left(1 - \alpha\right) H_{t-1}^{\alpha} \cdot \left(L_{t-1} + M_t^L\right)^{-\alpha-1} < 0 \tag{6.4}$$

where we define $M_t^i := \overline{M}_t^i/(1 + n_t)$. Notice that using $t - 1$ variables is permissible here as the production function is linearly homogeneous. One can easily see that $\lim_{M_t^L \to \infty} dw_t^H/dM_t^L = 0$.

6.1.3 The Pension System

Two general types of pension systems, Beveridgian and Bismarckian, will be considered in the following. In a Beveridgian system there are flat-rate benefits while in a Bismarckian system benefits depend on previous earnings.[2] In each period t the workers' contributions to the Beveridgian pension system are related to individual earnings w_t^i, $i = H, L$. The pension benefit paid to the retirees in the same period, however, depends on average earnings ω_t. Thus, the pension system's budget constraint before immigration can be written as

$$\tau_t \left(w_t^H H_t + w_t^L L_t\right) = q_t \omega_t \left(H_{t-1} + L_{t-1}\right) \tag{6.5}$$

where q is the replacement rate and τ the contribution rate to the pension system.[3] Recall that the per-capita pension benefit is defined as $p_t = q_t \cdot \omega_t$. After immigration has taken place we get

$$(1 + n) \tau_t \left\{w_t^H H_{t-1} + w_t^L \left(L_{t-1} + M_t^L\right)\right\} = p_t \left(H_{t-1} + L_{t-1}\right).$$

Using the definition of the average wage this simplifies to

$$(1 + n) \tau_t \left\{H_{t-1} + \left(L_{t-1} + M_t^L\right)\right\} = q_t \left(H_{t-1} + L_{t-1}\right). \tag{6.6}$$

Notice that this equation does not depend on wages. This is a typical feature of models of Beveridgian pension systems in which only the relative size of generations determines the relation between contributions and benefits.

As in the Beveridgian system contributions in the Bismarckian PAYG pension system are related to individual earnings in each period t. Pension benefits, however, depend on the previous period's 'individual' earnings, that is, there are two types of retirees: those who were skilled workers before retirement and those who were unskilled before retirement. In a system with individual accounts individual pension benefits are given by $q_t w_{t-1}^H$ and $q_t w_{t-1}^L$, respectively. The pension system's budget constraint is

$$\tau_t \left\{ w_t^H H_t + w_t^L \left(L_t + \overline{M}_t^L \right) \right\} = q_t \left(w_{t-1}^H H_{t-1} + w_{t-1}^L L_{t-1} \right) \qquad (6.7)$$

after immigration has taken place. Notice that the same replacement rate holds for all groups within one generation.

The time structure of the model is the following. Individuals born in period $t-1$ retire in t and receive a pension benefit. Workers born in t contribute to the pension system. All contributions are transferred directly to the retirees. At the beginning of period t, that is, before a new generation starts to work, all generations vote on the number of immigrants, taking into account the effect of this decision on their rest-of-life income. Immigration according to the agreed policy takes place immediately after the vote. Production is then carried out with domestic workers and immigrants. Hence, immigration has an impact on all current variables (w_t^H, w_t^L, τ_t, q_t and p_t). Variables in $t-1$ and $t+1$ remain unchanged as we assume immigration to take place only in period t.[4] Past variables cannot be changed anymore in a subsequent period. Neither do future variables change because the relative size of groups of workers does not change from period t to $t+1$. This is because there is no future immigration[5] and because natives and immigrants have the same reproduction rate.

Furthermore, we assume that there is no impact on one of the current variables due to immigration if it is fixed by regulations of the pension system. Whether and how any one of these variables is involved in the individual optimization problem depends heavily on the type of pension system considered.

6.2   VOTING IN A BEVERIDGIAN SYSTEM

6.2.1   Fixed-contribution Rate Regime

Under a fixed contribution rate regime, the replacement rate q_t is endogenously determined while the contribution rate is fixed at level $\bar{\tau}$. This leads to the following equation which can be derived from the pension system's budget constraint (6.6):

$$q_t = \frac{\overline{\tau}(1 + n_t)\left\{H_{t-1} + \left(L_{t-1} + M_t^L\right)\right\}}{H_{t-1} + L_{t-1}} \tag{6.8}$$

where $(H_{t-1} + L_{t-1} + M_t^L)/(H_{t-1} + L_{t-1})$ is analogous to the immigration ratio γ_t in equation (5.1). From (6.8) it follows that the replacement rate q_t grows due to reproduction of the domestic population and due to immigration.

Let us now consider the preferences of domestic groups with regard to unskilled immigration. Members of the working generation maximize their lifetime income[6] which is composed of current net wage income, $w_t^i(1 - \overline{\tau})$, $i = H, L$, and the future pension benefit, p_{t+1}, assuming $M_t^L \geq 0$:

$$\max_{M_t^L \geq 0} w_t^i(1 - \overline{\tau}) + p_{t+1}, i = H, L. \tag{6.9}$$

As we assume a one-time migration decision and no further immigration in the future group sizes as well as average wages remain unchanged in t and $t + 1$. The replacement rate remains unaffected. To see this consider period $t + 1$. From (6.8) follows

$$q_{t+1} = \overline{\tau}(1 + n_{t+1})$$

given that $H_{t+1} = (1 + n_{t+1})H_t$ and $L_{t+1} = (1 + n_{t+1})\left(L_t + M_t^L\right)$. This term is independent of immigration.[7] Notice the importance of the fact that immigrants behave just like natives. They are assumed to have the same fertility rate as natives and thus they have just as many offspring to support themselves in old age. If fertility rates differ, n_{t+1} would possibly depend on current immigration.[8] Therefore, the optimization problem (6.9) reduces to maximizing the current net wage income, $w_t^i(1 - \overline{\tau})$, with respect to M_t^L given that immigration is non-negative.

The retirees maximize their pension benefit p_t with respect to the level of immigration M_t^L according to

$$\max_{M_t^L \geq 0} q_t \omega_t = \frac{\overline{\tau}(1 + n_t)\left\{w_t^H H_{t-1} + w_t^L \left(L_{t-1} + M_t^L\right)\right\}}{H_{t-1} + L_{t-1}} \tag{6.10}$$

where we have used (6.8) and the definition of ω_t. From the optimization problems of the three groups of voters the individual preferences for immigration can be determined:[9]

Proposition 9 (Krieger, 2003, pp. 57–8) *Under a Beveridgian pension system with fixed contribution rates, the final voting outcome depends on the relative sizes of the three groups of voters. Skilled workers and retirees are in favor of unrestricted unskilled immigration while unskilled workers prefer zero immigration.*

The intuition for this result is rather simple. Given that the contribution rate is constant and that today's immigration has no effect on future pensions due to perfect assimilation of immigrants, maximizing the current net wage income, $w_t^i(1 - \bar{\tau})$, implies that only the effect on the wage rate is relevant for the young generation. Hence, skilled natives gain from unskilled immigration as they become a scarcer factor of production and their wages increase. For unskilled natives the opposite happens.

Retirees face three different effects which have to be weighted. The first effect of unskilled immigration is the direct (positive) impact of additional contributors to the pension system's total sum of contributions. The second effect is the indirect (positive) effect on the pension system because wages of the skilled rise as they become relatively scarcer. The third effect is the indirect decrease in contributions due to falling wages of the unskilled workers. However, for a Cobb-Douglas production function with the usual properties the second and third effects just offset each other. This leaves only the first effect which eventually makes retirees vote in favor of unrestricted unskilled immigration. The reason for this is the positive externality from an increasing number of contributors. We can interpret this result as an increase in the total sum of wages due to the immigration of an additional unskilled worker. Immigration is just a different form of fertility (recall Section 3.3).

Unless there are extreme fertility patterns, making either the old (very few offspring) or the unskilled (extremely numerous unskilled offspring) a majority, no group in society can dominate political decision-making. A coalition of groups is necessary in order to achieve the final voting outcome. Obviously, the coalition of skilled workers and retirees determines the political outcome of unrestricted immigration.

6.2.2   Fixed-replacement Rate Regime

In the fixed-replacement rate scenario, the exact opposite scenario of the previous case is assumed. The replacement rate is fixed at a certain level while the contribution rate is endogenously determined. From the Beveridgian budget constraint (6.6) it follows that

$$\tau_t = \frac{\bar{q}}{(1 + n_t)} \frac{H_{t-1} + L_{t-1}}{H_{t-1} + L_{t-1} + M_t^L} \tag{6.11}$$

if unskilled immigration takes place. With a fixed replacement rate an increasing number of contributors due to domestic reproduction or immigration leads to falling contribution rates. The effect on the preferences for immigration is not unambiguous as we will see in the following. The reason is that unskilled workers face falling contribution rates as well as falling gross wages. A priori it is not clear which effect dominates and thus whether this group's net income increases or falls.

This can be seen from the unskilled worker's maximization problem. Again, each group of the working generation maximizes lifetime income in period t. We assume that the replacement rate is fixed at the same level in every period, that is, $\bar{q} \equiv \bar{q}_{(t)} = \bar{q}_{(t+1)}$. Hence, as in the fixed-contribution rate regime the future pension benefit does not play a role in the optimization problem of the myopic workers.[10] There is, however, another difference to the fixed-contribution rate regime: both the wage level and the contribution rate depend on M_t^L. Hence, $w_t^L(1 - \tau_t)$ is to be maximized.

Proposition 10 (Krieger, 2003, p. 60) *Under the Beveridgian pension system with fixed replacement rate, unskilled native workers choose a positive but restricted level M_t^{L*} of immigration which is determined by*

$$\frac{d\left(w_t^L(1 - \tau_t)\right)}{dM_t^L} = 0 \iff \bar{q} = G^{BV}(M_t^{L*}; \alpha, n). \tag{6.12}$$

Skilled native workers prefer unrestricted immigration while retirees reject immigration. The median voter outcome is determined by the unskilled workers' position.

The formal derivation of function $G^{BV}(M_t^L; \alpha, n)$ in (6.12) can be found in Appendix C. In order to show that the unskilled workers' choice is an interior solution, we can turn to a graphical analysis. Function $G^{BV}(M_t^L; \alpha, n)$ can be drawn as a curve in the $M_t^L - \bar{q}$ space (see Figure 6.1). Intuitively, each point on the curve gives the level of unskilled immigration that exactly balances the positive and negative effects of immigration on unskilled workers' lifetime income, given a fixed replacement rate $\bar{q}$ and other shift parameters (α, n). We find that the first two derivatives of $G^{BV}(M_t^L; \alpha, n)$ with respect to immigration are positive (see Appendix C), hence the G^{BV}-curve is upward sloping if we fix the level of the partial output elasticity α and the fertility rate at, say, $\bar{\alpha}$ and $\bar{n}$. This is because a higher replacement rate causes ceteris paribus a higher total pension benefit. To avoid increases in contribution rates, more contributors and thus immigrants are needed.

The replacement rate $\bar{q}$ is exogenously given. The $G^{BV}(M_t^L; \bar{\alpha}, \bar{n})$ curve intersects $\bar{q}$ from below at the immigration level M_t^{L*}, which we call the critical level of M_t^L. For certain parameter values no intersection will occur because G^{BV} will be above $\bar{q}$ at $M_t^L = 0$ and zero immigration is the preferred level. Additional immigration is the preferred policy choice of the unskilled workers as long as $\bar{q} > G^{BV}(M_t^L; \alpha, n)$ because it raises lifetime income as the positive effect on contribution rates exceeds the negative wage effect. At the critical level the positive effect of immigration on net wages turns into a negative one, that is, for $M_t^L < M_t^{L*}$ the decrease in contribution rates more than offsets the decrease in gross wages. Hence, up to the critical level of immigration there exists a preference for additional immigration. Any higher level of immigration than M_t^{L*} will lead to a rejection of further immigration. A lower level is preferred in this case. The critical level M_t^{L*} must therefore be an interior solution, unless we have a situation in which G^{BV} and $\bar{q}$ do not intersect at all. Only if $M_t^L = M_t^{L*}$, is there no incentive to change the level of immigration.

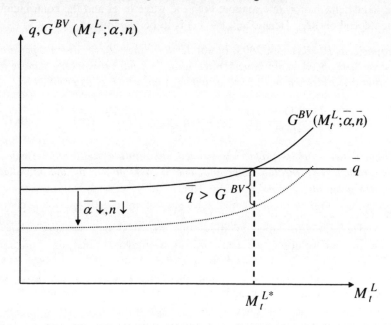

Source: Krieger (2003, p. 61).

Figure 6.1. *The unskilled workers' voting decision under the Beveridgian replacement-rate regime*

To gain some more insight into the preferences of unskilled workers we will consider some comparative statics, namely variations of $\bar{n}$, $\bar{q}$ and $\bar{\alpha}$. Let us assume that $\bar{q} = G^{BV}$ holds initially, that is, there is neither an advantage nor a disadvantage of immigration since net wages do not change. Function $G^{BV}(M_t^L; \bar{\alpha}, \bar{n})$ falls if either the reproduction rate $\bar{n}$ or the elasticity $\bar{\alpha}$ decreases.[11] Let us consider such a variation. We find that the $G^{BV}(M_t^L; \bar{\alpha}, \bar{n})$ curve shifts downwards and we get $\bar{q} > G^{BV}$ for M_t^{L*}. So again, additional immigration is wanted. The intuition for this result becomes clear if one recalls the definition of the contribution rate from equation (6.11). A decrease in the reproduction rate $\bar{n}$ increases the contribution rate because a constant total pension benefit is divided by fewer contributors. The higher contribution rate therefore leads ceteris paribus to a falling net wage. This negative effect can be offset by further immigration because this will increase the number of contributors and help to lower contributions per capita again.

A similar result follows from an exogenous variation of the replacement rate $\bar{q}$. At M_t^{L*}, an increase in $\bar{q}$ shifts the $\bar{q}$ line above the G^{BV} curve, so again $\bar{q} > G^{BV}$ and thus there is a preference for immigration. This can be explained from (6.11) as well: given an unchanged number of contributors a higher replacement rate increases total pension benefits unless immigration helps to relax the tax burden. Finally, if the partial elasticity of output α (with respect to skilled labor) decreases, the share of income of skilled workers and therefore their contributions to the pension system decrease. Hence, the average contributions of domestic workers decrease and contribution rates must increase. This problem can again be overcome only by the immigrants' additional contributions.

For skilled workers an unambiguous result can be derived. While unskilled workers have to weigh the positive effect of falling contribution rates with a negative wage effect, skilled workers' wage income increases for the given production function. Hence, they will support unrestricted immigration to their home country. Retirees maximize their pension benefits, $p_t = \bar{q}\omega_t$, with respect to immigration. Since the replacement rate is fixed, only the effect of immigration on the average wage matters. Because the average wage falls due to unskilled immigration retirees will reject unskilled immigration. Both skilled and unskilled workers gain at the expense of the retirees. In a model without different skill groups the (single) young generation will clearly be in favor of immigration.

According to the median voter theorem which ranks the alternative preferences with respect to the level of immigration, the median level is given by the unskilled workers' choice. The preferences of skilled workers and retirees will not gain a majority of votes. Hence, the final voting outcome is an interior solution in which a non-negative but restricted level of immigration is chosen.

Table 6.1 gives a summary of the results for the Beveridgian system. While the group of skilled workers gains in any case from unskilled immigration, comparing the fixed-contribution rate and the fixed-replacement rate regime we find that a change from one system to the other will turn the incentive to vote in favor of immigration upside down. In the fixed-contribution rate regime the retirees gain from increasing pension benefits while the unskilled workers face falling wages. Just the opposite holds for the fixed-replacement rate regime: the retirees now lose from falling average wages which are used to calculate their pension benefits. The unskilled workers still face falling wages but gain at the same time from falling contribution rates. From their perspective restricted immigration (up

Table 6.1. *Preferred level of immigration and voting outcome in the Beveridgian system*

Level of immigration in a Beveridgian system	Fixed-contribution rate regime	Fixed-replacement rate regime
Unskilled workers	zero	restricted $(0 < M_t^{L*} < \infty)$
Skilled workers	unrestricted	unrestricted
Retirees	unrestricted	zero
Voting outcome	unrestricted	restricted $(0 < M_t^{L*} < \infty)$
Compared to social optimum?	too high	too low

Source: Krieger (2003, p. 63).

to an optimal level) is favorable.

The voting outcome under neither of the two pension regimes corresponds to the social optimum, as described in Sections 4.1.2 and 5.1.5. While the young median voter internalizes all future contribution and benefit payments, he nevertheless does not take into account that there is another group of young voters with different preferences. Here, the group of unskilled workers ignores the fact that skilled workers prefer a higher level of immigration under both regimes. Socially optimal would have been to use a weighted average of both groups' choices. Hence, under the fixed-contribution rate regime the level of immigrants is too high compared to the social optimum while under the fixed-replacement rate regime it is too low.

6.3 VOTING IN A BISMARCKIAN SYSTEM

6.3.1 Fixed-contribution Rate Regime

From the budget constraint of the Bismarckian pension system (6.7) we derive the following equation for the replacement rate under a fixed-contribution rate regime:

$$q_t = \frac{\bar{\tau}(1 + n_t)\left(w_t^H H_{t-1} + w_t^L \left(L_{t-1} + M_t^L\right)\right)}{w_{t-1}^H H_{t-1} + w_{t-1}^L L_{t-1}} \tag{6.13}$$

Workers maximize today's net income, taking into account that their expected pension benefits in the second period are related to today's gross wages w_t^i which depend on immigration today. The optimization problem is

$$\max_{M_t^L \geq 0} \ w_t^i(1 - \bar{\tau}) + q_{t+1} \cdot w_t^i, \quad i = H, L. \tag{6.14}$$

It is important to investigate how the next period's replacement rate q_{t+1} behaves. According to (6.13), we get

$$q_{t+1} = \frac{\bar{\tau}\left(w_{t+1}^H H_{t+1} + w_{t+1}^L L_{t+1}\right)}{w_t^H H_t + w_t^L \left(L_t + M_t^L\right)} \tag{6.15}$$

where $H_{t+1} = (1 + n_{t+1})H_t$ and $L_{t+1} = (1 + n_{t+1})\left(L_t + M_t^L\right)$. Recall that we assumed no future immigration and that all groups of workers (including immigrants) have the same fertility rate. This implies that the relative group sizes do not change from period t to period $t + 1$. Hence, the marginal productivities of skilled and unskilled labor remain unchanged as well, that is, $w_t^i = w_{t+1}^i$. In (6.15) the bracketed terms can therefore be cancelled, leaving us with $q_{t+1} = (1 + n_{t+1})\bar{\tau}$. The unskilled worker's lifetime income turns out to be

$$w_t^L(1 - \bar{\tau}) + (1 + n_{t+1})\bar{\tau}w_t^L = w_t^L(1 + \bar{\tau}n_{t+1}), \tag{6.16}$$

that is, it consists of labor income and the contribution to the pension system compounded by the biological interest rate n_{t+1}. Based on maximizing (6.16) we can state the following proposition.

Proposition 11 (Krieger, 2003, p. 65) *Under a Bismarckian pension system with fixed contribution rates unskilled native workers reject immigration while skilled workers and retirees support it. The final voting outcome is therefore to support unrestricted immigration.*

Workers decide on immigration analogously to their decision under the Beveridgian system[12] because the effect of immigration on the pension benefit is a normal wage reaction. A wage reduction for unskilled labor implies also a reduction of the future pension benefit $q_{t+1} \cdot w_t^L$. The opposite holds for skilled workers.

The retirees simply maximize their expected post-migration pension benefit which is $p_t^i = q_t \cdot w_{t-1}^i$, $i = H, L$. It is necessary to use the i-index on the pension variable because the Bismarckian system is characterized by individual accounts. The pension benefit of formerly skilled retirees is related to the previous period's wages for the skilled. For formerly unskilled workers the analogous argument applies. The possibility of different votes on immigration policy has to be taken into account.

While w_{t-1}^i is determined in the past and not affected by immigration, closer inspection of q_t in (6.13) shows that (i) only the numerator is affected by immigration and (ii) the direct wage effects cancel out due to the Cobb-Douglas assumption. The maximization problem is equivalent to the Beveridgian one (one has to maximize $w_t^L M_t^L$) and leads to the same voting outcome, except that we have two distinct groups of retirees here but all group-specific terms will cancel out. Hence, both skilled and unskilled retirees will vote in the same way and favor unrestricted immigration. Hence, we can join the two groups of retirees to just one group as in the Beveridgian pension system. The reason for this surprising result is that pension benefits are calculated with respect to wages in the pre-immigration period $t - 1$. Immigration in t has an impact only on the replacement rate q_t which improves. Because q_t is the same for all retirees, the optimal immigration level guarantees that both $p_t^H = q_t w_{t-1}^H$ and $p_t^L = q_t w_{t-1}^L$ are maximized. Hence, the pension system is Bismarckian only in the sense that the basis upon which to calculate pensions, that is, the previous period's wage income, differs between workers. We can therefore conclude that there is no major difference in the outcome between Beveridgian and Bismarckian pension systems under the fixed-contribution rate regime. Theoretically, there is no need to explicitly distinguish between the two systems.

There is a further implication of the model that should be noted. We would expect that in our stylized Bismarckian system with individual accounts no intragenerational redistribution takes place. However, this may not be true because of a transmission effect via the joint replacement rate q_t. Let us imagine that there exist two distinct pension systems for skilled and unskilled workers with different replacement rates, say q_t^H and q_t^L. If unskilled immigration takes place in t, the wage of the skilled workers increases. With fixed contribution rates total contributions of the skilled and therefore the fictitious replacement rate q_t^H increase. Formerly skilled retirees gain from this effect because $p_t^H = q_t^H w_{t-1}^H$ increases. At the same time the wages of the unskilled workers decrease. In terms of total contributions of the unskilled this negative effect is partially offset by a higher number of contributors due to immigration. We can expect that in general the fictitious replacement rate q_t^L of the unskilled workers differs from q_t^H (this is not the case in the Cobb-Douglas scenario).

Assuming now that both groups are forced into a joint pension system, although replacement rates differ initially, implies that intragenerational redistribution between formerly skilled retirees and formerly unskilled retirees takes place even in the stylized Bismarckian system. Consider $q_t^H > q_t > q_t^L$, then redistribution takes place from skilled to unskilled workers. The pension benefit of the skilled decreases from p_t^H to $p_t^{H\prime} = q_t w_{t-1}^H$ while it increases for the unskilled.

6.3.2 Fixed-replacement Rate Regime

Fixing the replacement rate turns the system's budget constraint to

$$\tau_t = \frac{\overline{q}\left(w_{t-1}^H H_{t-1} + w_{t-1}^L L_{t-1}\right)}{(1+n_t)\left(w_t^H H_{t-1} + w_t^L \left(L_{t-1} + M_t^L\right)\right)}. \tag{6.17}$$

The fixed replacement rate goes along with different contribution rates for different periods. We have $\overline{q}_t = \tau_t(1+n_t)$ and $\overline{q}_{t+1} = \tau_{t+1}(1+n_{t+1})$ with $\overline{q} \equiv \overline{q}_{(t)} = \overline{q}_{(t+1)}$ and $\tau_t \neq \tau_{t+1}$. The differing contribution rates are of no concern for today's selfish generation, though. As before workers in period t maximize their lifetime income which is given by

$$w_t^i(1 - \tau_t) + \overline{q}_{(t+1)}w_t^i = w_t^i(1 + \overline{q} - \tau_t), \quad i = H, L. \tag{6.18}$$

As with the Beveridgian fixed-replacement rate regime both wage and contribution rate effects have to be considered. We will state the voting outcome for this pension regime in the following proposition. The formal derivation will be presented in Appendix C.

Proposition 12 (Krieger, 2003, p. 67) *Under the Bismarckian pension system with fixed replacement rate unskilled native workers choose a positive but restricted level of immigration M_t^{L**} which is given by*

$$\frac{d\left(w_t^L(1 + \overline{q} - \tau_t)\right)}{dM_t^L} = 0 \Longleftrightarrow \overline{q} = G^{BS}(M_t^{L**}; \overline{\alpha}, \overline{n}). \tag{6.19}$$

Skilled workers prefer unrestricted immigration while formerly skilled and unskilled retirees are indifferent with respect to immigration. For $H_t < L_t$ the unskilled workers' choice will be the median-voter outcome.

From lifetime income (6.18) we can conclude that three effects of immigration on native workers have to be considered. The term $(1 + \overline{q})$ describes a combination of two negative effects from falling wages due to immigration. On the one hand, today's wage income decreases. On the other hand, future pension benefits fall because the basis on which to calculate the benefits, today's gross wage, decreases while the replacement rate remains unchanged. A positive effect from immigration is the falling contribution rate. These effects can be combined in function $G^{BV}(M_t^L; \overline{\alpha}, \overline{n})$, which is again the starting point for a graphical analysis to derive the interior solution. The interpretation of $G^{BS}(M_t^L; \overline{\alpha}, \overline{n})$ is analogous to the one for $G^{BV}(M_t^L; \overline{\alpha}, \overline{n})$, that is, the curve is the locus in which positive and negative immigration effects on unskilled workers' lifetime income balance for given levels of $\overline{q}$ and the shift parameters.

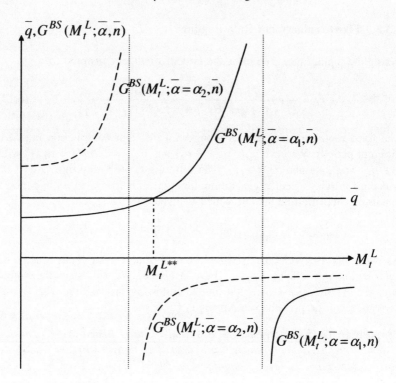

Source: Krieger (2003, p. 69).

Figure 6.2.   *The unskilled workers' voting decision under the Bismarckian replacement-rate regime*

Function $G^{BS}(M_t^L; \overline{\alpha}, \overline{n})$ is somewhat more complex than function $G^{BV}(M_t^L; \overline{\alpha}, \overline{n})$. This can also be seen from Figure 6.2. For a given α the function $G^{BS}(M_t^L; \overline{\alpha}, \overline{n})$ has two branches, one of them lying in the lower right quadrant of the coordinate system. This effect can only formally be shown, as for very large levels of immigration $G^{BS}(M_t^L; \overline{\alpha}, \overline{n})$ suddenly becomes negative. However, as this branch has no reasonable economic meaning we will not discuss this problem at length.[13] Even for rather extreme parameter values the negative branch starts only at very large levels of immigration which exceed the number of natives by far.

This leaves us with the branch of the function that lies in the positive quadrant. For sufficiently low values of M_t^L, $G^{BS}(M_t^L; \overline{\alpha}, \overline{n})$ increases with unskilled immigration. As long as immigration is below a critical value M_t^{L**} the positive effect from decreasing contribution rates due to immigration offsets the two negative effects related to falling gross wages. If, however, $M_t^L > M_t^{L**}$ the negative effects dominate and zero immigration is the voting outcome. Hence, we get a similar result as in the Beveridgian regime: for sufficiently low immigration rates unskilled workers are in favor of additional immigration. For too high rates they vote against further immigration. We therefore get an interior solution with some optimal positive level of immigration.

However, these results again depend critically on the chosen parameter values. The comparative statics show the same results as in the Beveridgian scenario: a lower birth rate, a lower elasticity α or a higher replacement rate ceteris paribus make the pension system costlier to the domestic population. The curves shift accordingly. Hence, there is an incentive to vote in favor of additional immigration. In Figure 6.2, we see that too high values of the output elasticity α lead to a situation in which no point of intersection exists. This is the case for α_2, but not for α_1 when $\alpha_2 > \alpha_1$. The optimal choice of unskilled workers is therefore zero immigration since $\bar{q} < G^{BS}(M_t^L; \bar{\alpha}, \bar{n})$ for any positive level of immigration.

Lemma 13 (Krieger, 2003, pp. 68–9) *Compared to the Beveridgian pension system under the Bismarckian system the critical level of immigration will be lower ($M_t^{L*} > M_t^{L**}$). If unskilled native workers vote for zero immigration this is more likely to happen under the Bismarckian system.*

These results follow easily from the fact that unskilled native workers face the additional negative effect from unskilled immigration on future pension benefits. It makes additional immigration under the Bismarckian system less attractive to domestic unskilled workers than under the Beveridgian system. A numerical analysis for different parameter values confirms this result.

Skilled workers again gain more, the higher the number of unskilled immigrants. They benefit from three different positive effects. The first two effects follow from the fact that skilled labor becomes scarcer and therefore wages increase. Today's earnings and future pension benefits increase. The third effect is again lower contribution rates.

The retirees maximize their pension benefit, which is $p_t^L = \bar{q} \cdot w_{t-1}^L$ and $p_t^H = \bar{q} \cdot w_{t-1}^H$, respectively. Since the replacement rate is fixed at $\bar{q}$ and the previous period's wages are not affected by today's immigration, retirees from both groups remain indifferent. They neither gain nor lose from unskilled immigration such that they can be ignored in the voting decision. The voting outcome depends only on relative group sizes. As we assume that there are more unskilled than skilled workers, the unskilled workers will be the majority and will vote against immigration.

Table 6.2 summarizes the results for the Bismarckian regime. Comparing the results from this section with those from Section 6.2.2, we find that skilled workers are clearly in favor of unskilled immigration because they will gain due to both higher wages and lower contribution rates. In the

Table 6.2.   *Preferred level of immigration and voting outcome in the Bismarckian system*

Level of immigration in a Bismarckian system	Fixed-contribution rate regime	Fixed-replacement rate regime
Unskilled workers	zero	restricted $(0 < M_t^{L**} < \infty)$
Skilled workers	unrestricted	unrestricted
Retirees (formerly unskilled)	unrestricted	indifferent
Retirees (formerly skilled)	unrestricted	indifferent
Voting outcome	unrestricted	restricted $(0 < M_t^{L**} < \infty)$
Compared to social optimum?	too high	too low

Source: Krieger (2003, p. 70).

Bismarckian pension system they additionally gain from increasing pension benefits. The retirees behave differently depending on the assumed pension system: in the Beveridgian system they vote against immigration because the average wage which is the basis for calculating pension benefits falls. In the Bismarckian system the basis of calculation is the previous period's wage which remains unaffected by immigration. Therefore, Bismarckian retirees are indifferent with regard to unskilled immigration.[14]

Although the argument is slightly different for the Beveridgian and the Bismarckian pension systems, we find that the unskilled workers are decisive for the voting outcome. In the Beveridgian system the median voter comes from the unskilled group while in the Bismarckian system the unskilled are the majority because the retirees do not participate in the election. Under both scenarios there are positive and negative effects of unskilled immigration on lifetime income. Unskilled workers gain from falling contribution rates and lose from falling gross wages. Assuming that all other variables are the same under both regimes, the additional negative wage effect on future pension benefits makes unskilled workers vote in favor of even less immigration under the Bismarckian system compared to the Beveridgian system ($M_t^{L**} < M_t^{L*}$). For the same reasons as in Section 6.2.2 the social optimum will not be achieved.

Finally, a possible extension of the model appears to be worth mentioning although it is not explicitly modeled. Consider a country with a Bismarckian system with fixed replacement rate. Assume that unemployment insurance exists and that unskilled immigrants replace unskilled native workers one by one because they slightly undercut natives' wages. Natives do not mind becoming unemployed though as they receive an equal transfer income from unemployment insurance or from welfare which is financed by the skilled (this is different from Section 5.3). This phenomenon can in fact be observed (see Sinn, 2002a). In terms of the voting outcome, as described in Table 6.2, this implies that both unskilled workers and retirees will be indifferent with respect to unskilled immigration while skilled workers will reject it. The reason is that, on the one hand, there is no longer a positive wage effect (the proportion of skilled and unskilled workers does not change) and on the other hand contributions to the unemployment-insurance system increase. The final voting outcome is therefore to reject unskilled immigration entirely, an even stronger result than before.

6.4   CHAPTER SUMMARY AND DISCUSSION

In Section 3.2, we argued that there exist different types of PAYG pension systems. We asked in this chapter whether these differences have an impact on the voting decisions of the citizens. Hence, we investigated the impact that different pension systems have on the outcome of a voting decision on immigration policy, given a median-voter model with three groups of voters: skilled workers, unskilled workers and retirees. Pension systems are either Beveridgian or Bismarckian with either fixed contribution rates or fixed replacement rates.

Under a fixed-contribution rate regime the increasing number of contributors due to immigration raises total revenues, which can be used to pay higher pension benefits to retirees. The working generations either gain or lose from immigration depending on whether they become the scarcer or the more abundant factor of production. As we have assumed unskilled immigration, unskilled workers are worse off from immigration while skilled workers are better off. These results hold regardless of whether we assume a Beveridgian or a Bismarckian pension system. Hence, we find that in both cases there is a majority of voters (skilled workers and retirees) who are in favor of immigration while only the unskilled workers vote against it. The voting outcome is to have unrestricted unskilled immigration.

Under the fixed-replacement rate regime the result is less obvious. Given the total pension benefit in this case, immigration leads to falling contribution rates. Skilled workers will clearly gain from unskilled immigration because of lower contribution rates and higher wages as they become the scarcer factor of production. For retirees a fixed replacement rate does not in any case guarantee unchanged pension benefits. Under the Beveridgian scenario benefits are calculated with respect to average wages, which fall due to immigration. Beveridgian retirees are against immigration while Bismarckian retirees remain indifferent.

The decisive voter under this regime is the unskilled worker, who faces opposing effects from unskilled immigration. If immigration is sufficiently low, the positive effect from falling contribution rates dominates the negative gross wage effect. If immigration is high, the opposite holds. The level of immigration will therefore be raised until both effects offset each other, that is, there exists an optimal positive level of immigration. There are some combinations of parameter values in which the negative impact on wages is always dominant. This is much more likely to happen under a Bismarckian system than under a Beveridgian system because falling wages have an additional negative effect on future pensions.

We can conclude that it makes a substantial difference whether one considers a pension system with fixed-contribution rates or with a fixed replacement rate. Incentives to vote in favor of immigration change for different groups under one or the other regime. At the same time, it does not make too much difference whether the system is Beveridgian or Bismarckian. The voting outcome and the incentives of the groups remain basically unchanged. Furthermore, we find that the voting outcome does not correspond to the social optimum. The social optimum is a weighted average of the preferred immigration choices of both skilled and unskilled workers. The voting outcome, on the other hand, is either determined by a coalition of skilled workers and retirees which excludes unskilled workers and leads to too much immigration or by the unskilled workers alone, which ignores the skilled workers' preferences for a higher number of immigrants.

To a certain degree these results are reflected in the positions of political parties and in the voting behavior of some groups. However, one has to be very careful here since there may be causality problems. Conservative parties often have relatively old members and supporters. Regarding pension issues their programs tend to be attractive to retirees and cohorts near retirement age. At the same time, these parties are usually not strong supporters of immigration flows. Left-wing parties not only have younger supporters but also a more liberal position regarding immigration. Parties with a trade-union background have to take care that immigration does not have negative wage and income effects which harm their typical voters.

Taking the assumptions of the model for granted, predictions about immigration policies in different countries should be possible, at least with regard to pension policy. In the last couple of years there was a tendency in many countries to tighten the link between contributions and benefits as we will argue in the next chapter. These countries' pension systems became more Bismarckian. Some countries like Sweden or Poland moved from a DB to a DC, that is, a fixed-contribution rate, regime. From our findings we expect that Bismarckian countries are becoming more reluctant to allow unskilled immigrants into the country while the new DC countries should become more liberal. Hence, depending on whether a move towards a Bismarckian system is accompanied by a move towards a DC system we can expect a more restrictive immigration policy or an ambiguous result which depends on the strength of the opposing effects.

Our exercise faces some limitations. First, our results depend on the use of Cobb-Douglas production technology, which is especially important for the size of wage effects. One also needs the assumption of the perfect assimilation hypothesis and the assumption of one-time immigration. Second, the voters must know which pension system they live in before they can reasonably decide on immigration issues. In the real world the distinction between the four different pension regimes is less clear-cut than shown in the model.

NOTES

1. This model has been introduced more thoroughly in Section 4.3.
2. The formal definition of Beveridgian and Bismarckian pension systems used in this paper follows Casamatta et al. (2000a); see also Section 3.3.3. We employ, however, a slight modification in the definition of the Bismarckian pension benefit by assuming that the benefit is related to previous (instead of current) wages.
3. We assume implicitly that the payroll tax rate of the Beveridgian system and the contribution rate of the Bismarckian system are equivalent. We will in both cases refer to it as contribution rate τ.
4. It should be noted that in the case of a Beveridgian pension system this assumption can be interpreted as myopic behavior of the young generation. Future immigration decisions are made by future generations. So, today's workers are myopic in the sense of believing that their immigration decision does not have an impact on the next generation's immigration decision. They will not consider future decisions in their maximization problem. In the Bismarckian system, in principle the same argument applies. However, future pension benefits are directly related to today's wage income. This is a fact that is known to all workers and can therefore not be ignored in the decision problem.
5. One gets the same result if the ratio of skilled and unskilled immigrants is the same as the ratio of skilled and unskilled natives (see Section 5.5).
6. We assume the discount rate between two periods to be zero.
7. This is also the reason why myopic voters will not consider future pension benefits in their maximization problem. It depends on variables which myopic workers believe they cannot influence. Hence, they will not include p_{t+1} in their optimization problem.
8. If we assume a different growth rate for immigrants, we can expect a conflict between domestic and incoming persons. For example, if immigrants have a

lower population growth rate than the natives, then the contributions per retiree raised in $t + 1$ are lower than without immigration. Some of the contributions raised from the natives will be shifted to retired immigrants. This will have an impact on the voting outcome.

9. The formal derivation of this result is briefly outlined in Appendix C.

10. Implicitly, a fixed-replacement rate implies that contribution rates may differ in both periods, that is, $\tau_t \neq \tau_{t+1}$. This is, however, not a concern for the workers because it will hurt only the next generation.

11. The respective derivatives are given in Appendix C.

12. See Appendix C to see that the same derivation of the optimum applies.

13. Details are nevertheless given in Appendix C.

14. Notice that for this common type of pension system the problem that the old generation may be hurt during the transition to a new steady state (see note 4 in Chapter 5) does not apply because retirees are at least indifferent with respect to immigration.

7. Redistribution and labor mobility

In Chapters 3 through 6 international labor mobility mainly took the form of immigration to a country. Our focus was the question of how immigrants affect national pension systems. In order to model this effect we assume away what immigrants think about the host country's pension system. It may be the case that they are not too happy about it. But even if this were the case, often other reasons to enter the country dominate. Implicitly we therefore assume that there is a rather steady inflow of workers to the host country which generates a positive externality to the host country's pension system.

Only rarely have we mentioned so far that citizens of typical target countries for immigrants may leave their home country as well. There is a variety of reasons why persons leave their home countries, one of them being differences in taxes and social systems. If countries are otherwise very similar, these differences may play an important role. Particularly in border regions richer people may consider moving to the neighboring country because of lower social security contributions and taxes. Poor people may be attracted by more generous transfer payments on the other side of the border. As these issues are most relevant in the context of the European Union, special emphasis will be given to this region in the following discussion.

Whenever individuals are internationally mobile the question arises whether migration flows caused by these differences will lead to a welfare improvement or whether they will generate inefficiencies. Answers to this question have been given by the theory of fiscal federalism or – considering countries and their social systems – by the theory of systems competition. The goal of this chapter is to introduce the basic arguments of these theories. Then, we will turn to the more specific question whether the results of these theories can also be derived when dealing with pension systems in open economies. Answers will be given by reviewing some of the recent literature on public pensions and labor mobility which will help us to understand a fundamental conflict regarding the desirability of policy harmonization between nations. Based on this knowledge, we will be able to investigate EU regulations on labor mobility and pension policy in the next chapter.

7.1 REDISTRIBUTIVE POLICY IN OPEN ECONOMIES

7.1.1 A General Fiscal Federalism Argument

The fiscal federalism theory provides criteria for the optimal level of government (centralized or decentralized) to which each public economic function should be assigned in a federation or an economic union. It deals, among other things, with such topics as tax competition in which countries compete for (highly) mobile factors of production. The systems competition theory is a very similar approach to tax competition theory. However, it implies much more fundamental changes for the countries and often takes a long time due to the large aggregates involved (see Sinn, 2003), for example, a country's entire social system instead of single parameters like tax rates. Since the general outcomes of both theories are equivalent, one can argue that systems competition is also a branch of fiscal federalism theory.[1]

The theories have some strong implications with regard to the level of redistribution in general.[2] Before we turn to redistribution within pension systems, we will give a brief outline of these arguments. The theory of fiscal federalism assumes a fundamental conflict. On the one hand, there are heterogeneous individuals who demand different amounts of public goods according to their preferences. The individual (private) provision of public goods, on the other hand, is inefficient due to the properties of the public good (non-excludability, non-rivalry). Public provision of public goods requires the inclusion of all users of the public goods, regardless of their individually preferred amount. In a sense, a uniform supply of public goods meets a heterogeneous demand (Kolmar, 1999, p. 45). Given this restriction, governments in each jurisdiction within an economic union like the EU have to optimally choose the level of the public good that maximizes regional welfare. Different jurisdictions may therefore provide different levels of the public good.

Even if jurisdictions are very small and placed at the lower end of the (national) governmental hierachy, for example, at the level of districts, the amount of public good may still be too uniform for some inhabitants. If the public good is social welfare requiring some redistribution (Pauly, 1973), there will always be some poor and some rich individuals with opposed preferences. The poor in a jurisdiction that has decided for a low level of social welfare would prefer the higher amount of this public good that may be offered in some other jurisdiction. Rich persons from the second region like the first region better and move in the opposite direction.

As long as there is no mobility between jurisdictions no problem arises because no interregional spillovers or externalities occur. If borders are open and people are (in principle) mobile but nobody moves, everybody's preferences regarding the public good seem to be met perfectly. This is Tiebout's (1956, 1961) world in which each individual has moved to the jurisdiction in which the supply of public goods is optimal from an individual's perspective (voting by feet). If necessary, this requires as many jurisdictions as there are individuals.

The more likely scenario, however, is that people start to migrate. This will have a direct effect on the possible level of redistribution in each jurisdiction. Having a relatively lower level of redistribution than other countries makes a jurisdiction less attractive to net recipients of the welfare system. At the same time lower taxes or contributions are attractive for net contributors, that is, rich individuals. If the change in contribution rates takes place unilaterally in only one country and if people are (perfectly) mobile, poor people would like to leave the country while rich people enter it. The potential transfer volume per recipient and thus national welfare increases. As all countries in an economic union face the same incentives, in equilibrium the level of redistribution will be sub-optimally low. The countries are caught in a prisoners' dilemma because international migration turns out to be harmful to them.

The reason is that public goods and redistribution cause interregional spillovers or externalities which result in migration. Increasing the level of redistribution in one region imposes a positive externality on other regions because due to migration these regions will have more rich contributors and less costly poor recipients in their welfare system. For less redistribution the opposite holds. What fiscal federalism theory tells us is that if there are many jurisdictions with different levels of public-good provision and if individuals are mobile interregionally, then either the differences in the redistributive system have to be levelled in order to eliminate the migration incentive or the public good has to be provided for a region that is sufficiently large to exclude the possibility of inefficient migration. This implies for the EU that if interregional spillovers from welfare systems occur leaving the responsibility for social policy at the level of member states (or even lower levels) may not be the optimal solution. Instead, one might think of transferring these competences to the next higher level, that is, to the EU.

7.1.2 A Simple Model of Fiscal Federalism

Let us briefly show in a very simple model which effects labor mobility has on redistributive systems[3] such as the pension system. Consider a small country with two types of (full-time) workers, skilled and unskilled, which are internationally immobile initially. We assume that this country and all other countries in the world are identical in all respects. In particular, each of them has a PAYG pension system which levies the same implicit tax on the workers. While intergenerational redistribution is obviously taking place, there may or may not be intragenerational redistribution. If there is intragenerational redistribution, it will be the same for all countries.[4]

Now we assume that the country under consideration unilaterally plans to increase the level of intragenerational redistribution unilaterally, for example, by increasing the flat-rate part of the pension benefit. If the skilled workers become perfectly mobile (unskilled workers remain immobile), they will immediately start to migrate to other regions because they want to avoid the higher implicit tax levied on them in comparison to an unskilled worker. Let us therefore assume for simplicity that the implicit tax is simply a per-unit tax τ imposed only on skilled workers.

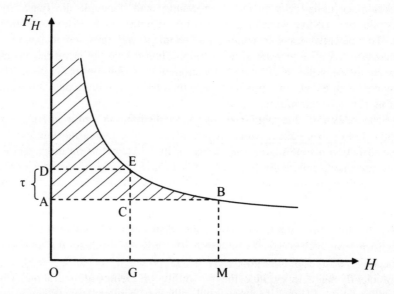

Figure 7.1.   The effect of international labor migration on redistribution

Two effects can be derived within this framework. First, for a small country the tax has no effect on skilled workers' after-tax income as they avoid taxation by migration. Second, the efficiency cost of taxation is therefore borne by the immobile unskilled workers alone. To see this, consider a constant returns-to-scale production function with two factors of production: $Y = F(H, L)$, where L is the number of unskilled workers and H the number of skilled workers at work in the country. This has to be distinguished from $\overline{H}$, the number of skilled natives. If both factors are immobile, their net-of-tax incomes are given by

$$Y_L = F_L + \tau \frac{H}{L} \quad \text{and} \quad Y_{\overline{H}} = F_H - \tau.$$

Redistribution via the tax or pension system equalizes net-of-tax incomes in the social optimum. Figure 7.1 represents the marginal productivity of skilled workers. The wage bill of skilled workers is given by rectangle $ABMO$ if no taxation takes place while the wage bill of unskilled workers is given by the shaded area. If skilled workers are mobile, they can always earn a fixed after-tax wage $\tilde{\omega}$, corresponding to A, on the world labor market. Let the tax τ be equal to DA, then a new equilibrium with F_H at level D is reached. Only G skilled workers remain in the country, that is, $\overline{H} - H$ skilled workers emigrate. All skilled workers earn a net wage independent of the tax. The immobile unskilled workers lose because the transfers they receive are smaller than their loss in wage income. The efficiency loss they have to carry is EBC. Notice that this welfare loss is a consequence of (inefficient) labor mobility alone, which is driven by differences in the redistributive systems. Redistribution becomes unsustainable under these circumstances.[5] In terms of the pension system this implies that no additional redistribution should be introduced by allowing for intragenerationally redistributive provisions if workers are internationally mobile.

7.1.3 Inefficient International Labor Allocation

The inefficient outcome caused by labor mobility can also be shown by considering the international allocation of labor in a model with two factors of production, K and N. Different implicit tax rates lead to an inefficient international labor allocation. If we make the simplifying assumptions that there are two countries, A and B, and that initially marginal productivities of labor and implicit taxes T_t^{imp} equalize internationally, a sudden increase in the tax rate in one of the countries, for example, through an increase in life expectancy, would create an incentive to leave this country. The young and mobile segment of the population would (at least in part) move to the country with the lower tax burden until the net incomes equalize again. As a consequence the marginal productivities of labor will fall apart such that the allocation of labor between the countries is no longer efficient and a welfare loss will occur. The migration incentive from the pension system may be characterized as artificial because it is not caused by productivity differences.

Figure 7.2 shows the effect graphically. The marginal productivity curves F_N^A and F_N^B intersect initially at F and determine the optimal international labor allocation N^* between countries A and B. However, in country A there exists a PAYG pension system which imposes an implicit tax on income. Accordingly, the marginal productivity curve is shifted downwards. Given the initial labor allocation N^*, a net income differential of $\overline{FJ}$ exists and induces some workers in country A to move to country B. Eventually, a

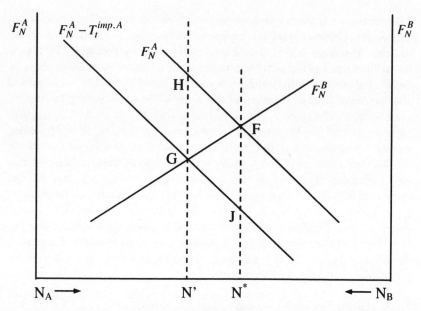

Figure 7.2.   International labor allocation and inefficient migration when a PAYG pension system exists

new equilibrium is reached at G where

$$F_N^A - T_t^{imp,A} = F_N^B.$$

The new labor allocation is given by N'. Because $F_N^A \neq F_N^B$ the allocation of labor is inefficient. The pension system in country A causes an inefficient (e)migration incentive. The welfare loss is given by the triangle FGH.

7.1.4   The Selection Principle

From a more general perspective, however, we cannot conclude that driving down redistributive measures is a problem per se. If redistribution takes place based on, for example, some rent-seeking or lobbying activity, systems competition may help to restore efficiency. Just as Tiebout (1956, 1961) argues, governments compete for workers by offering attractive tax and contribution rates. Their competition is analogous to competition in private markets and leads to an international welfare optimum. A problem arises, however, when government activity takes place according to the 'selection principle' (Sinn, 1997, 2003) and becomes unsustainable in systems competition. The selection principle states that the government steps in where the markets fail, for example, if there exist public goods or externalities or if asymmetric information leads to adverse selection. Then, the government does not replicate private activity but offers activities which will not be offered in private markets. This holds in particular for important fiscal activities by the state such as the redistribution of incomes. The main threat is that systems competition may drive down the redistributive system too far. There will be a less than optimal level of redistribution.

Recall our argument from Section 3.3.1 that low reproduction rates in many countries may be the consequence of existing PAYG pension systems because positive externalities are generated to childless individuals. In this case, the government often introduces incentives for child-bearing in the pension system. Erasing these incentives to comply with systems competition may worsen the situation of the pension system even further.

7.2 PENSION POLICY IN OPEN ECONOMIES – NOTES ON THE LITERATURE

The previous section has extracted two main consequences from the theory of redistributive taxation in open economies. First, the optimal level of redistribution is not sustainable in open economies with labor mobility because net contributors to the system have an incentive to avoid taxation by emigration. Second, if redistribution between mobile and immobile individuals is no longer sustainable, the burden of continuing redistributive measures has to be carried by immobile factors alone. In the following, we will investigate whether these results also apply to pension policy in open economies.[6] Two strands of the literature will be compared in order to show a fundamental conflict regarding policy harmonization. We will start by reviewing some general-equilibrium models that emphasize the role of policy harmonization to overcome efficiency losses from harmful labor migration. Then, we will consider public choice arguments which question the welfare-improving role of harmonization. The reason for this is that the political power of the old generation is no longer restricted by an exit option for the young generation.

7.2.1 Policy Harmonization and Global Efficiency

From the previous discussion we know that national governments may be forced to adjust their redistributive systems if factor mobility increases. Migration may turn out to be inefficient if it is driven solely by differences in the redistributive systems. In order to avoid the welfare losses that can be expected to occur under these circumstances, policy harmonization appears to be a possible countermeasure. It is hoped that this will help to maintain or to restore global efficiency.

Starting with Homburg and Richter (1993) some research has been done on general-equilibrium models which deal with the question of whether there is a need to harmonize social security contributions within an economic union like the EU. In their model the underlying pension system is a very simple PAYG system with contribution $\tau_t w_t$ per worker (N_t) and benefits $p_t w_t$ per retiree (N_{t-1}). A fixed-contribution rate regime is assumed, hence the pension system's budget equation is given by $p_t = \bar{\tau} \cdot D_t^{-1}$. Depending on the chosen contribution rates, pension benefits differ across countries. Workers are assumed to be mobile. Migration is a means of equalizing differences in lifetime utility between countries.

For an interregional equilibrium all migration incentives must be removed, that is, expected lifetime income must be equal in the countries under consideration, say A and B. Expected lifetime income is the sum of labor earnings and the implicit tax generated by the pension system. Hence, it is simply the right-hand side of the intertemporal budget constraint (3.14) of an individual born into a PAYG system. Furthermore, the allocation of labor is interregionally efficient if marginal productivities of labor are equalized in both regions. Hence, the condition for an efficiency-enhancing interregional equilibrium can be written as:

$$\bar{\tau}^A \cdot \left(\frac{r_{t+1} - n_{t+1}^A}{1 + r_{t+1}} \right) = \bar{\tau}^B \cdot \left(\frac{r_{t+1} - n_{t+1}^B}{1 + r_{t+1}} \right). \tag{7.1}$$

From (7.1) we can conclude that a time path of the allocation of people is interregionally efficient if and only if either one of the two following conditions holds: (i) $\bar{\tau}^h = 0$ for $h = A, B$, that is, the PAYG pension system is converted into a fully funded one,[7] or (ii) $\bar{\tau}^A = \bar{\tau}^B$ and $n_{t+1}^A = n_{t+1}^B$, that is, both contribution rates and expected population growth rates have to be equal across countries. This result can be achieved only coincidentally: population growth usually differs substantially between countries.

The harmonization of contribution rates is not sufficient to avoid inefficient migration here. Hence, national PAYG pension schemes will lead to an inefficient allocation of labor across countries because existing differences in the rates of return of the pension systems still create an artificial migration incentive. Labor is not allocated according to marginal productivities alone. Homburg and Richter conclude that only the integration of all pension systems can avoid these migration incentives.

Taking up Homburg and Richter's argument, Breyer and Kolmar (2002) come to a different conclusion. They find that the harmonization of contribution rates is actually sufficient for efficiency under the given assumptions. Homburg and Richter (1993) argued that the inefficiency comes from the fact that identical contribution rates go along with differing reproduction rates. But under perfect mobility from the first period of labor mobility onwards an efficient distribution of workers is reached if one assumes a constant size of each generation in the entire federation. This is because with harmonized contribution rates, perfect foresight and mobility of workers in each future period, it is a consistent belief of the individuals to assume that the country's population will not change in the future ($N_t^h = N_{t+i}^h \; \forall \; i \geq 1, h = A, B$) as this would distort the efficient allocation of workers.

In their model, Breyer and Kolmar (2002) furthermore relax the assumption of perfect mobility by introducing an immobile population segment. They find that depending on the assumed future mobility patterns, different policy requirements may be necessary to reach an efficient labor allocation. The harmonization of contribution rates may or may not be a necessary and sufficient condition for interregional efficiency. Often coordination has to be decided on 'before' migration but the coordination schemes depend on 'post-migration' marginal productivities. Therefore, it is the temporal structure of the problem and the underlying information structure that make it almost impossible to calculate the correct coordination scheme ex ante. We will return to these findings in the next chapter.

Regarding tax harmonization Breyer and Kolmar (2002) find that (in an unrestricted labor mobility framework) there is a strategic incentive to deviate unilaterally from any voluntary coordination agreement between different countries. A benevolent national planner who seeks to maximize national welfare chooses, by construction, the contribution rate that is optimal from his country's point of view, neglecting, however, external effects on other countries. This will not happen if a benevolent world planner chooses a single contribution rate in a consolidated pension system.

One should note that the results of the models discussed here strongly depend on the assumption of a place-of-residence principle of the pension systems (as is common in Europe), that is, the place of residence determines the pension system of which an individual becomes a member. Clearly, this may induce migration incentives if systems differ or change and when individuals decide to opt out of the existing social contract in their home country. Inefficient allocations due to national pension policies may be overcome if a dynastic origin principle is introduced as advocated by Sinn (1990). Each individual will choose a pension system at the beginning of his (working) life and has to stick to it later on. As the decision is once and for all time there is no longer the opportunity to escape from high implicit taxation. Then, all migration decisions will depend only on market wages in the different countries because all externalities of migration are fully internalized. Marginal productivities of labor will be equalized if all markets are competitive (see Kolmar, 1999, pp. 148–52) and the international allocation of labor will be efficient.

This is the same outcome that can be achieved if a consolidation of national pension systems to a unified European system takes place. A major difference between the two solutions is that the consolidation does not allow for any differences between countries and might, as argued above, conflict strongly with individual preferences. With the origin principle there is at least some choice left although at a very (possibly too) early stage in life. Highly risk-averse people could, for example, choose to live in a country with substantial redistribution while other less risk-averse individuals decide in favour of a country with a low level of redistribution. On the other hand, the practicability of this concept is very doubtful because this important decision demands too much from most people, particularly at a young age.

A second way of avoiding inefficiencies is to introduce a transfer system between member countries of an economic union, analogous to the one proposed by Wildasin (1991) for the case of static redistribution. This allows social security policy to remain as a national policy task. Workers who choose to reside in a low-contribution-rate country will cause a transfer from the host to the home country, which is used to compensate workers living in the country with high contribution rates. If an optimal transfer level is determined, the allocation of labor will not be distorted despite differing contribution rates (see Hange, 2001, pp. 113–4, or Kolmar, 1999, p. 152–5, for explicit solutions). This again does not seem to be a very realistic option because some countries will turn out to be net payers of transfers over long time intervals. These countries will hardly support a transfer system such that no unanimous vote, as required in the EU, in favor of the system can be expected.

7.2.2   Migration as a Restriction of the Power of Gerontocrats

Even successful policy harmonization that restores efficiency has some drawbacks. Public choice models for closed economies – such as Browning (1975) and succeeding models – assume that young workers have no influence on the political decision since they are not the median-voter generation. Therefore, older generations (gerontocrats or those close to retirement) have the power to introduce a suboptimally high level of redistribution. In contrast to this, the open-economy model by Haupt and Peters (2003) assumes that the young generation has an exit option. If the tax burden in the home country is getting too large, the young may emigrate to a neighboring country.[8] This limits the power of gerontocrats in a small open economy. National pension policy is endogenously determined and limited by the increasing labor mobility of the young.

A two-fold voting process is assumed for each country in the model:

first, there is a political decision ('voting by hand') on the amount of intergenerational redistribution, and second, the young generation will 'vote with its feet' on whether it will accept the redistributional decision. Haupt and Peters (2003) use a two-generations model with a simple PAYG pension system. The contribution rate is the exogenous choice variable of the retirees; the pension benefit is endogenously determined. Hence, for each country we have $p_t = \bar{\tau} \cdot w_t \cdot D_t^{-1}$ with D_t greater than 1 as we assume gerontocratic regimes in both countries ($N_{t-1} > N_t$). The two parts of the voting process have offsetting effects: the majority of retirees vote in favor of an increase of $\bar{\tau}$ while the minority of workers respond with emigration which causes an increase in the dependency rate (that is, D_t^{-1} falls). Hence, depending on the emigration elasticity,[9] retirees in the two countries will choose their payoff, that is, their pensions, like revenue-maximizing duopolists in Bertrand competition, holding constant the other country's contribution rate. By lowering the price, that is, the contribution rate, they induce higher demand. More workers enter the country and the dependency rate improves.

If one assumes myopic individuals, this framework is similar to the literature on tax competition, especially to the case of commodity taxation with Leviathan governments and mobile consumers (see Kanbur and Keen, 1993). Contribution rates are equivalent to taxes and lead to the well-known results from the literature on tax competition.[10] One finds a symmetric Nash equilibrium with identical contribution rates if the old generations are the same size in both countries. In this case, the gerontocrats have a strong incentive to harmonize contribution rates at a suboptimally high rate because with a single contribution rate in all countries workers cannot escape taxation through emigration. Hence, in the context of this model, harmonization turns out to be harmful because the old generation is no longer restricted by the young generation's exit option.

If the old generations differ in size, the 'larger' country will choose a higher contribution rate. This is because the migration elasticity is higher in a small country. Lowering the rates in the small country will decrease the total contributions collected from the natives only by a small amount. At the same time a large amount of additional contributions can be raised from immigrants if the small country undercuts its neighbor. The gain is sufficiently high to offset the losses. This reasoning is simply reversed for the large country. Due to the fact that the small country has positive net immigration, the median voter in the small country receives a higher pension benefit than the neighbor median voter. Contributions per retiree are higher than in the large country.

An additional element enters the model by assuming rational individuals who anticipate the effect of today's decisions on their future pension payments. The Nash contribution rates are higher than in the case of myopic migrants. A high contribution rate today (which benefits today's retirees) forces many workers to emigrate to the other country. Due to this, the number of retirees in the next period will be low (then, the country is small).[11] However, the retirees in a small country receive higher pension benefits than the retirees in a large country. Hence, today's workers are less averse to high rates since they expect higher pensions in the next period. This induces an incentive to raise contribution rates in the first period.

These results are clearly in contrast to the discussion in the previous section where a benevolent world planner tries to avoid inefficient migration by eliminating artificial migration incentives such as different implicit tax rates. A consolidation or harmonization is an appropriate means to achieve this goal. From Haupt and Peters' (2003) model, on the other hand, we learn that migration and social competition may be disadvantageous for a gerontocratic median-voter generation. Pensions are unambiguously reduced compared to the case without labor mobility. Interregional coordination can then be used to improve the median voter's position.

Comparing the normative and positive approaches in the models discussed above one can conclude that the benevolent planner approach neglects the fact that policy coordination has to be supported by the populations of all member countries if we realistically assume democratic societies. Policy coordination by benevolent planners assumes that no group of individuals in any of the countries will be worse off. The positive analysis in Haupt and Peters (2003), however, shows that coordination is just a means for the old generation to improve their situation at the expense of the young generation.[12] This is certainly not a Pareto improvement in the strict sense that all individuals (including the working generation) are made better off.

Basically, this discussion boils down to the question of whether one believes that less competition (consolidation, origin principle) or more competition (no coordination) leads to stronger distortions when compared to the efficient outcome. In the first case, the lack of escape possibilities allows the political process to play a dominant negative role; in the second case, inefficient migration causes benevolent national governments to behave in harmful ways from a world-planner perspective. Clearly, there is always hope that a consolidated European pension system would be administered by benevolent politicians but some caution seems to be appropriate.

Between the two polar cases of having hardly any competition and having strong competition, the principle of delayed integration, suggested by the Wissenschaftlicher Beirat beim Bundesfinanzministerium (2000),[13] might be a promising middle course. Here all migrants within and from outside the EU are allowed to enter the destination country's welfare system only after a delay of some years. Before that, they remain members of the welfare systems of their home countries such that during the first years redistributive measures cannot induce migration incentives, only (marginal) productivities matter for the migration decision. In the short run, systems competition between EU member states is mostly excluded such that inefficiencies from migration are weakened. In principle, different implicit taxes can still play a role but they are certainly less important for long-run migration. Much more important in the long run, particularly with regard to the increasing median age of voters, is whether there still exists an exit option for young persons in case of a Leviathan government or gerontocrats planning excessive taxation. This option is still available under the principle of delayed integration.

7.3 CHAPTER SUMMARY

Sustaining redistribution in an open economy with international labor mobility is a difficult task. Those who benefit from a tax-transfer system are attracted by generous welfare states and those who are net contributors want to flee to low-tax countries. Under systems competition, a suboptimally low level of redistribution has to be feared. If the redistributive systems remain unchanged and if the relatively lower number of contributors is ignored, the burden has to be carried by the immobile factors of production. Often the burden falls on those who should actually be beneficiaries of the system such as the immobile poor or retirees.

These problems also apply to redistributive pension systems. When implicit taxes between the pension systems differ an artificial migration incentive is generated. The optimal international labor allocation is distorted and an efficiency loss results. If it is mainly the young contributors to the pension system who leave the country, the sustainability of the pension system is threatened. Several solutions to these problems have been proposed, ranging from a consolidation of national pension systems into a supranational system to the introduction of a dynastic origin principle or a fiscal transfer system between countries. Most of the solutions appear to be too difficult to implement due to a lack of political support. There may also be doubts as to whether a centralized system always performs efficiently. In the worst case gerontocratic power is extended to an entire economic union.

If the need for harmonization is nevertheless acknowledged, two main possibilities seem to be politically feasible. The international harmonization of contribution rates in the sense of an equalization, however, will only under certain conditions be sufficient to restore global efficiency. Delayed integration cannot solve the problems entirely but it is a reasonable compromise between reducing artificial migration incentives and not entirely eliminating the exit option for net contributors to the social systems.

In the next chapter, we will apply these theoretical findings to the European Union. We will ask whether EU regulations support artificial migration incentives and whether these incentives actually exist or not.

NOTES

1. In the following, we will not explicitly distinguish between these terms.
2. The following arguments can be traced back to Stigler (1957), Musgrave (1971), Oates (1972) and many others.
3. This argument follows Cremer et al. (1996). Other models dealing with pensions and labor mobility with one immobile factor are Konrad (1995) and Hange (2000).
4. We assume away any distortions of the labor–leisure choice if redistribution takes place. This can be done by assuming an exogenous labor supply.
5. An analogous argument can be made if unskilled workers are mobile. These workers will move to the country with the most generous transfer payments (or with a high level of intragenerational redistribution). However, this will very soon undermine the financial feasibility of the system.
6. This section partly follows Krieger (2001).
7. If the total population in the economic union is fixed, rational governments with perfect foresight will set $\bar{\tau}_t^h = 0$ at the outset. This is because a country that gains population will find it increasingly difficult to keep the implicit tax non-negative, that is, to keep the growth rate above the interest rate. Even if the contribution rate is continuously lowered, population growth will come to a halt when the other country is completely deserted. Then, $\bar{\tau}_t^h$ is zero and an implicit tax has to be paid (see Schneider, 1996).
8. See also von Hagen and Walz (1995) for a very similar model with the shadow economy as an additional exit option. Breyer and Stolte (2001) investigate changes in the labor–leisure choice of young workers trying to avoid excessive taxation through the old generation.
9. The migration decision depends on two variables. First, it is the comparison of lifetime incomes that creates a migration incentive. Second, people have different intensities of attachment-to-home which strengthens or weakens the incentive (see Mansoorian and Myers, 1993).
10. See, for example, Kanbur and Keen (1993) for the case of commodity taxation and Wilson (1991) or Bucovetsky (1991) for the case of capital taxation.
11. A doomsday scenario as in Konrad (1995) is assumed. Since the world ends after period 2, the generation born in the last period will migrate myopically.
12. The same argument can be made if we assume a Leviathan government instead of a gerontocracy.
13. See also Richter (2002) and Sinn (2002b).

8. Pension policy in the European Union

One of the most important goals of European integration is to promote the mobility of factors of production. In the long run, it is hoped to bring the European Union to a higher growth path. At the same time pension systems of the EU member states differ in design and in internal rates of return. This implies that the predictions of fiscal federalism and systems competition theory from the previous chapter may apply. According to these theories the mobile segments of the population will follow artificial migration incentives and will ceteris paribus move to countries with more attractive pension systems. Redistribution will no longer be sustainable.

The important question that arises from these findings is whether the EU member states are at risk of being harmed by systems competition. Is there inefficient labor mobility and do member states engage in some kind of tax competition to attract immigrants or to avoid emigration? In order to give preliminary answers to these questions it is important to investigate European pension regulations first. Are there any countermeasures that help to avoid the problems or is policy coordination between member states too weak? In this chapter, we will consider the most important EU pension regulations and come to the conclusion that inefficient migration cannot effectively be avoided.

However, while a too weak regulatory framework is a necessary condition for harmful systems competition the problems may not necessarily arise if migration incentives are relatively small. We will therefore make use of the concept of the 'net public pension wealth' to evaluate the performance of national pension systems. The differences in the estimates suggest that substantial migration incentives generated by the pension systems exist although pension systems are only one of several factors that influence the migration decision. On the other hand, recent migration flows are so small that a direct impact from the existence of pension systems on migration can hardly be deduced. At most, indirect evidence that systems competition is at work can be found if the latest pension reforms in European countries are compared. There is a reform trend towards more funding and to a tighter link between contributions and benefits, that is, to reduce the level of redistribution.

131

8.1 THE REGULATION OF PENSION POLICY AT THE EUROPEAN LEVEL

Let us start our discussion by outlining the role that pension policy plays at the European level. It should be noted that social policy in general is allocated at the national level, that is, the member states are responsible for their national social policy alone. However, there are some important areas in social policy which are influenced by EU policy. In the following, we will describe the most important rules that are laid down in EU treaties and regulations.

8.1.1 European Pension Policy: The Treaties

In order to achieve one of the foremost goals of the European Union and its predecessors, the 'raising of the standard of living and quality of life' (Article 2 ToR), four basic freedoms of movement have been laid down in the Treaty of Rome (ToR) from 1958 and in the Treaty of the European Community from 1993 (Maastricht Treaty):[1] the freedom of movement of individuals, capital, goods and services. Since the passing of the Single European Act in 1986, freedom of movement is no longer a theoretical right but the EU has explicitly committed itself to actively removing legislative barriers to mobility. From an economic perspective freedom of movement is the prerequisite of an efficient (regional) allocation of factors of production.

Articles 48–58 ToR[2] deal with the freedom of movement of individuals. Our main interest, the mobility of employed persons, is laid down in Art. 48–51 ToR. While Art. 48 ToR rules out any discrimination based on nationality, Art. 49 ToR requires the abolition of any legislative or administrative restrictions and obstacles to movement. Most relevant for the field of social policy, however, is Art. 51 ToR which states that

> The Council shall (...) adopt such measures in the field of social security as are necessary to provide freedom of movement for workers; to this end, it shall make arrangements to secure for migrant workers and their dependants:
> (a) aggregation, for the purpose of acquiring and retaining the right to benefit and of calculating the amount of benefit, of all periods taken into account under the laws of the several countries;
> (b) payment of benefits to persons resident in the territories of Member States.

While this article is very general, holding for all 'classical' branches of the social system, old-age security is certainly at the heart of it. The acquisition of pension claims and the payment of pension benefits must be organized in such a way that they do not impede migration. A restriction of mobility would obviously occur if potential migrants feared that by taking employment in other countries with differing pension systems they would either not acquire pension claims at all or receive fewer benefits than they could expect when being equivalently employed in their home countries.

8.1.2 European Pension Policy: The Regulations

In addition to the treaties with more general rules, regulations contain implementation rules. Council Regulation (EEC) No. 1408/71 and the implementing Council Regulation (EEC) No. 574/72 lay down the details of Art. 51 ToR. They define, in particular, which individuals can be considered as members of a social system. In order to secure the acquisition of (pension) claims and payments of (pension) benefits, Regulation 1408/71 states that

- non-discrimination must hold, that is, for immigrants from other EU member states the same rules of the social systems apply as for domestic citizens (Art. 3, No. I, Regulation (EEC) 1408/71);
- contribution times in different countries accumulate in the case of benefit payments depending on the number of years of membership, that is, a country's social system has to accept contribution periods in other countries' social systems (according to these systems' rules) as if they were made in this country (Arts. 18, 38, 45, 64 and 72, Reg. (EEC) 1408/71);
- benefit payments can be exported to any member state, that is, benefit recipients do not have to live in the country of the social system that is responsible for the payments (Art. 10, Reg. (EEC) 1408/71).

From the last point (and from Art. 51(b) ToR) one can conclude in turn that only those countries to which social systems contributions were made are responsible for benefit payments, regardless of the place of residence of the recipient. Retirees from northern Europe living, for example, in Spain do not receive any pension benefits from the Spanish pension system unless they were contributors to this system during some period of their working life. Any benefit payments are ultimately made by the pension system of the retiree's home country. Recall Section 3.3.3 to see that this regulation is the reason why it is reasonable to consider only the migration of young workers but not retirees in pension-migration models. Regulation (EEC) 574/72 includes mostly procedural and administrative issues.

The previous description shows that neither Art. 51 ToR nor the relevant regulations aim at harmonizing the member states' social systems. Each country's legislation is still fully responsible for domestic social policy unless its provisions discriminate against other EU citizens. In this sense, this part of the EU framework regarding social issues can hardly be considered a truly independent EU social policy. Instead, it is a means of facilitating the free movement of citizens and thus mainly an appendix to national social policy and EU economic policy.

Most of the pension provisions within the EU date back to the Treaty of Rome. No fundamental advances towards a common European pension policy have been made since. Obviously there was no urgent need for changes. Only recently a first small step towards further coordination has been set at the top of the agenda although it is hardly recognized by the public. The European Commission and the member states initiated a process based on the so-called 'open method of coordination' in which mutually agreed objectives with regard to social policy are defined. Based on these objectives, peer review enables member states to examine and learn from best practice in Europe (see the articles in Verband Deutscher Rentenversicherungsträger, 2002).

8.2   AN EVALUATION OF EUROPEAN PENSION POLICY

Combining our findings from Chapter 7 and from the previous section we can now evaluate – from a theoretical perspective – whether inefficient labor migration between EU member states has to be feared. In order to do so, we need some information on the level of policy coordination that is optimal to avoid inefficiencies and on the actual level of coordination. If these levels differ, efficiency losses have to be feared. Therefore, it is useful to first define four different levels of policy coordination for social policy in general and pension policy in particular (see Kolmar, 1999, p. 130):

- The weakest form is 'cooperation' between countries. This includes, for example, the possibility of transfering claims and benefits as well as efforts to allow for a simple and smooth transferability.

- 'Coordination' implies some institutionalized connection between the parameters of the member states' pension systems. Two different forms of coordination may occur: 'Point coordination' implies that one or more parameters of the pension system has to be set in a predetermined and fixed ratio to a certain benchmark. If there is 'level coordination', certain minimum or maximum levels are set for all countries.

- 'Harmonization' is a special case of coordination where all parameters of the pension system are to be set at the same level in all countries.

- 'Integration' or 'consolidation' is given if all national pension systems are transferred into a single, uniform European pension system.

Considering these four levels of policy coordination one can conclude that European social and pension policy is best characterized by the lowest level of policy coordination, that is, by a 'cooperation' between member states. Even if in practice some obstacles to the transferability of claims and benefits still exist, living in countries with different pension laws does not cause any major obstacles to the acquisition of claims to future benefits. With the open method of coordination one can expect that the situation will improve further.

However, since pension policy is still the sole responsibility of member states, fundamental differences with regard to the parameters of pension systems remain between countries. This can easily be seen from the following example. Considering Homburg and Richter's (1993) framework, the difference between countries boils down to a comparison of implicit taxes which rely on two parameters, the contribution rate and the fertility rate. Even if contribution rates do not differ substantially, fertility differences are quite significant: in 2000, the total fertility rate for Germany was 36 per cent below the French and 20 per cent below the British. For Italy, the situation was even worse. The French total fertility rate was about 50 and the British 32 per cent higher as we learned from Table 2.1. The internal rates of return of the German and the Italian pension system are therefore particularly low compared to the ones in some of the neighboring countries.

If differences of this kind exist, there is potentially an incentive for labor migration between EU member states, given the fact that the existing level of policy coordination in the EU cannot prevent artificial migration incentives. If the net-income differentials or rate of return differences persist for too long, people will start to move, thereby inducing the previously discussed problems. Eventually, governments have to react either unilaterally or within the EU. Übelmesser (2004b) argues precisely along these lines. To her, harmonization in the EU is suboptimally low such that 'a more courageous approach leading to a more pronounced involvement of the European level is (...) needed' (Übelmesser, 2004b, p. 718).

But what should this approach look like? Does it imply a consolidation of pension systems? The advantage of a single uniform European tax-transfer policy is that no rich individual can escape from taxation and no poor individual can gain simply by moving to another EU member state.[3] The EU level is the only one at which all interregional spillovers are internalized and no distortions from inefficient migration have to be feared. There are, however, major disadvantages to this solution as well. Any solution involving a centralized decision maker can hardly take account of individual preferences. This also holds if differing national pension systems are considered. Citizens of the UK have a preference for (or at least live in the tradition of) a Beveridgian pension system while most continental Europeans prefer Bismarckian-style systems. It is most difficult to merge these two systems into one that all Europeans can agree upon. But even with similar pension systems, an agreement may be difficult if redistribution between members from different countries can be expected. In a consolidated system, French retirees would face lower benefits due to low fertility rates in Germany and Italy. Finally, abstaining from any exit option may lead to suboptimally high levels of redistribution as discussed in Chapter 7.

Hence, the consolidation of pension systems does not appear to be the first-best solution to choose. In fact, there are even institutional barriers to this policy because within the EU the subsidiarity principle applies. It requires that responsibilities are given to the lowest possible level in governmental hierachy that allows non-distorting decision-making. While the level of cooperation is obviously too low in this hierachy, one has to investigate whether the next higher level of coordination, that is, either point or level coordination of the social systems, will suffice to achieve the goal of avoiding distortions.

Übelmesser (2004b) tries to identify the most decentralized structure which allows an efficient international labor allocation to be achieved. Based on Breyer and Kolmar (2002) she concludes that the relevant mobility scenarios for the EU are given by restricted mobility today and either restricted or unrestricted mobility in the future. For either of these scenarios a coordination or equalization of contribution rates across countries is a necessary and sufficient condition for efficiency. For a proof of this assertion we refer to Breyer and Kolmar (2002). However, in some cases the information problem regarding post-migration marginal productivities, as discussed in Section 7.2.1, comes up. This may happen if the mobile segment in population is too small to compensate (through migration) for fertility differences between countries. This problem, however, may be solved by promoting the mobility of workers even more until the segment of mobile workers is sufficiently large. Hence, point coordination can in general achieve efficiency. A consolidation of the member states' pension systems into a unified European system is not required.

From comparing the optimal level of harmonization as described by Übelmesser (2004b) and the current state we can therefore conclude that the level of harmonization is suboptimally low and further steps towards a coordination of contribution rates will be necessary in the future.[4] The open method of coordination is not sufficient to guarantee global efficiency; it may even be harmful if it makes inefficient migration easier.

8.3 DO EU MEMBER STATES' PENSION SYSTEMS INDUCE MIGRATION INCENTIVES?

In the previous section, we argued from a theoretical perspective that the differences between the pension systems of EU member states may generate migration incentives. If these incentives are sufficiently strong, EU pension regulations will not be able to prevent an inefficient international labor allocation and there will be welfare losses for the entire EU. In this section we will turn to the important empirical question whether the discussion about differences in the pension systems is actually relevant. We will ask whether there are sufficiently large differences between pension systems that may make migration decisions reasonable. If there are only small differences, there is no urgent need for further harmonization. In order to evaluate potential migration incentives, we will present some estimates of the net public pension wealth (Feldstein, 1974; Wildasin, 1999).

8.3.1 Net Public Pension Wealth

Net public pension wealth (NPPW) is defined as gross public pension wealth minus the present discounted value of the contributions to the public pension scheme. Gross public pension wealth is just the present discounted value of expected retirement benefits. Hence, the NPPW tells us whether, in present value terms, a persons pays more into or receives more out of the pension system. This implies that the NPPW is simply the negative net direct contribution X to the pension system that was defined in (3.23): $NPPW = -X$. More generally, we define the NPPW to be

$$NPPW_0 = \sum_{t=R}^{D} \frac{p}{(1+r)^t} - \sum_{t=0}^{R} \frac{\tau w}{(1+r)^t} \tag{8.1}$$

for a person at the beginning of his career (period 0) where R is the (certain) age of retirement and D the (certain) end of life. If the person lives for two periods, we can rewrite (8.1) by using $p^{PAYG} = (1+n)\tau w$ and get

$$NPPW = \frac{p}{1+r} - \tau w = \frac{(1+n)\tau w}{1+r} - \tau w = \tau w \cdot \frac{n-r}{1+r} \tag{8.2}$$

which is just the implicit tax from (3.16). This is an intuitive result: only in a dynamically inefficient state with $n > r$ does the pension system contribute positively to the personal wealth of a PAYG system's member. Whenever $n < r$ the member will make a net contribution to the pension system which equals the implicit tax. Hence, in general we expect estimates of the NPPW to be negative numbers.

However, in real-world pension systems sometimes a positive NPPW can be observed. Depending on the rules of the pension systems some groups in society may have a positive NPPW despite dynamic efficiency. This is particularly true when intragenerational redistribution takes place. The NPPW of low-earning individuals may be positive when flat-rate benefits play an important role. Furthermore, if the NPPW is calculated for an older person, it is more likely to be positive – or at least it is less negative – as past contributions are sunk.

8.3.2   Estimating the Net Public Pension Wealth for Different European Countries

The previous section's discussion gives an impression of the difficulties of estimating the NPPW for different countries. One has to take into account not only differences between contribution and fertility rates, as equation (7.1) for the interregional equilibrium suggests, but also differences in the institutional design of the pension system and interpersonal differences. It may be the case that certain groups in society are severely burdened by the pension system while the rest of the society is in a rather comfortable situation compared to other countries.

This may be a problem insofar as Sinn (1998) points out that 'marginal' mobility is sufficient to set fiscal competition in motion, that is, governments already feel the political pressure of factor mobility if only a few contributors to the social systems react to differences in the (factor) incomes. As soon as some people from countries with social systems which are unfavorable to them decide to move to other countries, the entire system starts to get unbalanced. For more and more persons the situation becomes worse and incentives for migration become stronger.

Wildasin's (1999) estimates of the NPPW in seven European countries try to consider interpersonal differences by considering different prototype persons. These persons differ by age and family status. Some results are shown in Table 8.1 but have to be interpreted carefully due to the long-run nature of the underlying assumptions and predictions about the future parameters of the pension systems. The numbers are the absolute gain or loss of expected lifetime income in Euros or the relative gain or loss in terms of lifetime income, respectively. As expected, in most cases a loss has to be accepted by the members of the pension system. There will be lower pension benefits in present value terms compared to the previous contributions to the system. However, older persons face a lower implicit tax on their rest-of-life income than persons aged 20. This effect follows immediately from the fact that past contributions are sunk. Nevertheless, there are obvious differences between countries. In Italy, France and

Table 8.1. Estimated net public pension wealth for seven European countries in Euro and in per cent of lifetime income

| Country | 20 years old | | | |
| | single | | married | |
	Euro	%	Euro	%
Belgium	−30 152	−13	−28 224	−12
Denmark	−11 438	−3	−7 289	−2
France	−13 634	−6	−9 652	−4
Germany	−53 059	−16	−53 059	−16
Italy	−28 698	−13	−28 698	−13
Luxembourg	−33 543	−11	−33 543	−11
Netherlands	−91 018	−31	−87 810	−30
Country	40 years old			
	single		married	
	Euro	%	Euro	%
Belgium	−20 240	−8	−15 503	−6
Denmark	−3 707	−1	6 701	2
France	15 558	8	24 786	12
Germany	−38 758	−11	−38 758	−11
Italy	18 173	9	18 173	9
Luxembourg	−15 939	−5	−15 939	−5
Netherlands	−84 439	−28	−76 772	−25

Source: Wildasin (1999, p. 265).

Denmark (only for married persons) the pension system is so favorable for older persons that the NPPW is positive at age 40. Furthermore, we find that in some countries (Belgium, Denmark, France, the Netherlands) married persons gain from special advantages in the pension rules compared to unmarried persons.

A direct comparison of the NPPW in the countries under consideration shows substantial differences. While a Danish single person aged 20 would lose only 3 per cent of lifetime income in the Danish pension system, the same person would lose 31 per cent of lifetime income in the Netherlands. In absolute numbers, an unmarried or married German aged 20 loses more than €53 000 of lifetime wealth in present value terms while in France it is only €13 634 and €9 652, respectively. Assuming that workers earn the same income everywhere there obviously exists a substantial financial incentive to emigrate from countries with high implicit taxation to countries with low implicit taxation.

An exemplary estimate of this financial incentive can be found in Table 8.2, which shows how many per cent of lifetime income a German can gain

Table 8.2. Estimated change of net public pension wealth following migration from Germany to other European countries in Euro and in per cent of lifetime income

| | 20 years old | | | |
| Migration from | single | | married | |
Germany to:	Euro	%	Euro	%
Belgium	9 134	3	11 942	3
Denmark	42 906	12	47 055	14
France	33 394	10	37 375	11
Italy	12 631	4	12 631	4
Luxembourg	14 115	4	14 115	4
Netherlands	-52 672	-15	-49 464	-14
	40 years old			
Migration from	single		married	
Germany to:	Euro	%	Euro	%
Belgium	8 371	2	12 205	3
Denmark	39 957	11	45 740	13
France	53 756	15	58 883	17
Italy	40 835	12	40 835	12
Luxembourg	14 770	4	14 770	4
Netherlands	-54 874	-16	-50 615	-15

Source: Wildasin (1999, p. 268).

from moving to another European country. Since the NPPW in Germany is – in comparison to other countries – highly negative, there exists a fiscal incentive to leave Germany and to move to other countries, except for the Netherlands where the implicit tax is even higher. A single person aged 20 will gain about 12 per cent of lifetime income by moving to Denmark and 10 per cent by moving to France, equivalent to about €43 000 and €33 000, respectively. Comparable numbers can be found for other individuals and other countries (see Wildasin, 1999). These numbers indicate that there exist substantial differences in implicit taxation between European countries which may give rise to harmful migration decisions, in particular in border regions.

A second effect of these results should not be neglected. The measures of the NPPW or the implicit taxes can also be seen as valuable information for immigrants coming from outside the EU who are interested in knowing which destination country is ceteris paribus most attractive in terms of the pension system. If these immigrants are indifferent with respect to their future host country, they are more likely to move to a country like Denmark than to the Netherlands.

It is rather difficult for most people to estimate the performance of their home country's or their future host country's pension system correctly. This task becomes even more difficult if a comparison with other countries' pension systems is to be made. However, it seems nevertheless unlikely that the differences between the EU member countries remain unobserved. The media spreads the word and international personnel in border-region firms compare net incomes and expected average pension benefits. Sometimes people simply have the wish to opt out of their national social system because they are not satisfied with its performance. In particular high-skilled employees will then be much more willing to seriously consider their international options. If they believe that there is a better place to live, mobility at the margin will occur. A survey study by Boeri et al. (2001) shows that the willingness to (partly) opt out of the home country's pension system is twice as high in Italy and Germany as in France. Considering the fertility differences this result is not surprising.

While all these arguments may give rise to a migration of European citizens the actual number of migrants in Europe is low. We will turn to this observation in the next section.

8.4   MIGRATION IN EUROPE

In the following, we will show that migration flows between EU countries are relatively small. There are obviously only small incentives in the EU – from wage differentials to differing social systems – that induce people to leave their home countries. Migration costs appear to be rather high but we will argue that there is nevertheless indirect evidence for marginal mobility.

8.4.1   Migration Flows in Europe

Table 8.3 shows details on migration to selected EU member states. In addition to total number of immigrants in 1997 the share of foreign immigrants in total domestic population by region of origin is presented. Except for the small country of Luxembourg total immigration from all countries of the world accounts for less than 1 per cent of total population. The most important immigration countries in the EU are Germany and Austria, which have a high share of immigrants from 'other' European countries, that is, mainly from central and eastern Europe (see also Chapter 9) and Turkey. The weighted average for all EU member states is 0.36 per cent of total population (excludes Ireland due to lack of data). In the US, this immigration share was only slightly higher at 0.37 per cent in 2002 (US Department of Homeland Security, 2003, p. 11; own calculations). A

comparison of these numbers is, however, slightly misleading because of the
much higher barriers for immigration to the US compared to the very small
barriers for migration within the EU. Mobility between US states, on the
other hand, is very high because there are no legal or language barriers at
all.

*Table 8.3.   Total number and share of immigrants by region of origin
              (1997)*

Country:	A	D	F	I	LUX	NL	UK
Total Population	8.1	82.0	58.5	57.5	0.4	15.6	58.2
Total Immigration	56.9	615.3	65.8	143.2	9.5	77.8	187.0
Foreign immigrants by region of origin in % of total population							
EU-15	0.14	0.18	0.01	0.02	1.75	0.13	0.10
Other Europe	0.45	0.35	0.01	0.08	0.22	0.08	0.02
Africa	0.03	0.04	0.06	0.09	0.07	0.06	0.03
America	0.03	0.04	0.01	0.03	0.10	0.06	0.03
Asia	0.06	0.13	0.02	0.04	0.09	0.07	0.10
Rest of the World	0.00	0.01	0.00	0.00	0.03	0.11	0.04
Total Share	0.71	0.75	0.11	0.25	2.26	0.50	0.32

Notes: Total population in millions; total immigration in thousands; Rest of the
world includes Oceania, stateless persons and persons with unknown nationality.

Source: Eurostat (2000, pp. 40-1 and 122-9); own calculations.

The share of immigrants from other EU countries hardly exceeds 0.2 per
cent of the total population. Exceptions are Belgium and Luxembourg where
the EU institutions and the financial sector attract European employees, and
Ireland with the booming Dublin region. The weighted average is about
0.09 per cent of total population, which is a quarter of the total immigration
share. Also the total number of migrants of 342 000 for the entire EU in
1997, from which 44 per cent moved to Germany, appears to be negligible.
Notice, however, two important qualifications. First, the numbers presented
here may underestimate the actual numbers of migrants somewhat as not all
of them register in the host countries. Second and even more important, the
EU is actively promoting labor mobility. This, however, is a process that
takes some time because people need to get used to the idea and have to
learn about the new opportunities. For today's young generation it is already
much more natural to work abroad. Hence, it can be expected that the
migration flows will become larger in the future with all the consequences
that were discussed above.

8.4.2 Migration Costs

If hardly any migration flows can be observed, one could argue that there exists a migration equilibrium within the EU. Each individual worker may already have achieved his utility maximum. This, however, does not appear to be too reasonable an assumption given the existing differences in wages and the tax-transfer system. In the following, we will therefore briefly formulate some thoughts as to why there has as yet been so little migration. The main argument is certainly the existence of migration costs, which may take very different forms and will certainly go far beyond the costs of hiring a removal company.

So far, our theoretical discussion has abstracted from the migration costs which are necessarily incurred if an individual wants to take advantage of, for example, a wage differential with a neighboring country or a more favorable pension system in that country. These costs seem to be quite substantial as even the largest income differential which existed in the EU prior to the EU eastern enlargement did not induce noticeable migration flows.[5] Hence, migration costs must include far more than just monetary costs. In an abstract sense, these (not directly measurable) extra costs can be interpreted as utility losses caused by a strong attachment-to-home or home bias. Being raised in a certain country involves the acquisition of (home) country-specific human capital which helps to cope with this country's manners and customs. Migration implies giving up this specific human capital. At the same time, the need to invest in new and different (host) country-specific human capital is a costly task. An analogous argument can be made for social relationships. The stock of human capital rises with age such that the opportunity cost of giving up this capital stock by leaving the country becomes larger. This may be seen as an additional argument why it is reasonable to model only mobility of the young but not the old and why in fact mainly young people migrate (recall Section 3.3.3).

In terms of the social systems we may argue that in most countries there is a preference for a certain type of social or pension system. If the existing pension system of a country corresponds to a large degree to the preferences of its citizens, then the citizens will dislike moving from their preferred choice to a less preferred system. Again a certain migration cost is involved, here in terms of a utility loss.

This argument is similar to Tiebout's (1956, 1961) because individuals have chosen the jurisdiction that offers the level of redistribution (public good) that is closest to their own preferences. Unlike in Tiebout's model, however, no one has voted with their feet here. Hence, it would be more appropriate to argue with long-standing social norms and traditions which people are born into. In other words, people get used to the existing system and most of them cannot imagine improving their situation in an alternative social system. This is even more the case at a more general level: most individuals have only a rough idea of the functioning of their home country's tax and welfare systems and hardly take advantage of all available benefits and exemptions. To find out about the differences in other countries requires extensive knowledge. Even in the economic literature, there are (so far) few attempts of comparisons of this type.[6] Under these circumstances staying in their home country appears to be the superior choice for many (risk-averse) people instead of taking the risky chance of migrating.

Therefore, the attempt to find out whether differences in pension systems contribute to the small migration flows involves major conceptional (and empirical) problems. Not only are pension systems one of several potential influential variables, it is even difficult to extract a single measure that describes pension systems in an appropriate way. Including all pillars of the pension system and all forms of redistribution at the same time makes a calculation even more difficult. It is also not always possible to clearly deduce the implicit and explicit tax burden that is involved with the pension system. Often, there are special tax treatments which are favorable for retirees and which should be added to the pension benefit. Since these transfers are paid from general tax revenues there is an explicit tax burden from the pension system as well.

A preliminary empirical observation by Jousten and Pestieau (2002) might explain why migration induced by the welfare state may not play any role at all. It can be shown that countries with a large degree of intragenerational redistribution in the pension system do not rely solely on the PAYG pension system but have a rather large funded pillar as well. In countries with little intragenerational redistribution, however, one finds that the PAYG system has a dominant role. It is quite possible that these two redistributive effects offset each other to a certain degree such that the differences between countries are smaller than suspected (Jousten and Pestieau, 2002). A comprehensive empirical analysis of this hypothesis has yet to be conducted.

8.4.3   Indirect Evidence for Marginal Mobility

While we cannot deduce any direct evidence that differences in pension systems cause noticeable migration flows, there may at least be some indirect evidence that systems competition is working, that is, that there is mobility at the margin which leads to changes in pension systems. In order to do so it is instructive to consider recent reform steps regarding the pension systems in EU member states.

Let us again consider the institutional differences between pension systems from Section 3.2. Lindbeck and Persson (2003) suggest a three-dimensional classification with distinctions between DB vs. DC systems, funded vs. unfunded systems and actuarial vs. non-actuarial systems. According to the fiscal federalism and the systems competition theory, international labor mobility at the margin suffices to induce financing problems to redistributive systems such that redistribution can no longer be sustained. In Lindbeck and Persson's (2003) classification the last two categories involve redistribution. The more funding and the more actuarial fairness there is, the less redistribution is involved in a pension system. By becoming more Bismarckian pension systems involve less intragenerational redistribution. This makes a pension system more attractive to those who are averse to (strong) redistribution or it reduces the disadvantage compared to systems with a strong Bismarckian component. At the same time, the system becomes less attractive to poor people. This effect holds even more when intergenerational redistribution is avoided as well (funded systems).[7] Hence, if there is mobility at the margin which induces people to migrate in the expected direction, we would expect that pension reforms will go into the direction of less redistribution. If ageing is expected to lower pension benefits below the poverty line, one could introduce a basic pension financed from general tax revenues which would then reduce actuarial fairness.

Consider Figure 8.1 to see whether there is any evidence from an international comparison of pension systems that may indicate the effects of systems competition. Unfortunately, there are no thorough empirical studies on this topic. The diagram depicts only the first pillar of the pension system, which is the public pension system, in different European countries. Hardly any country has a dominant funded part in the first pillar; instead almost every public pension system is PAYG. Some systems, such as the Netherlands, Ireland or the UK, are more Beveridgian in having flat benefits while others are more Bismarckian. Regarding pension reforms the diagram exhibits a clear movement in a south-eastern direction, that is, towards systems which have a larger degree of funding and/or a higher level of actuarial fairness. A change towards more funding can be made, for example, by setting up a special fund in the public pillar that collects extra contributions today to soften the imbalance of the budget in the years of most severe ageing (around 2030–50). Actuarial fairness can be strengthened if, for example, not only selected years of contributions are used to calculate the pension benefit but all years of contributions.[8] Sweden and Italy are the most prominent examples of taking rather radical reform steps as both countries are moving towards notional defined-contribution (NDC) pension systems[9] from classical DB systems. In Germany, the latest reforms (not exhibited in the graph) differed slightly from most other European experience. The reason is that in Germany a Bismarckian pension

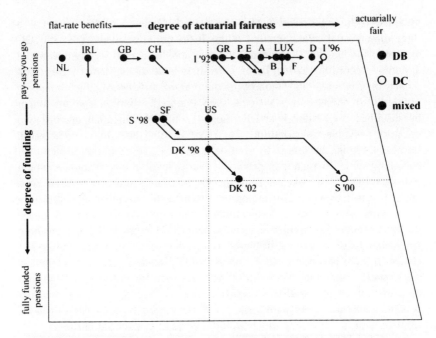

Notes: DB = defined-benefit system, DC = defined-contribution system; A = Austria, B = Belgium, CH = Switzerland, D = Germany, DK = Denmark, E = Spain, F = France, GB = United Kingdom, GR = Greece, I = Italy, IRL = Ireland, LUX = Luxembourg, NL = Netherlands, S = Sweden, SF = Finland, US = United States.

Source: Werding (2003, p. 14).

Figure 8.1. *Characteristics of public pension schemes and directions of recent change, 1990–2002*

system already exists. Therefore, the German pension system took first steps towards more funding (in the second and third pillar) only.

These observations are in line with the predictions from the systems competition model. By introducing more funding and by reducing non-actuarially fair regulations, the level of redistribution has been reduced. One should, however, be aware that the observations from Figure 8.1 are not conclusive empirical evidence proving a causal relationship between international labor mobility and the change in the design of pension systems. This can easily be seen from the following observation: the ratio of old-age pension benefits in the domestic product of all EU member states (except for the Netherlands) increased between 1990 and 1996 (Jousten and Pestieau, 2002). In this respect no harmful systems competition is indicated. There might be other objections as well. A reduction of the level of redistribution may also be explained as an attempt to reduce the shadow economy or distortions of the labor–leisure choice (this is an analogous argument to the marginal mobility argument). And more funding may be useful to better diversify demographic and capital-market risks. Further arguments can be found but nevertheless the observed changes in the pension systems give at least a first indirect indication that systems competition may be at work.

If one accepts the assertion that systems competition takes place in the EU, one should note another aspect. So far, we have implicitly assumed that pension reforms are an implication of marginal mobility. One could, however, also argue that some countries have decided to voluntarily enter into or even start systems competition to gain an advantage for their pension systems. They recognize that a reduction of redistribution makes pension systems more attractive to the desired type of immigrants, namely high-earning EU citizens. This group can quickly and easily be integrated such that the positive externality on the domestic pension system is particularly high. This strategy is, however, dangerous and may end up in a prisoners' dilemma situation.

8.5   CHAPTER SUMMARY

Empirical observations show that implicit taxes and the net public pension wealth differ between European countries. The differences appear to be very substantial such that a change to a more favorable pension system may be a profitable option. Given this observation, one has to fear that the predictions of the fiscal federalism and the systems competition theory may come true. Artificial migration incentives generated by the pension systems lead to inefficient migration flows. Because potential net contributors try to avoid high implicit (and explicit) taxation and because transfer recipients try to gain from the most generous social systems, redistribution will no longer be sustainable. Mobility at the margin suffices to start this process and the EU regulatory framework with respect to pensions is such that it cannot avoid inefficiencies.

However, there is no direct conclusive evidence yet that systems competition has induced substantial migration flows between EU member states. In fact, there is hardly any migration flow to be observed. The reason is that migration costs in a very broad sense, which also include utility losses from migration, still impede labor mobility. Compared to these costs migration incentives – from wage differentials to social system differences – appear to be small. Unless the migration incentives become relatively larger migration flows will remain negligible.

It would nevertheless be an illusion to conclude that systems competition is not a threat to welfare states. People first need to learn about the new opportunities that labor mobility offers particularly in the EU where mobility is heavily promoted. Today's young generation is already much more mobile than older generations and future generations will be even more so. But even with small migration flows there will be marginal mobility effects which should suffice to start systems competition. This competition works in the long run or as Sinn (2003, pp. 4–5) states: 'Often the migration responses are so slow that a long period of time can elapse before a country is forced to react to a policy move of another country. (...) It may take decades before the forces (...) become visible.' In this sense, we may have to interpret the fact that all major pension reforms in Europe over the last decade involved a reduction of (intragenerational) redistribution as an outcome of systems competition.

If systems competition in the EU has so far worked very slowly, this may change in the future, however. The EU eastern enlargement will bring about new challenges. This will be the topic of the next chapter.

NOTES

1. All following citations from treaties and regulations are taken from the EU's internet resources; see European Union (2004).
2. The succeeding Treaty of Amsterdam (1997) assigns Art. 39–48 to these provisions.
3. It is nevertheless possible to move outside the EU.
4. It is very important to notice that this discussion is based on the social policy practice of the EU and its member states. This implies among other things that the place-of-residence principle holds, that is, the place of residence determines which pension system an individual becomes a member of. It follows immediately that immigration incentives through jurisdictional differences are relevant. However, other principles, such as the concept of delayed integration, may lead to favorable results as well and may be easier to implement.
5. For male employees in the manufacturing sector the income differential between Germany and Portugal was €25 000 per year in 1998 (Statistisches Bundesamt, 2000, pp. 11–2).
6. Wildasin (1999) is a notable exception.
7. Even for the DB vs. DC distinction one can argue analogously. In a DB system ageing necessarily leads to increasing contribution rates which cannot be avoided by the young contributors. In particular, high-earning young individuals may therefore consider moving to a DC country. While here the future pension benefit is likely to be rather low due to the ageing process, today's tax burden is expected to remain constant in the long run or even to

fall to a lower level. Those who prefer a rather high old-age income have the opportunity to save privately an additional amount while others may prefer to forgo this possibility. The advantage is that additional choices are available under the DC system which do not exist under the DB system.

8. Several countries have used only the last five years before retirement to calculate the pension claim (for example, the pension claim is 70 per cent of the average income of the last five years) or even the years with the highest contributions. This benefits persons with volatile annual incomes during working life which are rather low on average, while it hurts those who paid steadily high contributions over, say, 30 years. Actuarial fairness therefore requires the pension claim to be calculated based on the entire working life's average income.

9. Notional defined-contribution system have recently gained some attention because they combine aspects of both FF and more traditional PAYG-DB systems. NDC systems are based on PAYG financing. However, an individual notional (unfunded or virtual) account is established for each worker. This implies a rather tight link between retirement benefits and payroll contributions which shows a close resemblance to the concept of a Bismarckian pension system. The attractive feature is that – at least in the long run – benefits and contributions are kept in balance by keeping the contribution rate constant. For details, see Williamson and Williams (2003). A further discussion of this topic can be found in Chapter 9.

9. Pension policy and the EU eastern enlargement

In 2004, eight central and eastern European countries joined the European Union. Due to the existing differences in national per-capita incomes large inflows of workers from these countries – a 'trek westwards' (Straubhaar, 2001) – were expected. While it is too early yet to evaluate whether these flows have started, projections assume that about two to five million persons will migrate to the previous EU (EU-15) over the next 15 years. Compared to the findings of the previous chapter indicating little migration within the EU, this would imply a fundamental change.

Immigration is therefore an important topic in the political debate of some western European countries, in particular in Austria and Germany, which are assumed to become the main target countries for migrants. For this reason, some countries advocated a seven-year transitional period of restricted freedom of movement for citizens of the accession countries (a similar instrument was used during the southern enlargement).[1] Many people fear that otherwise migrants will not only move westwards to find jobs and to enter the labor markets but that they will 'migrate into the social security systems', thereby causing a burden on the domestic population.

Recalling our previous discussion this concern appears to be somewhat surprising, at least when it comes to pension systems. The migrants from eastern Europe will become members of western European pension systems and thus generate a positive externality to the EU-15 population. Unless this positive effect is substantially reduced by very low skill levels or fertility rates, high unemployment probabilities of the immigrants and so on, there is little reason to fear immigration from the accession countries in this area. Clearly, we cannot exclude negative effects in other branches of the welfare system, congested public infrastructure or falling wages for some skill groups but a negative impact on the pension system is unlikely.

While there is little doubt that the Austrian and German pension systems will gain from immigration, an interesting question is rarely asked and still open to debate. This question arises when we consider the migrants' perspective of the target countries' pension systems, in particular the German one: as Germany is one of the most rapidly ageing countries in

150

the EU why would an immigrant want to become a member of the German pension system – of all pension systems? While the large wage differential is certainly a good reason to migrate to Germany, the German pension system is probably not. The entrance fee to the German system appears to be especially high because due to the demographic development the expected internal rate of return is very low compared to the pension systems of most immigrants' home countries. Therefore, it is rather unattractive to leave the old and enter the new pension system.

In this chapter (based on Krieger and Sauer, 2004) we will investigate differences in the pension systems of the main source and target countries for east–west migration after the EU enlargement, that is, Poland, Hungary, the Czech Republic and Germany, respectively. To consider only Germany in this chapter is justified by the fact that Germany alone is expected to absorb two-thirds of eastern European migrants to the EU-15. We find that the expected immigration is clearly beneficial to the German pension system, not only because of an increase in the number of contributors but also – among other things – because of an improvement in the age structure of contributors. On the other hand, for immigrants there is a burden because in their home countries dependency rates are more favorable and the newly reformed pension systems involve less inter- and intragenerational redistribution.

Before we start with a comparison of pension systems in Germany and the accession countries, we will discuss the effects of labor mobility between an economic union and a group of accession countries in a small model. We will apply some findings from previous chapters to make the model more realistic. Furthermore, we will allow for a negative pension effect in the accession country due to emigration of young workers. The model may be seen as an extension of the framework developed by Homburg and Richter (1993) and will disclose the effects of immigration on natives and immigrants. One surprising result is that, with a sufficiently large wage differential, immigration flows may be so large that a positive pension effect benefits both natives and immigrants in the target country.

After having introduced the model, we will briefly review the estimates of the expected future immigration flows following the EU eastern enlargement. Details will furthermore be given on the age and skill distribution of eastern European immigrants. Finally, the differences in the pension systems in the four countries under consideration will be investigated and discussed.

9.1 A SIMPLE MODEL DETERMINING THE LABOR ALLOCATION AFTER THE EU EASTERN ENLARGEMENT

Let us consider the case of a country which is on the verge of joining an economic union. Both the joining country and the economic union have a PAYG pension system. The economic union is ageing at a relatively faster rate, that is, the population growth rate is lower. Furthermore, we assume that at the time of joining the economic union workers of the joining country are attracted by a substantial wage differential which is sufficiently large to override negative incentives imposed by the pension system. Migrants will enter the country despite the fact that they have to enter the pension system. If the wage differential were small, though, it would be unattractive to migrate from an individual migrant's perspective. However, we will show that a sufficiently large number of migrants may lead to falling contribution rates which are attractive for both natives and immigrants.

Let there be two countries where country A is the core area (economic union) and country B is the joining country and let $n_t^i \equiv N_t^i/N_{t-1}^i - 1$, $i = A, B$, be the respective population growth rates. The ratio N_t^i/N_{t-1}^i is the inverse of the dependency rate and the output of each economy is given by $Y_t^i = F(N_t^i, K_t^i)$. In a framework which is similar to Homburg and Richter (1993; see Section 7.2.1) individuals maximize lifetime utility and face the following intertemporal budget constraint:[2]

$$c_t^y + \frac{c_{t+1}^o}{1 + r_{t+1}} = w_t^i + \bar{p}\frac{n_t^i - r_{t+1}}{(1 + r_{t+1})(1 + n_t^i)} \quad \text{for} \quad i = A, B, \quad (9.1)$$

which implicitly assumes a fixed-benefit system in which countries define the pension benefit as exogenously given while the contribution rate adjusts endogenously. This assumption appears to be appropriate if one recalls Figure 3.1, which shows that most European pension systems are DB systems. Notice that this assumption is in contrast to the original model by Homburg and Richter (1993) which is based on a fixed-contribution rate regime. We assume the following simple budget equation for each country's pension system:[3]

$$p_t^i \cdot N_{t-1}^i = \tau_t^i \cdot N_t^i \quad \Rightarrow \quad \tau_t^i = \bar{p} \cdot \frac{N_t^i}{N_{t-1}^i}. \quad (9.2)$$

Migration of workers from the joining country may start as soon as borders are open. As usual retirees are assumed to be immobile in the sense that they receive pension benefits from their home country. In order to induce migration flows it is necessary that the location-dependent income which is the right-hand side of (9.1) is larger in the core area than in the joining country:

$$w_t^A + \overline{p}\frac{n_t^A - r_{t+1}}{(1 + r_{t+1})(1 + n_t^A)} > w_t^B + \overline{p}\frac{n_t^B - r_{t+1}}{(1 + r_{t+1})(1 + n_t^B)} \quad (9.3)$$

Migration takes place until the migration equilibrium is achieved. Substituting for n^i and τ_t^i leads to the following proposition.

Proposition 14 (Krieger and Sauer, 2004, p. 7) *In the migration equilibrium, given by*

$$w_t^A - \overline{p}\left[\frac{N_{t-1}^A}{N_t^A} - \frac{N_{t-1}^B}{N_t^B}\right] = w_t^B, \quad (9.4)$$

no more migration flows occur because wages net of the effects induced by fertility differences equalize.

We simply assume here, instead of explicitly adding a term which measures migration cost, that the core area's wage rate is net of migration cost (from the perspective of a potential migrant). The bracketed term measures the difference in the national pension systems by comparing national dependency rates and is determined by the difference in the fertility of domestic population. If fertility is lower in the core area, as we will assume in the following, the incentive to leave the joining country is lowered. The bracketed term corresponds to the difference of both countries' net public pension wealth, that is, $\Delta NPPW$, or the difference in implicit taxes. In a sense, it measures the effective entrance fee because the immigrant will be released from his home country's implicit tax burden but at the same time will be subject to the target country's implicit tax.

The wage differential decreases with a larger number of migrants because marginal productivities of labor adjust in both countries. Eventually marginal productivities of labor should equalize, taking into account the pension differential. At the outset, wage differentials – for example, between Germany and the EU accession countries – are probably much larger than the differences in the pension systems, thus the negative impact will not matter too much. Nevertheless, the effect of the pension system is negative for each single individual as it reduces the expected income gain from migration. This can be seen from Figure 9.1 where marginal productivities for two regions are exhibited.

The marginal productivity curve in the core area (F_N^A) is shifted downwards by the negative pension effect. This results in the curve denoted by PP. The wage differential is smaller at the outset when the number of young migrants M is zero ($M_0 = 0$). An artificial migration disincentive is created which leads to a lower than optimal number of migrants, that is, M^P instead of M^*. The welfare loss is given by the triangle EFG.[4]

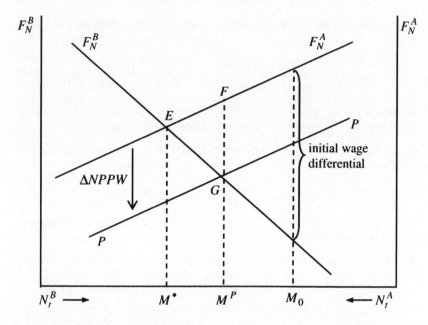

Source: Krieger and Sauer (2004, p. 8).

Figure 9.1. International allocation of workers given a large initial wage differential and a PAYG pension system

So far, our analysis has not explicitly taken into account that migration has a positive effect on the core area's pension system because the number of contributors increases and a negative effect on the joining country's pension system in which fewer contributors remain. Under the given pension system contribution rates can fall in the economic union according to (9.2). However, we assume that contribution rates at the outset are more favorable in the joining country (recall that fertility rates in the core area are lower). Therefore, a single migrant will not change the relative performance of the pension systems substantially and will still consider the new pension system as a burden. But if there is a sufficiently large number of migrants the performance of the pension system will improve noticeably in the core area and worsen in the joining country. At some point, the core area's pension system will do even better than the joining country's. The contribution rates will be lower. The pension systems have identical contribution rates if the bracketed term in (9.4) vanishes.

Lemma 15 (Krieger and Sauer, 2004, p. 9) *Contribution   rates   in   both* *countries equalize when the break-even level of migration is reached:*

$$\overline{M} = \frac{N_{t-1}^A N_{t-1}^B \left(n_t^B - n_t^A\right)}{N_{t-1}^A + N_{t-1}^B}.$$ (9.5)

This result follows when in (9.4) migration flows are taken into account. Then,

$$\frac{N_{t-1}^A}{N_t^A + \overline{M}} = \frac{N_{t-1}^B}{N_t^B - \overline{M}}$$

can be solved for $\overline{M}$, considering $n_t^i \equiv N_t^i / N_{t-1}^i - 1$.

Any migration level beyond $\overline{M}$ will positively add to the wage differential and create an additional positive migration incentive. This can be seen from Figure 9.2 where the QQ line intersects the marginal productivity curve of country A at the break-even migration level $\overline{M}$.[5] If – due to a large wage differential – more migration than $\overline{M}$ takes place, the new optimal migration level will be M^{**} which is beyond the welfare optimal level in a world without pension systems (M^*). Again the existence of a PAYG system generates an artificial migration incentive although into an unexpected direction when compared to the systems competition results from Section 7.1.

Notice that the break-even level may also lie to the left of M^*. In this case, shown by the RR curve, the impact of the pension system is negative for all migrants as $\overline{M}' > M^*$. The implicit tax must be larger initially under this scenario compared to the previous one. The optimal migration level M^{***} is below M^*. The reason is that net wages equalize when the NPPW difference is still negative. This scenario is analogous to the case discussed in Figure 9.1.

Figure 9.3 shows once more the derivation of the break-even migration level, here in terms of contribution rates to the pension system. The curves are derived from the equation for the contribution rate given by (9.2), taking migration into account.[6] Again, both pension systems are equal at migration level $\overline{M}$ where both contribution rates are the same. If all citizens of country B are moving to the core area, the minimum contribution rate $\tau_t^{A,min}$ can be reached in country A. To the left of $\overline{M}$ the contribution rate in the core area is higher than in the joining country, so entering the pension system is not (yet) attractive; only the wage differential induces migration.

Here, a problem of coordination failure may arise because a single potential migrant does not consider the positive externality he induces on other potential migrants. A single migrant will not noticeably change the core area's pension system; a sufficiently large number of migrants, however, will induce contribution rates to fall below the joining country's level. Both the citizens of the core area and the immigrants will gain from

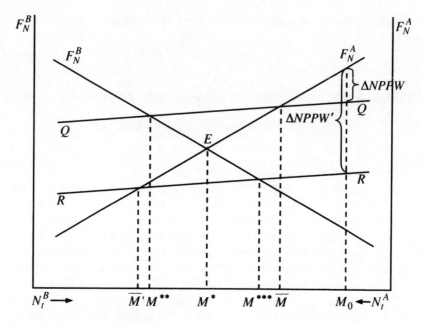

Source: Krieger and Sauer (2004, p. 9).

Figure 9.2.   International allocation of workers in the case of endogenous determination of the contribution rate

this reduction in contribution rates. Whether this happens or not depends on whether the wage differential is large enough to induce at least $\overline{M}$ potential migrants to move.

It should be noted that this result follows from the fixed-pension benefit assumption because this allows both natives and immigrants to gain from immigration. Furthermore, we assume the migration equilibrium to be stable, at least in the short run.[7] Long-run stability is much more difficult to guarantee.[8] The problem that arises is with the next generation that has to pay for an increased number of retirees. If the fertility of immigrants is still relatively higher after entering the core area, it is the immigrants' children who will face too high contribution rates compared to a scenario without migration in the preceeding period. Some children may therefore consider migrating back to country B in $t+1$ where the number of retirees is lower due to migration in t. The process of migration and re-migration may extend to all future periods. However, this is not a major concern of today's migrants.

Let us now assume that the joining country's pension system does not fix the pension benefit but the contribution rate as is the case in a notional

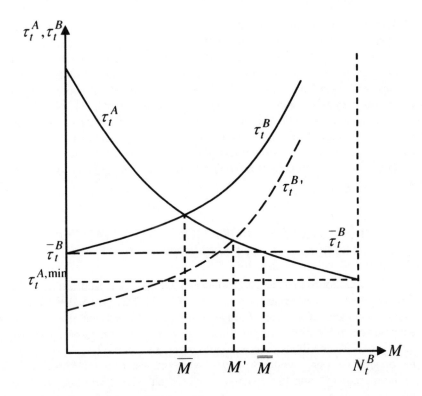

Source: Krieger and Sauer (2004, p. 10).

Figure 9.3.   The change in national contribution rates caused by international labor migration

defined-contribution system. The contribution rate is now $\overline{\overline{\tau}}_t^B$, regardless of the number of migrants. Therefore, more migrants, $\overline{\overline{M}}$, are needed to break even as can be seen from Figure 9.3. The cost of migration has to be paid for by country B's retirees who will receive lower benefits.

Finally, we can assume that the joining country's pension system consists not only of a PAYG pillar but also of a funded pillar, leaving the replacement income $\overline{p}$ unchanged. The funded pillar will cover a share $\varkappa$ of the pension benefit. If dynamic efficiency holds ($r > n$), contributions τ_t^B can fall by more than $\varkappa$ because contributions to the funded pillar yield a higher return. Therefore, contributions in the joining country are relatively lower than in the core area. This leads to a downward shift of the τ_t^B-curve in Figure 9.3 to a new $\tau_t^{B\prime}$-curve. Hence, the new break-even level of migration is M' which shows that the difference between the two pension systems is larger under this scenario.

Summarizing our findings we conclude that if there is a relatively low number of migrants these migrants will face a burden by entering the core area's pension system, assuming a higher reproduction rate in the joining country. If, however, the number is sufficiently large both immigrants and natives will gain from migration. Moving from a system with defined contribution rates or with a larger funded pillar to a system without these features tends to increase the burden. This lowers the possible income gain compared to a situation without pension systems at all. The pension system causes an artificial migration disincentive which leads to a too low (but nevertheless quite substantial) migration from the joining country to the core area.

9.2   THE EXPECTED MIGRATION POTENTIAL FOLLOW-ING THE EU EASTERN ENLARGEMENT

There is little doubt that the EU eastern enlargement will lead to migration flows from the accession countries to the EU-15. This will induce a gain to the members of western European pension systems via the positive externality that we discussed previously. However, we do not know whether the positive effect will also accrue to the immigrants themselves according to the previous section's model. Countries which choose to impose restrictions on immigration during the seven-year transitional period will share only a little in this gain.

The size of the positive externality depends on two aspects. In addition to a quantitative effect from having additional contributors (with an above average number of children), the 'quality' of immigrants plays a role as well. High skill levels, low unemployment probabilities and a fast integration add to the positive effect of immigration. In the following, we will investigate what can be expected from EU eastern enlargement in this regard. In order to do so we will briefly summarize three major studies on east–west migration which estimate the number of expected immigrants. Furthermore, we add data on important differences between the major source and destination countries of migrants, that is, Poland, Hungary, the Czech Republic and Germany, respectively. This information deals mostly with the qualitative characteristic of the immigrants.

Studies on east–west migration were conducted by Bauer and Zimmermann (1999), the European Integration Consortium (2001) and Sinn et al. (2001), respectively. While the first study is concerned with immigration into the entire EU, the latter two studies concentrate primarily on the expected inflow of migrants into Germany. However, a comparison of the studies is nevertheless possible as in the past more than two thirds of the immigrants from the 10 central and eastern European countries[9] (CEECs) applying for membership in the EU-15 went to Germany (European Integration Consortium, 2001, p. 104). Forecasts of future migration potential assume that this distribution of migrants across EU countries will remain constant over time. Therefore, Germany is expected to be the main destination country for immigration.

The estimates of the potential immigration into Germany range from two million up to five million persons in the first 15 years after accession, depending on the underlying forecast model and the chosen scenario. The results represent only rough estimates due to definition and statistical problems as well as problems in capturing the individual factors influencing migration decisions (Brücker, 2001a). Furthermore all estimations are based on econometric models using historical data taking into account the experience from past migration to Germany, especially in the context of the EU southern enlargement which may not be able to give a sufficiently exact base for estimating the future migration potential from the CEECs.

The most important explanatory variable for migration in the estimation models is the income differential between source and target countries, expressed as the difference in GDP per capita in purchasing power parities (ppp). This corresponds to the wage differential in the previous section's model. In 1998, for Poland, Hungary and the Czech Republic, respectively, this measure was 33, 40 and 47 per cent of the EU-15's (Brücker, 2001b, p. 7). It does not account for tax payments and transfers influencing disposable income (Flaig, 2001), so a comprehensive perspective considering long-term disposable income is missing. Sinn et al. (2001) consider potential net contributions to or benefits out of German social security systems to migrants to show that fiscal activity can distort migration decisions in the way that was discussed in previous chapters. Surveys conducted in some CEECs find evidence for a significant impact of differences in social security systems on migration decisions (Bauer and Zimmermann, 1999, pp. 97–100). Other studies argue that there is no empirical evidence for the relevance of social security systems in the migration decision (Brücker et al., 2000, p. 325).

Despite this ambiguity the findings are in line with our basic argument. In the first place, it is the wage differential which drives migration decisions. Whether or not the pension system has, among other things, a positive or negative impact on expected incomes depends on the total number of migrants. These effects are difficult to predict (or even to recognize) and potential migrants may therefore neglect or misjudge them, leading to ambiguous empirical evidence. This may turn out to be a costly mistake as Wildasin's (1999) estimates of the NPPW and the potential gains and losses from migration in Section 8.3.2 show.

In the following we will turn to some of the qualitative factors which have an impact on pension systems. In particular, we consider the age distributions and fertility rates in Germany, in the accession countries and among potential migrants. Furthermore, we will look at skill distributions and unemployment probabilities. Notice that – in particular with regard to fertility rates – the case of Germany may be an extreme example. For other EU member states (like Austria) the following findings will most likely be less pronounced.

Table 9.1.   Selected demographic projections for Poland, Hungary, the Czech Republic and Germany

			POL	HUN	CZ	GER
	males	2000	69.9	66.8	71.5	74.7
Life expectancy		2050	78.5	74.6	75.2	80.0
at birth	females	2000	78.2	75.2	78.4	80.8
		2050	84.7	81.1	81.5	85.0
Annual growth rate of working-age population		2000–50	-0.45	-0.67	-0.77	-0.46
Annual growth rate of elderly population		2000–50	1.55	0.71	1.17	0.93
Old-age dependency		2000	20.4	23.7	21.9	26.6
rate (65/20-65)		2000–35	38.4	34.9	42.3	54.1
in %		2035–50	55.2	47.2	57.5	53.2

Source: Krieger and Sauer (2004, p. 14).

Age structures of the population in the EU member countries and in the CEECs differ significantly. Although birth rates have fallen considerably since the beginning of transition in the CEEC-10 (but are expected to recover in the future), the average age of the workforce will remain rather low for the next one or two decades in comparison with the German and EU level (European Integration Consortium, 2001, p. 25). This is because of relatively high birth rates before 1990. Almost every CEEC has relatively smaller age groups beyond age 65 and relatively larger cohorts for ages 0 to 14 (Bauer and Zimmermann, 1999, pp. 42–3). Table 9.1 lists selected demographic projections for Poland, Hungary, the Czech Republic and Germany.[10] For pension systems the average annual growth rate of the working-age population is important. Abstracting from the problem of unemployment this rate is negative for all countries and therefore reduces the effect of the positive growth of the wage rate. The internal return of the PAYG pillar is going to be lowered. On a 2000–50 time horizon the (working-age) population growth rate is less negative in Germany than in

Hungary and the Czech Republic because fertility will stabilize earlier at a low level. But this result changes for other time horizons. Recall also that the growth rate of wages has to be added to the population growth rate in order to realistically calculate the implicit return. During the economic catch-up process in the CEECs growth rates will be higher than in Germany, thus the possible disadvantage for the two countries will (at least partly) be offset.

In addition to the reproduction pattern of a society, the development of longevity plays an important role as well. According to Table 9.1 life expectancy at birth is expected to increase in all countries and for both sexes. It is much more instructive, however, to consider the dependency rate which was used in equation (9.4) of the model to measure differences in pension systems. Figure 9.4 shows that the ageing process in Germany is far more advanced than in the accession countries. The 25 per cent level will be reached in Germany in 2007 but only in 2018, 2020 and 2023, respectively, in the other countries. When the dependency rate peaks in Germany at about 44 per cent in 2035, even the next most advanced country, the Czech Republic, reaches only about 35 per cent. Only at the very end of the projection's time horizon may the accession countries catch up (if the predictions for this distant time period are still reliable). In terms of the implicit return on pension contributions the change from an accession country's PAYG pension system to the German one does not appear to be an attractive choice, at least in the short run, which is most relevant for the discussion of the EU enlargement.

Usually, immigration improves not only the dependency rate but the entire age structure of the target country. Empirically, a relatively higher mobility of younger people in comparison to older people can be observed which can be explained on the basis of human capital theory as expected lifetime gains from migrating are smaller for older people (Bauer and Zimmermann, 1999, p. 15). The younger age groups are on average more prone to migration and they have in most CEECs a larger share in the population compared to the EU-15. Hence, it can be expected that the potential migrants from the CEEC-10 are on average considerably younger than the population in the target countries. This assumption is confirmed by empirical results based on microanalytical surveys which show that 57.7 per cent of the potential emigrants from the Czech Republic, 54.3 per cent from Hungary and 51.1 per cent from Poland are younger than 30 (Fassmann and Münz, 2002, p. 77). A further indicator for the plausibility of this assumption is the current age structure of already immigrated employees from the CEECs to EU-15: on average, these workers are significantly younger than nationals and foreign workers in the EU. In the EU-15 on average only 55 per cent of all workers are aged 25–44 while among workers from the CEECs the share

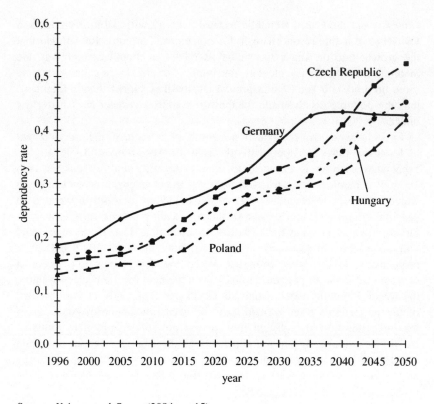

Source: Krieger and Sauer (2004, p. 15).

Figure 9.4. *Projected old-age dependency rates (65+/0–64) in Germany, Poland, Hungary and the Czech Republic*

is almost 70 per cent (European Integration Consortium, 2001, p. 55) .

The migration probability of old, unemployed or poor people is below average. This is partly because they are less mobile and partly because they have fewer opportunities than other population groups to enter the labor markets or the social security systems of western European countries. Our discussion in the previous chapter shows that EU pension regulations effectively prevent migration of retirees into more generous social systems. The mobility of unemployed and poor people is limited by their reduced ability to pay movement costs as a result of their relatively low income. These costs even rise if possible immigration into unemployment has to be taken into account. The participation of unemployed and poor immigrants in the general social security system of the destination country is usually prevented by several safety measures. Only very basic social assistance may be applicable. In Germany, for example, a means-tested social assistance cannot be claimed by immigrants without German citizenship. Beyond that, the need for means-tested social assistance by such an immigrant can justify his expulsion from Germany even if he has EU citizenship (Sinn et al., 2001, pp. 155–7).

Regarding skill distribution one should consider the qualification level of potential migrants from the CEEC-10: on average, one can expect a rather high education level of migrants from CEEC-10, even in comparison to that of the population in the EU-15. This can be explained first by the generally high education levels in the CEECs compared to other countries with similar per capita incomes (see, for example, European Integration Consortium, 2001, p. 26). Sinn et al. (2001, p. 71) emphasize that the general education level in the CEEC will increase further in the future. Second, as human capital theory points out, it can be expected that the average qualification level of migrants is higher than the overall qualification level in a given source country. The individual migration probability is positively correlated with higher education which enhances individuals' ability to collect and process information, thereby reducing the risks and costs of migration (Bauer and Zimmermann, 1999, p. 15). Empirically, it can be observed that migrants who emigrated from the CEEC-10 in the past have a higher endowment of human capital in comparison to migrants from other countries to EU-15, possibly even in comparison to the EU-15 (see, for example, European Integration Consortium, 2001, p. 55).[11] Surveys show that 55.1 per cent of the potential emigrants from the Czech Republic, 57.2 per cent from Hungary and 50.5 per cent from Poland have a secondary or tertiary education (Fassmann and Münz, 2002, pp. 77–8).

Much past migration to Germany took place at a time of higher economic growth and employment levels in Germany (Brücker et al., 2000), that is, in a time of high demand for a foreign workforce, especially for low-skilled workers. As general economic conditions have worsened in the meantime and due to technological and structural changes in the economy, the low-skilled migrant labor market is characterized by an ongoing decrease in demand and a corresponding rise in the unemployment rate and/or decreasing wages (Sinn et al., 2001, pp. 65–70). Immigration into unemployment causes high migration costs as migrants who are unemployed immediately after immigration receive hardly any public transfers in the target country. Decreasing wages in the low-skill labor market segment lower the income gap for low-skilled workers between sending and receiving countries. Therefore there are low and decreasing migration incentives for low-skill workers from the CEEC-10 (Sinn et al., 2001, p. 101).[12]

In sum, empirical evidence indicates that within the CEECs the highest potential mobility prevails within the younger population groups, especially when they have a relatively high education level (Sinn et al., 2001, p. 104).

Therefore we can conclude that the German and other western European pension systems may gain substantially from eastern European immigrants not only because of the previously described quantitative effect but also because of the qualitative effects.

On the other hand, Germany suffers from a particularly rapid ageing process. Hence, it most likely imposes a burden on individual migrants from the accession countries (at least for low levels of total migration according to the model). If this is the case, migrants will prefer not to enter the German pension system if they have a choice. Schnabel (2000) shows that among young cohorts of self-employed Germans who are not mandatory members of the German public pension system, voluntary participation is close to zero. With regard to migrants the same attitude can be expected. Only if immigration is sufficiently large, according to our model, may the German pension system be viewed as having a positive impact on immigrants, but the projections show that very large numbers of immigrants are needed to stabilize the age structure of the German population and thus possibly to drive down contribution rates. While according to the estimations presented in this section an average yearly inflow of 130 000 to 330 000 persons from the accession countries is expected over the next 15 years, the United Nations' (2000, p. 37) estimate requires an average yearly immigration of 324 000 persons to Germany and 863 000 to the EU-15 just to keep total population constant until 2050. For a constant dependency rate, however, the number needs to be much higher. This indicates that immigration flows sufficiently large to exceed the break-even level of our model can hardly be expected. Therefore, the pension system will most likely impose a burden on immigrants.

9.3   A COMPARISON OF PENSION SYSTEMS IN EAST-ERN EUROPE AND GERMANY

The analysis in the previous section allows for a very general comparison of the EU-15 and the CEEC-10 countries with regard to economic and demographic conditions and the effects of potential migration. But we learned before that the institutional characteristics of pension systems may have a substantial impact as well. Therefore, our analysis in this section will investigate in even more detail the institutional characteristics of the pension systems of different countries. In this context it will be necessary to focus on single countries as all European countries have distinct pension systems. The four countries Poland, Hungary, the Czech Republic and Germany are an obvious choice as these countries are the most important source and target countries of migrants.

The analysis of institutional details allows us to derive further evidence on whether it is favorable for eastern European migrants to enter the pension system of other countries such as Germany. Again, we argue that immigration is favorable if the implicit tax can be lowered compared to the burden borne in the home country. This may be the case for relatively higher fertility rates in the target country but also for a lower level of redistribution.

In the following, we will not only briefly describe the pension systems and reforms in these countries but also take a closer look at the relative sizes of the pillars of the pension systems and at the design of the PAYG pillar. Both have a potential impact on the individual migrant's NPPW. Assuming that an immigrant is young and relatively well educated as argued in the previous section, a relatively lower level of funding makes the target country's pension system less attractive. Furthermore, migrating from countries with a defined-contribution system (NDC) to a country with a defined-benefit system (DB) or from a Bismarckian to a Beveridgian pension system (implying more intragenerational redistribution) is likely to impose an additional burden on the individual migrant.

9.3.1 The Pension Systems of Poland, Hungary, the Czech Republic and Germany

Although there were also country-specific reasons why pension reforms became necessary in CEECs in the 1990s, some general features can be extracted that hold for all countries. After the breakdown of the socialist economies, the former pension systems could no longer be sustained. The systems were often considered as unfair and ineffective and faced major financing problems due to sharply increasing unemployment, bankruptcies and problems of collecting contributions. Public confidence in the pension systems was extremely low. Since fundamental reforms take time and need to be backed by strong public support, in the beginning only gradual reforms were introduced to overcome the most pressing problems. However, this was not sufficient to keep up the sustainability in the long run when the ageing of societies would become the main challenge. Hence, in the second half of the 1990s fundamental reforms were introduced in Poland and Hungary, a step which is yet to be taken in the Czech Republic. Obviously, the situation is different for the mature German pension system where for political reasons only gradual reforms are possible. Here, the very rapid ageing process is the main challenge.

Poland
In Poland, a new pension system was introduced in 1999. It replaced the existing PAYG system with a three-pillar system. The new first pillar is

an NDC system which bases benefits on individual contributions during working years. The contribution rate is fixed by law at 12.22 per cent and will be the same for all future cohorts; hence, in principle the government refrains from the possibility of changing contribution rates.[13] Pension benefits will therefore adjust endogenously to changes in the underlying parameters. Like the first pillar, the second pillar is mandatory. It consists of individual, privately managed savings accounts. The contribution rate is fixed at a level of 7.3 per cent, so the total contribution rate from both mandatory parts is 19.52 per cent of gross earnings. All contributions to licensed pension funds are paid equally by employers and employees. The third pillar is savings or voluntary contributions to private pension funds, for example, long-term savings plans or occupational-pension programs.

Hungary

The Hungarian pension reform introduced a new pension system in 1998 in which the old one-pillar mandatory PAYG system was replaced by a three-pillar pension system. The basis for the first pillar of the new pension system was a reformed and downsized version of the earlier defined-benefit PAYG pension system. In addition to the change of the indexation formula, several redistributive elements were removed from the benefit formula as it was one of the main goals of the reform to tighten the link between contributions and benefits. The total contribution rate in the reformed pension system is 30 per cent for all workers, shared by employees and employers. Starting in 2002, 22 percentage points of the total contribution rate have to be paid into the unfunded pillar and 8 percentage points into the funded pillar. In the second pillar mandatory contributions are to be placed in pension funds which are legally structured in a similar way as the previously existing third-pillar mutual benefit funds (Palacios and Rocha, 1998). The main difference is, however, that at the time of retirement the accumulated capital becomes part of a real insurance pool that shares mortality risk (Augusztinovics et al., 2002, p. 40). The third pillar consists of the typical voluntary private pension scheme which is mainly constructed based on mutual associations.

Czech Republic

In contrast to Poland and Hungary, the Czech Republic has not (yet) conducted a fundamental systemic reform of its pension system. Instead, a number of gradual reforms were enacted in the course of the 1990s which aimed at improving the existing public PAYG pension system and complementing it with a voluntary private pillar (Müller, 2002, p. 113).[14] So far, it seems that the reforms are not sufficient to guarantee long-run stability.

The first pillar is PAYG financed and of the DB type. It mixes flat-rate and earnings-related pension benefits (Laursen, 2000). The inclusion of this basic flat-rate redistributive element in the public pension system stands in contrast to the Polish or Hungarian systems where intragenerational redistribution has been transferred from the pension system to the state budget. The total contribution rate is 26 per cent of gross wages, 19.5 percentage points being paid by the employers and 6.5 by the employee. The first pillar of the pension system is supplemented by a voluntary defined-contribution-type pension fund system introduced in 1994. There is a minimum contribution per month and certain minimum participation times (Jelínek and Schneider, 1999, pp. 260–61). The government subsidizes participation in private pension funds. A person contributing to a fund receives a subsidy of up to 40 per cent.

Germany
Until very recently, the German pension system has basically been a one-pillar, defined-benefit PAYG system of the Bismarckian type with a tight link between contributions and benefits. On average, 85 per cent of old-age income originate from the public pension pillar. Less than 5 per cent are covered by (voluntary) occupational pensions and about 10 per cent by savings, earnings and family transfers (Börsch-Supan, 2001, p. 15). In the public pillar contributions are mandatory for almost all dependent workers (except for certain groups like civil servants); about 90 per cent of the workforce are covered by it (Börsch-Supan et al., 2001, p. 165). The contribution rate of 19.5 per cent is levied equally on employees and employers. Furthermore, there is a substantial federal grant to the pension system. The goal of the recent pension reform is to keep the contribution rate below a long-run level of 22 per cent. In principle, this implies that the net replacement rate is free to adjust but the government de facto guarantees that the level will not fall below 67 per cent. In order to allow members of the pension system to make up the (anticipated) decrease in the replacement rate of about 3 percentage points, a supplementary voluntary private pension scheme has been introduced. The government supports these old-age savings with subsidies or tax deductions.

9.3.2   Comparing Different Aspects of the Pension Systems

Table 9.2 presents the main characteristics of the pension systems under consideration. Except for Poland all countries have defined-benefit systems, so only potential Polish migrants face the problem of migrating into a 'different' type of pension system. We argued in Section 8.4 that the Polish NDC system has some advantages to migrants compared to a DB system.

With regard to intragenerational redistribution little changes by migrating from Poland or Hungary to Germany since all three pension systems are Bismarckian. Only for potential Czech migrants does this criterion matter. If the migrant expects to be rather high earning (at least in the future), he may find the German pension system more attractive in this respect. The NPPW may improve.

Furthermore, the relative size of unfunded and funded pension pillars can be considered. Although the estimates in the Table 9.2 are rather rough, the funded pillar in all three accession countries exceeds the German one by far. For Poland, the projections show that a slightly higher replacement income is expected from the second pillar than from the first pillar. In Hungary, there is a legal guarantee that the second-pillar benefit cannot be lower than 25 per cent of the first-pillar benefit, while in the Czech Republic the government target is a level of 17–27 per cent. Müller (1997, p. 227) expects about one quarter to one third of old-age income in eastern European countries to come from funded sources. Compared to this, the new German funded pillar remains small. Only 5 to 10 per cent of the replacement income will be covered by it.

Table 9.2.   Selected characteristics of the pension systems

	POL	HUN	CZ	GER
First pillar (PAYG)				
financing method	NDC	DB	DB	DB
intragen. redistribution	Bism.	Bism.	some Bev.	Bism.
Second pillar (FF)				
mand. or vol.?	mand.	mand.	vol.	vol.
Expected replacement income in %				
total	62	~57	65–7	70
from 1st pillar	30	45	55–60	67
from 2nd pillar	32	min. 11.25	10–5	3
(second pillar)/(total)	>50	min. 25	17–27	~5
Expected public pension spending in %				
2000	10.8	6.0	7.8	11.8
2050	8.3	7.2	14.6	16.9

Note: Based on a full career average worker; Bism. = Bismarckian; Bev. = Beveridgian; mand. = mandatory; vol. = voluntary.

Source: Krieger and Sauer (2004), p. 24.

The relative size of the first two pillars may also be used as a first measure of the level of redistribution within the pension system because the second funded pillar does not usually involve redistributive elements while the first pillar does. Especially if coming to a foreign country without ethnic or family ties – which could be considered as social and information networks – the willingness of migrants to participate in inter- and intragenerational redistribution as net contributors, that is, to pay the entrance fee, is low (unless the personal implicit tax burden is reduced). This holds even more if migration is considered to be only temporary because even under EU regulations problems of transferability may arise.

A further measure for the level of intergenerational redistribution is the amount of public pension spending relative to GDP. It shows the overall size of the PAYG pillar and indicates once more its importance in Germany: the share will increase from 11.8 per cent in 2000 to 16.9 per cent in 2050. A similar development (though at a lower level) will occur in the Czech Republic where the increase will be from 7.8 to 14.6 per cent. It is striking that this happens in countries which introduced only gradual reforms and hints at the necessity for further reforms in the future. In marked contrast are Hungary and Poland where the share is projected to remain almost constant or even to decrease: in Hungary from 6.0 to 7.2 per cent and in Poland from 10.8 to 8.3 per cent (Dang et al., 2001). This is due to the fact that the replacement income will increasingly come from the funded pillar and less from the PAYG pillar.

From the demographic risk displayed in this projection for Germany (and the Czech Republic) follows a certain political risk. It is difficult to predict which groups in society may eventually lose from the reforms. It is certainly preferable to be a member of a pension system which can be considered as relatively stable without prospects of major reforms in the future. However, Bismarckian systems substantially reduce the political risk because contributions are considered to be legal claims to property rights. The German constitutional court, for example, has strengthened the property-rights character of contributions in several verdicts.

Finally, having a relatively large PAYG pillar also implies relatively large implicit tax payments with the consequence of rather low internal rates of return. The average return on contributions to the whole three-pillar pension system can therefore be expected to be lower than in a country with a smaller first pillar.

Regarding the return on contributions one can expect that the rates of return on government bonds in the eastern European countries will be above the German ones for some time because economic growth will be higher as a result of an economic convergence process (for example, Fassmann and Münz, 2002, pp. 90–5). Notice, however, that higher rates of return on investment imply higher implicit tax rates as well according to (3.17). Furthermore, risk of default or inflation will remain relatively higher. Eventually, rates will converge to western European levels (especially if the eastern European countries enter the EMU).

The internal rate of return of the German PAYG system will worsen further in the future if immigration does not take place. While German wages grow roughly at the same speed as long-run productivity growth and while fertility is low, eastern European wages are increasing relatively faster during the catch-up process which had already begun at the end of the last decade (Sinn et al., 2001, pp. 34–8) and will only slowly converge to the EU-15 level (Fassmann and Münz, 2002, pp. 90–5). Therefore, we can expect that the average return on contributions in the German pension system will not exceed that of the accession countries in the foreseeable future. This will certainly not make the German system a very attractive choice for eastern European immigrants.

9.4   CONCLUSIONS

With the upcoming EU eastern enlargement large immigration flows can be expected. While for the target countries immigration may not be considered as beneficial in all respects it will certainly help to soften the financing problems of pension systems in the EU-15 and particularly in Germany. The larger the inflow of immigrants and the easier their integration, the larger will be the positive externality and thus the gain for the domestic population. In particular, migrants from countries such as Poland, Hungary and the Czech Republic appear to be rather attractive from the perspective of western target countries. This is because the expected immigrants are young and well educated according to the projections discussed in this chapter.

But taking the often neglected perspective of an immigrant things look different if the immigrant has to enter a pension system with a relatively higher implicit taxation. The model in this chapter shows that a difference in implicit taxes or the NPPW of two DB systems due to a more rapid ageing process in the target country most likely imposes a burden on the immigrant. The burden will be even larger when the pension system in the source country is an NDC system or has a relatively large funded pillar compared to a DB system with little funding in the target country. Only in the special case of substantial migration flows beyond a break-even level (induced by large wage differentials) may immigrants benefit from their own migration decision because contribution rates fall below their home country's level. While usually pension systems create a migration disincentive, here a migration incentive occurs although fertility rates are relatively lower in the target country.

This outcome, however, appears to be rather unlikely in the context of EU enlargement. Migration will hardly be sufficient to induce the effect.

Instead, one would rather expect that migrants who were members of the newly reformed eastern European pension systems will not be too happy to enter the pension system of a rapidly ageing country such as Germany. The Polish pension system, for example, has a PAYG and a funded pillar of almost equal size. Furthermore, the PAYG pillar is organized as an NDC system. Together with the prospects of high economic growth during the time of economic catch-up this implies rather low implicit taxes on contributions to the pension system as a whole. The internal rate of return of the Polish pension system is therefore certainly not lower but possibly higher that of the German pension system. Although to a somewhat lesser degree, this applies to Hungary and the Czech Republic as well. Hence, if substantial east–west migration is going to take place, this is due to large existing wage differentials and possibly to benefits in other branches of the welfare system but hardly because of the pension system.

NOTES

1. The EU member states agreed on restrictions to the freedom of movement according to the two plus three plus two rule. Each member state is allowed to keep the existing restrictions on immigration for another two years after the enlargement. Thereafter, the restrictions can be extended for another three and then another two years; however, only after an examination of their necessity.
2. Here, c_t^y is consumption during the working life, c_{t+1}^o is consumption during retirement and w_{t+1}^i is the country-specific wage rate.
3. The pension benefits can be assumed to differ by a fixed fraction $\overline{\vartheta}$ between both countries, but for simplicity we will set $\overline{\vartheta} = 1$.
4. Notice that the argument is equivalent to the one derived from Figure 7.2.
5. The derivation of the QQ curve is explained in Appendix D.
6. The derivation of the curves in Figure 9.3 is explained in Appendix D.
7. For this to hold, the increase in the number of contributors in country A must reduce wages more than contributions to the pension system. Otherwise, all workers in the joining country will immediately move to country A (leaving country B deserted) as all of them will unambiguously gain from migration.
8. See Hange (2001, pp. 74–9) for a discussion of this issue.
9. Bulgaria, the Czech Republic, Estonia, Hungary, Latvia, Lithuania, Poland, Romania, Slovakia and Slovenia.
10. Note that these projections already include some net migration (see Dang et al., 2001).
11. That migrants from the CEECs are mostly employed in the low skilled sector (European Integration Consortium, 2001, pp. 56–7) only seemingly contradicts this fact: It is the result of limited access to labor markets in the EU-15 as certificates and qualification records are not acknowledged by the EU-15 authorities (for example, Sinn et al., 2001, p. 48). It can be expected, however,

that the accession process will lead to an approval of these records, that is, that existing labor market barriers to higher educated jobs will be removed.

12. Some groups of low-skilled workers will nevertheless be welcomed in western Europe, for example, nurses and agricultural workers.

13. At least, increases in contribution rates can be excluded. The rates may eventually be reduced when the pension system has matured (Chlon et al., 1999, p. 21).

14. As there is no mandatory private pillar the Czech Republic has basically a two-pillar system.

10. Concluding remarks

The ageing of societies is one of the greatest challenges to industrialized countries. While life expectancy increases further, birth rates will remain low or even fall. This development is a major threat to all social systems that are related to the age structure of the population. In an ageing society, more resources are needed to meet pension claims or to come up with the increasing costs for health services. If the number of contributors is small and decreasing, severe financing problems in these branches of the social system can be expected.

Starting from this observation, one of the goals of this study was to investigate whether immigration is in fact – and as often argued – a potential solution to the ageing problem in western countries. Closely related to this is the question whether there will be a sufficiently large number of immigrants in a country in order to cope with the outcome of the ageing process, that is, the question whether a sufficiently large number of immigrants will be allowed into the country by the domestic population and whether there are enough foreigners who are interested in entering the pension system of a rapidly ageing country. In this context, we finally turned to the question whether countries may engage in harmful competition for mobile workers in order to attract new members for their social systems.

The first result of our investigation will disappoint all who believe that immigration is the solution to the ageing problem: Although immigration has a positive effect on the pension system, the number of immigrants needed to resolve the pension crisis is simply too large to be manageable. Any immigrant entering a country with a PAYG pension system will generate a positive externality for domestic members of the pension system. This externality comes either as a reduction in contribution rates or as an increase in pension benefits or as a combination of both. Estimates show that the externality is substantial but at a time when the ageing problem is most severe each country needs several million immigrants per year to stabilize the pension system. It is unrealistic to believe that these numbers can be achieved. However, an active immigration policy may nevertheless help to keep the parameters of the pension system at manageable levels. In particular during a transitional period in which a more successful family policy may be introduced or the capital stock in a new funded pension

173

pillar is built up, this form of immigration will allow for some relief. This, however, requires major reform steps immediately because the time frame for this sort of reform is rather short in most countries.

An active immigration policy is very difficult to implement if it requires more than just opening up the borders to allow more immigrants into the country. It will be necessary that immigrants – in addition to immigration for humanitarian reasons – are carefully selected based on qualification. The 'ideal' immigrant fits perfectly into those occupations which are believed to stimulate economic growth. However, it can hardly be expected that many of these persons will be attracted as there is fierce competition for the small number of them. With sufficient efforts to integrate less qualified immigrants there will nevertheless be substantial gains which will make natives more favorable towards immgration. Otherwise support for immigration will be low.

The support for immigration may also be rather low – despite the welfare gain for the entire society of the target country – if the gains accrue only to a minority of citizens while the majority suffer from immigration. For example, under a fixed-contribution rate pension regime retirees gain from an increased number of contributors due to immigration. At the same time, the working generation may lose if intragenerational redistribution in favor of immigrants and their children takes place. The majority of workers will therefore reject immigration unless some of the retirees' gain is transferred to them. This is a very relevant problem in politics if parties are supported or influenced by certain interest groups. Left-wing parties which are often supported by trade unions are rather reluctant to allow, for example, craftsmen onto construction sites in their country. On the other hand, conservative parties may not support immigration because many of their voters fear an increasing cultural distance.

Regarding voting decisions another important result has been derived. Only under special circumstances will the voting outcome correspond to the social optimum when a decision is to be made on the parameters of the pension system. Only a young individual, representative of all as yet unborn generations, will internalize all future benefits and contributions and choose a level of immigration corresponding to the social optimum. But a young individual will hardly be the decisive median voter because future generations cannot vote. If, for example, immigration leads to higher net incomes from falling contribution rates but also to lower pension benefits due to a falling average wage, a young person gains for a longer time period from higher net wages than the median voter. Therefore, the latter will choose a suboptimally low level of immigration.

But even if the young generation has a majority of votes, the outcome may not be welfare optimal. This happens if members of the young generation are affected to a different degree by immigration. If immigrants are unskilled, skilled natives support immigration while unskilled natives may want to restrict or even abandon it. The unskilled may turn out to have the decisive vote here but since they ignore the positive effect on young skilled workers they choose a suboptimally low level of immigration as well. Since both a defined-benefit regime and unskilled immigration are not too far from describing real-world pension systems in most western countries, solving the ageing problems via immigration policy becomes more difficult. Democratic societies need to be aware of these sorts of built-in restrictions which lead to deviations from the social optimum and which result whenever gains and losses accrue to different groups. Politics rarely adopts a benevolent-planner perspective in which the goal is to achieve a welfare maximum for the entire society.

At least within the EU migration cannot be restricted by national policy because one of the foremost goals of European politics is to abolish restrictions on mobility. Unrestricted labor mobility between similar countries leads to different problems and challenges, though. In particular, two issues have to be mentioned here. First, while immigration policy is an important political topic, it is often neglected that natives may emigrate from a country because of worsening conditions. Second, redistribution in a country becomes much more difficult if people migrate to countries which offer better conditions to them. These findings are particularly disturbing for a country with a relatively large social system. If a social system becomes more expensive compared to some neighboring country and if migration costs are not overly high, net contributors may think of migrating. In terms of the pension system a rapid ageing process increases the burden on contributors substantially, so individuals may consider moving to a country with higher fertility rates. In Europe, young and high-skilled workers have become much more mobile in recent years and much more willing to improve their personal living conditions by migration.

If young net contributors to the social systems leave the country, balancing the budget becomes more and more difficult. The problem gets even more severe if net beneficiaries of social systems from other countries are attracted to migrate into the seemingly more generous domestic social system. Adjusting to this development most often leads to a reduction in the level of redistribution. Countries engage in a systems competition in order to keep at least their net contributors in the country. The consequence is that there will be less redistribution than a country would opt for without the effect of labor mobility. In terms of international pension systems, one finds that all major reforms in the last decade have led to less redistribution. Most pension systems have become more Bismarckian. For countries with a long Bismarckian tradition this imposes a threat. For them an active family and immigration policy is getting even more important.

There is a second policy measure which may help to restrict at least harmful systems competition although it will not help to solve the ageing problem. With a coordination of national pension policies in the EU artificial migration incentives generated by differences in the pension systems can be avoided. It has been shown that an equalization of contribution rates will be a necessary and sufficient condition in order to achieve an efficient international labor allocation. Migration decisions will then depend only on differences in the marginal productivities of labor, not on the level of implicit taxes. However, European politics has not yet moved to this topic; instead one has introduced a coordination process based on the 'open method of coordination'. This process will even out differences between national pension regulations and thus reduce barriers to labor mobility. Given that without a coordination of contribution rates increasing labor mobility will facilitate harmful systems competition this is a rather problematic policy instrument.

This holds even more when eight central and eastern European countries become members of the EU in May 2004. It is expected that large migration flows will occur following the enlargement. There is some debate whether these migration flows are harmful for the target countries (mainly Germany) or not. It seems, however, that the majority of migrants are well-educated and committed to quickly finding jobs. Poor immigrants are usually excluded from most social benefits in the target countries anyway. Hence, overall a positive effect from east–west migration can be expected. In particular, the pension system will benefit substantially from these immigrants. Nevertheless, several European countries have opted for restrictions upon the freedom of movement of migrants. While this may help to prevent some temporary problems in some parts of the labor market, the positive effects on the pension system are forgone. One can only hope that this is the correct choice and that the costs of allowing immigrants from eastern Europe into the country will in fact be greater than the benefits. This, however, will be decided only in the future.

In sum, our discussion in this book shows that immigration policy offers some chances to ease the ageing problem which threatens the industrialized world. However, there are also many uncertainties. Most likely voters and governments will not agree on the measures necessary to maximize social welfare.

Appendix A: Unfunded pension systems, ageing societies and immigration

DERIVING THE GOLDEN-RULE PATH OF AN ECONOMY

In order to derive the golden-rule path of an economy we will use a simple OLG model (based on Wellisch, 1999, pp. 9-14) with two overlapping generations in each period t, workers N_t and retirees N_{t-1}. There is a constant population growth rate n. Workers inelastically supply one unit of labor while retirees do not work at all. A homogeneous private good is produced with a linearly homogeneous production technology given by

$$F(K_t, N_t) = N_t F\left(\frac{K_t}{N_t}, 1\right) \equiv N_t f(k_t), \qquad (A.1)$$

where K_t is capital input and $k_t := K_t/N_t$ is the capital-labor ratio. The function $f(k_t)$ is the output per effective unit of labor. Total output in the economy can be used for workers' consumption, retirees' consumption and net investment given by

$$I_t = K_{t+1} - K_t. \qquad (A.2)$$

It is assumed that there is no depreciation, so net investment equals gross investment. Notice that investment becomes effective only after one period has elapsed. In period t consumption of workers is c_t and consumption of retirees is z_t. The (closed) economy's budget constraint tells us that no more than the production can be consumed:

$$F(K_t, N_t) = c_t \cdot N_t + z_t \cdot N_{t-1} + I_t. \qquad (A.3)$$

Dividing (A.3) by N_t gives the production function per effective unit of labor. Given $N_t = (1 + n)N_{t-1}$ for all periods t, we get

$$f(k_t) = c_t + \frac{z_t \cdot N_{t-1}}{N_t} + \frac{K_{t+1}}{N_t} - k_t = c_t + \frac{z_t}{(1+n)} + (1+n)k_{t+1} - k_t. \quad (A.4)$$

In the long run the dynamic economy described by (A.4) converges to the steady state. In this state, neither the capital-labor ratio nor consumption will change anymore, that is, $k_t = k_{t+1} = k$, $c_t = c_{t+1} = c$ and $z_t = z_{t+1} = z$ for all t. The long-run production function per effective unit of labor (A.4) is therefore given by

$$f(k) = c + \frac{z}{(1+n)} + nk. \tag{A.5}$$

The utility of a representative individual who decides on consumption and investment is

$$U(c; z) = U\left(c; (1+n)\left[f(k) - c - nk\right]\right), \tag{A.6}$$

where we made use of (A.5) to substitute z. Utility is maximized with respect to c and k and leads to the following first-order conditions:

$$U_c/U_z = 1 + n, \tag{A.7a}$$

$$f_k(k) = n. \tag{A.7b}$$

Condition (A.7a) tells us that the (intertemporal) marginal rate of substitution between consumption today and future consumption must equal the population growth rate. In terms of future consumption the marginal cost of reducing consumption during working life is $1 + n$ as for a given capital-labor ratio there are n additional consumers in the next period. Condition (A.7b) describes the 'golden-rule path of capital accumulation'. In the long run, the marginal productivity of capital should equal the population growth rate, which maximizes consumption possibilities in each period and for each generation. Compared to the steady state, for $f_k(k) < n$ the capital-labor ratio increases such that there is an 'over-accumulation' of capital. Reducing investment allows consumption to increase and at least one generation is better off. The economy is 'dynamically inefficient' as a Pareto improvement is possible. Analogously, for $f_k(k) > n$ the economy is 'dynamically efficient'.

INTRODUCTORY GIFT AND IMPLICIT TAXES

Sinn (2000) argues that the introductory gift to the first generation of retirees equals the present value of the implicit taxes that have to be paid by all future generations. In order to show this we can regard the total pension claims of the old generation at any point in time as the implicit debt of the PAYG system:

$$\Delta_t^{imp} = p_t \cdot N_{t-1}. \tag{A.8}$$

Now $p_{t+1} = \tau_{t+1} \cdot w_{t+1} \cdot \frac{N_{t+1}}{N_t}$ from (3.7) can be substituted into $S_t^{imp} = (p_{t+1})/(1 + r_{t+1})$ from (3.19). It follows that

$$S_t^{imp} \cdot N_t \equiv \frac{\tau_{t+1} \cdot w_{t+1} \cdot N_{t+1}}{1 + r_{t+1}} \qquad (A.9)$$

or

$$S_t^{imp} \cdot N_t \equiv \frac{T_{t+1}^{imp} \cdot N_{t+1}}{1 + r_{t+1}} + \frac{S_{t+1}^{imp} \cdot N_{t+1}}{1 + r_{t+1}}, \qquad (A.10)$$

if $\tau_{t+1} \cdot w_{t+1}$ is replaced according to (3.18). Equation (A.10) should hold for any period $t + j$, $j \geq 1$, as well, so

$$S_{t+j}^{imp} \cdot N_{t+j} \equiv \frac{T_{t+j+1}^{imp} \cdot N_{t+j+1}}{1 + r_{t+j+1}} + \frac{S_{t+j+1}^{imp} \cdot N_{t+j+1}}{1 + r_{t+j+1}}. \qquad (A.11)$$

Combining (3.6), (3.18) and (A.8) gives

$$\Delta_t = T_t^{imp} N_t + S_t^{imp} N_t, \qquad (A.12)$$

into which (A.10) can be inserted:

$$\Delta_t = T_t^{imp} N_t + \frac{T_{t+1}^{imp} \cdot N_{t+1}}{1 + r_{t+1}} + \frac{S_{t+1}^{imp} \cdot N_{t+1}}{1 + r_{t+1}} \qquad (A.13)$$

where the last term can be replaced by (A.11) for $j = 2$. Continuing for $j \geq 3$, the implicit savings term can eventually be eliminated and we end up with

$$\Delta_t^{imp} = \sum_{j=t}^{\infty} T_j^{imp} N_j R_j, \qquad (A.14)$$

where R_j is the discount factor for calculating period t's value of a tax paid in period j. If one assumes that the elements of the sum in (A.14) converge, it follows that the present value of the implicit taxes to be paid by all subsequent generations equals the value of the implicit government debt. This holds for any point in time as long the pension system exists. If we consider the introduction of a PAYG pension system and assume $\Delta_0^{imp} = p_0 N_0^{\text{retirees}}$, we get

$$\Delta_0^{imp} = \sum_{j=0}^{\infty} t_j^{imp} \tau_j w_j N_j R_j = \sum_{j=0}^{\infty} \frac{r_j - i_j}{1 + r_j} \tau_j w_j N_j R_j \qquad (A.15)$$

which proves the initial claim.

NO EFFICIENCY GAIN FROM A TRANSITION FROM FF TO PAYG

In this appendix we will investigate formally whether a Pareto improving transition from a PAYG to an FF pension system is possible when some of the implicit debt of the PAYG system is shifted to future generations by issuing (explicit) government debt. We assume that the transition takes place in period 0 by financing the entire implicit debt in the PAYG system through issuing explicit government debt, which we will denote as Δ_t^{exp}. Any interest payments for the debt are levied as taxes t_t^{exp}. Consider now how debt changes between two periods:

$$\Delta_{t+1}^{exp} = (1 + r_{t+1}) \left(\Delta_t^{exp} - t_t^{exp} N_t \right) \tag{A.16}$$

which we can solve for Δ_t^{exp}:

$$\Delta_t^{exp} = t_t^{exp} N_t + \frac{\Delta_{t+1}^{exp}}{1 + r_{t+1}}. \tag{A.17}$$

This expression holds for any period, that is, we get

$$\Delta_{t+j}^{exp} = t_{t+j}^{exp} N_{t+j} + \frac{\Delta_{t+j+1}^{exp}}{1 + r_{t+j+1}} \tag{A.18}$$

for $t + j$, $j \geq 1$. Now insert (A.18) into (A.17) to get

$$\Delta_t^{exp} = t_t^{exp} N_t + \frac{t_{t+j}^{exp} N_{t+j}}{1 + r_{t+1}} + \frac{\Delta_{t+j+1}^{exp}}{(1 + r_{t+1}) (1 + r_{t+2})} \tag{A.19}$$

and repeat this procedure for all following periods $t + j$, $j \geq 2$. We end up with

$$\Delta_t^{exp} = \sum_{j=t}^{\infty} t_j^{exp} N_j R_j, \tag{A.20}$$

which is just the same term as for the implicit debt given in the previous appendix in (A.14), if implicit debt equals explicit debt at the outset. This, however, was what we assumed. Hence, we find that the present value of the tax burden after the transition does not differ from the implicit debt of the PAYG pension system.

DERIVING THE VALUE OF AN IMMIGRANT

As before, we start out by showing the effect of a new-born child on the pension system, before we present an analogous effect for immigration. The basis for the analysis is an OLG model with three generations, generation t being born in period $t - 1$, working in t and receiving pension benefits in $t + 1$.

Let n_{t+1}^T be the average number of children of a member of generation t, r_{t+1} the rate of return on an investment in period t and w_t the income of a descendant in period t, which is a multiple of his parents' lifetime income. Furthermore, we define the number of descendants in generation t that one member of generation 0 has as

$$N_t^T \equiv \prod_{i=1}^{t} n_i^T.$$

Analogously, we can derive the wage income of members of generation t relative to the income prevailing in generation 0:

$$W_t \equiv \prod_{i=1}^{t} w_i.$$

The discount factor for cash flows can be written as

$$R_t \equiv \prod_{i=1}^{t} \frac{1}{1 + r_i}.$$

Finally, we normalize these values to be 1 in period 0, that is, $N_0^T = W_0 = R_0 = 1$. Let X_t be the direct net contribution to the pension system in present value terms for a member of generation t:

$$X_t = \tau_t^{LS} - \frac{p_{t+1}}{1 + r_{t+1}}, \tag{A.21}$$

where τ_t^{LS} is here the total (lifetime) contribution to the pension system and

$$p_{t+1} = n_t^T \cdot w_t \cdot \tau_t^{LS} \tag{A.22}$$

is the pension benefit of a member of generation t. Combining (A.21) and (A.22), we get a familiar expression:

$$X_t = \tau_t^{LS} \left(1 - \frac{n_{t+1}^T \cdot w_{t+1}}{1 + r_{t+1}} \right), \tag{A.23}$$

which tells us that the net contribution of a member of generation t to the pension system is positive if the rate of return on the capital market exceeds the internal rate of return of the PAYG pension system. If we replace τ_t^{LS} by $w_t \tau_t$ in (A.21) and take the pension benefit $p_{t+1} = (1 + n_t)\tau_t w_t$ as in (3.7), we end up with $\tau_t w_t (r_{t+1} - n_{t+1})/(1 + r_{t+1})$ which is the expression for the implicit tax. Hence, the net contribution of a child to the pension system corresponds to the implicit debt in the sense that an additional child reduces the implicit debt. Servicing the implicit debt becomes easier for the recent members of the system.

It is now possible to extend equation (A.23) to take into consideration that new members of the pension system, that is, new-born children, have children themselves. Hence, any new-born child will found a dynasty of potential contributors to the pension system that will never cease to exist. Making use of the definitions of N_t^T, W_t and R_t, we can convert (A.23) into an expression for the period 0 value of the direct net contribution of a member of generation t (notice that $n_{t+1} = N_{t+1}/N_t$, $w_{t+1} = W_{t+1}/W_t$ and $1/(1 + r_{t+1}) = R_{t+1}/R_t$.):

$$X_t^0 = X_t R_t = \tau_t^{LS} \left(R_t - \frac{N_{t+1}^T W_{t+1} R_{t+1}}{N_t^T W_t} \right). \qquad \text{(A.24)}$$

Let us now introduce the simplifying assumption that contributions to the pension system grow in proportion to wages such that we can write $\tau_t^{LS} = \tau_0^{LS} \cdot W_t$ or

$$X_t^0 = X_t R_t = \tau_0^{LS} \left(R_t W_t - \frac{N_{t+1}^T W_{t+1} R_{t+1}}{N_t^T} \right). \qquad \text{(A.25)}$$

Equation (A.25) gives the total direct net contribution of one member of generation t that is descended from an individual born in generation 0. However, the individual born in period 0 has not only one descendant living in period t. Instead the individual born in period 0 founded a dynastic chain of generations which leads to a total of N_t descendants in period t, assuming 'normal' reproduction behavior. Hence, if an additional child was born in period 0, the present value of the total direct net contributions of all his descendants, that is, of the dynasty founded by him, is

$$V_0 = \sum_{t=0}^{\infty} X_t^0 N_t^T$$

$$= \tau_0^{LS} \left(\begin{array}{c} N_0^T W_0 R_0 - N_1^T W_1 R_1 + N_1^T W_1 R_1 \\ - N_2^T W_2 R_2 + N_2^T W_2 R_2 - \ldots \end{array} \right) = \tau_0^{LS}. \qquad \text{(A.26)}$$

Appendix B: The political economy of pension policy and immigration

---

DERIVING THE VOTING OUTCOME OF THE BROWNING MODEL

In the following we will derive the voting outcome of the Browning model. The optimization problem and the basic assumptions have been laid down in Section 4.1.2, so we can start by presenting the first-order conditions here. For the young generation the optimality conditions for the choice variables s_t^y, s_{t+1}^o and τ will be given by

$$\frac{\partial U^y}{\partial s_t^y} = -U_{c_t^y} + U_{z_{t+2}} \cdot (1+r)^2 \leq 0, \; s_t^y \geq 0, \; s_t^y \cdot \frac{\partial U^y}{\partial s_t^y} = 0, \qquad \text{(B.1a)}$$

$$\frac{\partial U^y}{\partial s_{t+1}^o} = -U_{c_{t+1}^o} + U_{z_{t+2}} \cdot (1+r) \leq 0,$$

$$s_{t+1}^o \geq 0, \; s_{t+1}^o \cdot \frac{\partial U^y}{\partial s_{t+1}^o} = 0, \qquad \text{(B.1b)}$$

$$\frac{\partial U^y}{\partial \tau} = -U_{c_t^y} - U_{c_{t+1}^o} + U_{z_{t+2}}(1+n)(2+n) \leq 0,$$

$$\tau \geq 0, \; \tau \cdot \frac{\partial U^y}{\partial \tau} = 0. \qquad \text{(B.1c)}$$

Conditions (B.1a) through (B.1b) can be summarized. We can ask under which circumstances young workers will choose a positive contribution rate ($\tau > 0$). For this to hold, the first part of (B.1b) must hold with equality. If we plug in (B.1a) and (B.1b), that is, $U_{c_t^y} \geq U_{z_{t+2}} \cdot (1+r)^2$ and $U_{c_{t+1}^o} \geq U_{z_{t+2}} \cdot (1+r)$, we get the following simple condition:

$$\tau \geq 0 \iff (1+n)(2+n) \geq (1+r)(2+r) \iff n \geq r \qquad \text{(B.2)}$$

which is the familiar condition for dynamic inefficiency. This should immediately be obvious: if no implicit debt is to be repaid (for example, if a PAYG pension system is newly introduced), workers will pay contributions to a PAYG pension system only if it yields a higher return than an FF pension system.

The old workers' first-order conditions can be derived in a similar way, except that consumption at a young age will no longer be taken into account. The optimization problem consists of maximizing (4.3) from Section 4.1.2 with respect to individual budget constraints similar to (4.6) and (4.7) but shifted by one period. The Kuhn-Tucker first-order conditions are given by

$$\frac{\partial U^o}{\partial s_t^o} = -U_{c_t^o} + U_{z_{t+1}} \cdot (1+r) \le 0,\ s_t^o \ge 0,\ s_t^o \cdot \frac{\partial U^o}{\partial s_t^o} = 0, \qquad \text{(B.3a)}$$

$$\frac{\partial U^o}{\partial \tau} = -U_{c_t^o} + U_{z_{t+1}}(1+n)(2+n) \le 0,\ \tau \ge 0,\ \tau \cdot \frac{\partial U^o}{\partial \tau} = 0. \qquad \text{(B.3b)}$$

Summarizing both conditions and asking again for a condition for positive contributions, we get

$$\tau \ge 0 \iff (1+n)(2+n) \ge (1+r) \qquad \text{(B.4)}$$

which is less restrictive than (B.2) because the right-hand side of (B.4) is smaller than $(1+r)(2+r)$. In order to see which generation will choose a higher contribution rate, let us first assume that both generations will choose a positive contribution rate, that is, both (B.2) and (B.4) hold with strict inequality. We will call the optimal choice variables of the young generation s^{y*}, s^{o*} and τ^*. Hence, (B.1b) can be written as

$$U_{c^y}\left[(1-\tau^*)w - s^{y*}\right] + U_{c^o}\left[(1-\tau^*)w - s^{o*}\right] = (1+n)(2+n)$$
$$\times U_z\left[\tau^*w(1+n)(2+n) + (1+r)^2 s^{y*} + (1+r)s^{o*}\right]. \qquad \text{(B.5)}$$

Let the optimal choice variables of the old generation be s^{o**} and τ^{**} and assume that old workers, by deciding on savings, behaved in the past like young workers today, that is, $s_{t-1}^y = s^{y*}$. We can now plug the optimal variables of the young workers into the old workers' optimality condition (B.3b). This gives

$$U_{c^o}\left[(1-\tau^*)w - s^{o*}\right] \gtreqless (1+n)(2+n)$$
$$\times U_z\left[\tau^*w(1+n)(2+n) + (1+r)^2 s^{y*} + (1+r)s^{o*}\right]. \qquad \text{(B.6)}$$

Comparing (B.5) and (B.6), we find that both optimality conditions are identical except for the first term on the left-hand side of (B.5). Since $U_{c^y} > 0$, the left-hand side of (B.6) is smaller than the left-hand side of

(B.5) while both right-hand sides are equal. This implies a strict inequality ($<$) in (B.6) which, however, violates (B.3b). Hence, the first part of (B.3b) holds with equality only if the optimal choice variables s^{o**} and τ^{**} differ from s^{o*} and τ^*. In fact, τ^{**} has to be larger than τ^* because only then will $U_{c^o}[(1 - \tau^{**})w - s^{o**}] > U_{c^o}[(1 - \tau^*)w - s^{o*}]$ which is necessary to simultaneously ensure strict equality in both (B.5) and (B.6). The same would be the case if $s^{o**} > s^{o*}(> 0)$. However, this situation cannot occur. If (B.2) holds with strict inequality (in order to ensure $\tau^* > 0$), the same follows for (B.4). This implies that – if (B.3b) holds with equality – (B.3a) must holds with strict inequality which is possible if and only if $s^{o**} = 0$. Hence, we get $s^{o**} \leq s^{o*}$ which contradicts $s^{o**} > s^{o*}$.

Consider finally retirees who maximize (4.4) from Section 4.1.2 with respect only to the contribution rate as this group does not save anymore. Retirees can influence their consumption by increasing pension benefits via higher contribution rates according to budget constraint (4.1). The higher the contribution rate, the larger benefits are and thus consumption in retirement. Hence, retirees will always choose the highest possible contribution rate which is 100 per cent. Summarizing the results for the three groups in society leads to Proposition 5.

THE DYNAMICS OF THE RS MODEL

To investigate the dynamics of the RS model if factor prices can adjust, we need to determine the capital-labor ratio $k_t = K_t/N_t$ of the following constant-returns-to-scale production function:

$$F(K_t, N_t) \equiv N_t \cdot f(k_t) \tag{B.7}$$

with the following factor price equations:

$$r_t = f'(k_t) - 1 \tag{B.8}$$

and

$$w_t = f(k_t) - (1 + r_t)k_t. \tag{B.9}$$

The aggregate stock of capital in period 0 is denoted by K_0. N_0 is given by (4.11) when $t = 0$, so the capital-labor ratio in that period is

$$k_0 = K_0/N_0. \tag{B.10}$$

To investigate k_t for $t \geq 1$, we need further information. Preferences are given by a log-linear utility function:

$$u(c_t, c_{t+1}) = \log c_t + \delta \log c_{t+1} \tag{B.11}$$

where $\delta < 1$ is the subjective intertemporal discount factor. The individual intertemporal budget constraint is given by

$$c_t + \frac{c_{t+1}}{1+r} = \varpi_t(1-\tau) + \frac{p_{t+1}}{1+r} \tag{B.12}$$

where ϖ is the worker's before-tax income, depending on whether he is skilled or not, τ is the contribution rate and p the pension benefit which are related through the pension system. Individual savings are then given by

$$\varsigma_t = \frac{\delta}{1+\delta}\varpi_{t-1}(1-\tau) + \frac{p_t}{(1+\delta)(1+r)} \tag{B.13}$$

and help to determine the capital stock in period $t+1$. The aggregate capital stock differs from other periods by including savings of the immigrants as well. Considering both the effective labor supply of natives and immigrants (in the income term of (B.12)) and the total number of workers $1+m$ (in the pension term of (B.12)), we get

$$K_1 = \frac{\delta}{1+\delta}w_0(1-\tau)N_0 + \frac{p_1(1+m)}{(1+\delta)(1+r)} \tag{B.14}$$

where w is the wage rate per unit of effective labor. The capital-labor ratio turns out to be

$$k_1 = \frac{1}{N_1}\left(\frac{\delta}{1+\delta}w_0(1-\tau)N_0 + \frac{p_1(1+m)}{(1+\delta)(1+r)}\right). \tag{B.15}$$

For any following period labor supply is given by

$$N_t = (1+m)(1+n)^t N_1, \quad t \geq 1. \tag{B.16}$$

Applying $p_t = (1+n)\tau w_t N_t$ from (4.14) and changing indices in (B.15) to $t-1$ and t, respectively, we get the capital-labor ratio for all periods $t \geq 2$:

$$k_t = \frac{\delta w_{t-1}(1-\tau)}{(1+\delta)(1+n)} + \frac{(1+n)\tau w_t}{(1+\delta)(1+r)}. \tag{B.17}$$

Comparing (B.10), (B.15) and (B.17), we find that the dynamics of k_t differ from period 2 in the sense that the capital-labor ratio no longer depends on immigration. This is because of the assumption of perfect assimilation.

Appendix C: Voting on immigration when pension systems differ

---

DERIVING THE VOTING OUTCOME OF THE FIXED CONTRIBUTION-RATE REGIME

Given the existence of a non-negativity constraint the optimization problems in this chapter have to be solved by using the Kuhn-Tucker method. For the Beveridgian pension system with fixed contribution rates from optimization problem (6.9) there follow the first-order conditions

$$\frac{d(w_t^i(1-\bar{\tau}))}{dM_t^L} \leq 0, \quad M_t^L \geq 0, \quad \frac{d(w_t^i(1-\bar{\tau}))}{dM_t^L} \cdot M_t^L = 0.$$

Under this scenario the variation of w_t^i due to immigration is decisive as τ is fixed. Since $dw_t^L/dM_t^L < 0$, in order to meet the Kuhn-Tucker conditions for unskilled workers $M_t^L = 0$ has to be chosen. For skilled workers the opposite is true as $\lim_{M_t^L \to \infty} dw_t^H/dM_t^L = 0$. They prefer the highest possible level of immigration, that is, there is an infinite number of immigrants ($M_t^L \to \infty$). The term 'infinite' should not, however, be taken too literally. While $M_t^L \to \infty$ is necessary to ensure that the Kuhn-Tucker conditions hold, the realistic meaning is that this group prefers unrestricted immigration or simply 'open borders'.

Notice that this derivation holds in principle also for the Bismarckian pension system with fixed contribution rates. The only difference is that the workers' lifetime income is given by $w_t^L(1 + \bar{\tau}n_{t+1})$ according to (6.16).

For retirees, the first of the Kuhn-Tucker conditions of optimization problem (6.10) is given by

$$\frac{d(q_t \cdot \omega_t)}{dM_t^L} = w_t^L + \frac{dw_t^H}{dM_t^L}H_{t-1} + \frac{dw_t^L}{dM_t^L}\left(L_{t-1} + M_t^L\right) \leq 0. \quad \text{(C.1)}$$

For a Cobb-Douglas production function (6.2) the second and the third terms of (C.1) cancel out:

$$\frac{d(q_t\omega_t)}{dM_t^L} = (1-\alpha)\left(H_{t-1}/(L_{t-1} + M_t^L)\right)^\alpha \geq 0.$$

Only if M_t^L approaches infinity can the optimality condition be met $(\lim_{M_t^L \to \infty} d(q_t \omega_t)/dM_t^L = 0)$.

Analogously for the Bismarckian system. The optimization problem leads to the (first) Kuhn-Tucker conditions for each of the two groups. We get

$$\frac{\bar{\tau}(1+n)}{w_{t-1}^H H_{t-1} + w_{t-1}^L L_{t-1}}$$
$$\times \left(w_t^L + \frac{dw_t^H}{dM_t^L} H_{t-1} + \frac{dw_t^L}{dM_t^L} \left(L_{t-1} + M_t^L \right) \right) w_{t-1}^i \leq 0 \quad \text{(C.2)}$$

for $i = H, L$. Cancelling the other (positive) terms leaves us with the bracketed expression which is the same as in (C.1); thus the same interpretation applies.

DERIVING THE OPTIMALITY CONDITION OF THE BEVERIDGIAN FIXED REPLACEMENT-RATE REGIME

For a fixed replacement rate $\bar{q}$ and the future average wage the expected future pension benefit of today's workers is given. The optimization problem reduces to maximizing net wage $w_t^L(1 - \tau_t)$, which includes the endogenous contribution rate. For unskilled workers the first of the Kuhn-Tucker conditions is given by

$$\frac{d\left(w_t^L(1 - \tau_t)\right)}{dM_t^L} = (1 - \tau_t)\frac{dw_t^L}{dM_t^L} + \frac{w_t^L \tau_t}{H_{t-1} + L_{t-1} + M_t^L} \leq 0. \quad \text{(C.3)}$$

The interior solution with $d\left(w_t^L(1 - \tau_t)\right)/dM_t^L = 0$ and $0 < M_t^L < \infty$ follows by rewriting (C.3), given w_t^L and dw_t^L/dM_t^L as well as τ_t according to (6.11):

$$\left(1 - \frac{\bar{q}}{(1+n_t)} \cdot \frac{H_{t-1} + L_{t-1}}{H_{t-1} + L_{t-1} + M_t^L} \right) \alpha \left(1 - \alpha \right) H_{t-1}^\alpha$$
$$\times \left(L_{t-1} + M_t^L \right)^{-\alpha - 1} = \frac{(1 - \alpha) H_{t-1}^\alpha \left(L_{t-1} + M_t^L \right)^{-\alpha}}{H_{t-1} + L_{t-1} + M_t^L}$$
$$\times \frac{\bar{q}}{(1+n_t)} \cdot \frac{H_{t-1} + L_{t-1}}{H_{t-1} + L_{t-1} + M_t^L} \quad \text{(C.4)}$$

which can be solved for $\bar{q}$. This results in

$$\bar{q} = \frac{1}{F} \cdot \alpha \left(1 + n_t \right) \left(H_{t-1} + L_{t-1} + M_t^L \right)^2 \quad \text{(C.5)}$$

where $F = (H_{t-1} + L_{t-1}) \left[(1 + \alpha) \left(L_{t-1} + M_t^L \right) + \alpha H_{t-1} \right]$. The right-hand side of (C.5) is $G^{BV} (M_t^L; \overline{\alpha}, \overline{n})$. The first derivative of $G^{BV} (M_t^L; \overline{\alpha}, \overline{n})$ with respect to the level of unskilled immigration is

$$\frac{dG^{BV} (M_t^L; \overline{\alpha}, \overline{n})}{dM_t^L} = \frac{1}{F^2} \alpha (1 + n_t) \left(H_{t-1} + L_{t-1} + M_t^L \right)^2$$
$$\times \left[\left(L_{t-1} + M_t^L - H_{t-1} \right) + \alpha \left(H_{t-1} + L_{t-1} + M_t^L \right) \right] > 0 \quad \text{(C.6)}$$

because $L_{t-1} > H_{t-1}$. The second derivative turns out to be

$$\frac{d^2 G^{BV} (M_t^L; \overline{\alpha}, \overline{n})}{d \left(M_t^L \right)^2} = \frac{2}{F^2} \alpha (1 + n_t) (H_{t-1})^2 > 0. \quad \text{(C.7)}$$

The derivatives with respect to the shift parameters $\overline{\alpha}$ and $\overline{n}$ are

$$\frac{dG^{BV} (M_t^L; \overline{\alpha}, \overline{n})}{d\overline{\alpha}}$$
$$= \frac{1}{F^2} (1 + n_t) \left(H_{t-1} + L_{t-1} + M_t^L \right)^2 \left(L_{t-1} + M_t^L \right) > 0 \quad \text{(C.8)}$$

and

$$\frac{dG^{BV} (M_t^L; \overline{\alpha}, \overline{n})}{d\overline{n}} = \frac{1}{F^2} \alpha \left(H_{t-1} + L_{t-1} + M_t^L \right)^2 > 0 \quad \text{(C.9)}$$

DERIVING THE OPTIMALITY CONDITION OF THE BISMARCKIAN FIXED REPLACEMENT-RATE REGIME

From (6.18) we first consider the optimal choice of an unskilled worker by deriving the first of the relevant Kuhn–Tucker conditions:

$$\frac{d \left(w_t^L (1 + \overline{q} - \tau_t) \right)}{dM_t^L} = (1 + \overline{q} - \tau_t) \frac{dw_t^L}{dM_t^L} + w_t^L \frac{d(1 + \overline{q} - \tau_t)}{dM_t^L} \leq 0. \quad \text{(C.10)}$$

In order to show the interior solution, that is, $d \left(w_t^L (1 + \overline{q} - \tau_t) \right) / dM_t^L = 0$ and $0 < M_t^L < \infty$, we rewrite equation (C.10) as

$$(1 + \overline{q} - \tau_t) \frac{dw_t^L}{dM_t^L} \leq -\tau_t w_t^L \frac{\frac{dw_t^H}{dM_t^L} H_{t-1} + \frac{dw_t^L}{dM_t^L} \left(L_{t-1} + M_t^L \right) + w_t^L}{w_t^H H_{t-1} + w_t^L \left(L_{t-1} + M_t^L \right)}. \quad \text{(C.11)}$$

Plugging w_t^H, w_{t-1}^H, w_t^L and w_{t-1}^L into (6.17) gives

$$\tau_t = \frac{\bar{q}\left(w_{t-1}^H H_{t-1} + w_{t-1}^L L_{t-1}\right)}{(1+n_t)\left(w_t^H H_{t-1} + w_t^L\left(L_{t-1} + M_t^L\right)\right)}$$

$$= \frac{\bar{q}}{(1+n_t)}\left(\frac{L_{t-1}}{L_{t-1} + M_t^L}\right)^{1-\alpha}. \quad (C.12)$$

Together with w_t^H, w_t^L, dw_t^H/dM_t^L and dw_t^L/dM_t^L this can be inserted into (C.11). Hence,

$$\frac{d\left(w_t^L(1+\bar{q}-\tau_t)\right)}{dM_t^L} = 0$$

$$\Longleftrightarrow \alpha(1+\bar{q}) - \alpha\frac{\bar{q}}{(1+n_t)}\left(\frac{L_{t-1}}{L_{t-1}+M_t^L}\right)^{1-\alpha}$$

$$= (1-\alpha)\frac{\bar{q}}{(1+n_t)}\left(\frac{L_{t-1}}{L_{t-1}+M_t^L}\right)^{1-\alpha} \quad (C.13)$$

which can be solved for $\bar{q}$:

$$\bar{q} = \frac{\alpha(1+n_t)}{\left(\frac{L_{t-1}}{L_{t-1}+M_t^L}\right)^{1-\alpha} - \alpha(1+n_t)}. \quad (C.14)$$

The ratio on the right-hand side of (C.14) is function $G^{BS}(M_t^L; \bar{\alpha}, \bar{n})$. Turning to the skilled workers, the first of the Kuhn-Tucker conditions is

$$\frac{d\left(w_t^H(1+\bar{q}-\tau_t)\right)}{dM_t^L} = (1+\bar{q}-\tau_t)\frac{dw_t^H}{dM_t^L} + w_t^H\frac{d(1+\bar{q}-\tau_t)}{dM_t^L} \leq 0. \quad (C.15)$$

Both terms are non-negative. It is obvious that the first term becomes zero if immigration approaches infinity. Employing the Cobb-Douglas production function we find that this holds for the second term, too. We get

$$\lim_{M_t^L \to \infty} w_t^H\frac{d(1+\bar{q}-\tau_t)}{dM_t^L} = \frac{\alpha(1-\alpha)\bar{q}}{1+n_t}\frac{H_{t-1}^{\alpha-1}L_{t-1}^{1-\alpha}}{L_{t-1}+M_t^L} = 0.$$

Appendix D: Pension policy and the EU eastern enlargement

DERIVING THE QQ CURVE

In order to derive the QQ curve in Figure 9.2 consider the net wage in country A. At the outset there is a positive difference between the $NPPW$s of both countries which lowers the marginal product of labor in country A, that is, $F_N^A - \Delta NPPW$. The marginal product F_N^A falls if immigration takes place. $\Delta NPPW$, however, is reduced since

$$\frac{d(\Delta NPPW)}{dM} = -\bar{p} \left[\frac{N_{t-1}^A}{(N_t^A + M)^2} + \frac{N_{t-1}^B}{(N_t^B - M)^2} \right] < 0.$$

Therefore, the QQ curve approaches the F_N^A-curve as M increases and eventually goes beyond it.

DERIVING THE CURVES IN FIGURE 9.3

Introducing migration M into (9.2) gives

$$\tau_t^A = \frac{\bar{p} N_{t-1}^A}{(N_t^A + M)} \quad \text{and} \quad \tau_t^B = \frac{\bar{p} N_{t-1}^B}{(N_t^B - M)}$$

with the derivatives

$$\frac{d\tau_t^A}{dM} = -\bar{p} \frac{N_{t-1}^A}{(N_t^A + M)^2} < 0 \quad \text{and} \quad \frac{d\tau_t^B}{dM} = \bar{p} \frac{N_{t-1}^B}{(N_t^B - M)^2} > 0$$

which leads to the curves shown in the graph. At the maximum possible migration level, L_t^B, the following holds

$$\tau_t^A = \bar{p} \frac{N_{t-1}^A}{N_t^A + N_t^B} \equiv \tau_t^{A,min}$$

and τ_t^B approaches infinity as the denominator is zero.

References

Aaron, H. (1966), 'The Social Insurance Paradox', *Canadian Journal of Economics and Political Science*, pp. 371–4.

Auerbach, A. J., J. Gokhale and L. J. Kotlikoff (1991), 'Generational Accounts: A Meaningful Alternative to Deficit Accounting', in *Tax Policy and the Economy*, D. F. Bradford (ed.), MIT Press, Cambridge, MA, pp. 55–110.

Auerbach, A. J., J. Gokhale and L. J. Kotlikoff (1992), 'Generational Accounting: A New Approach to Understanding the Effects of Fiscal Policy on Savings', *Scandinavian Journal of Economics*, 94, 303–18.

Auerbach, A. J. and P. Oreopoulos (1999), 'Analyzing the Fiscal Impact of US Immigration', *American Economic Review, Papers and Proceedings*, 89, 176–80.

Augusztinovics, M., R. I. Gál, Á. Matits, L. Máté, A. Simonovits and J. Stahl (2002), 'The Hungarian Pension System Before and After the 1998 Reform', in *Pension Reform in Central and Eastern Europe – Volume 1*, E. Fultz (ed.), International Labour Office, Budapest, pp. 25–93.

Azariadis, C. and L. Lambertini (2003), 'The Fiscal Politics of Big Governments: Do Coalitions Matter?', in *Economics for an Imperfect World: Essays in Honor of Joseph E. Stiglitz*, R. J. Arnott, B. C. Greenwald, S. M. R. Kanbur and B. Nalebuff (eds.), MIT Press, Cambridge, MA, pp. 367–85.

Bauer, T. K. (1998), *Arbeitsmarkteffekte der Migration und Einwanderungspolitik: Eine Analyse für die Bundesrepublik Deutschland*. Physica, Heidelberg.

Bauer, T. K. and K. F. Zimmermann (1999), 'Assessment of Possible Migration Pressure and its Labour Market Impact Following EU Enlargement to Central and Eastern Europe', IZA Research Report No. 3, Bonn.

Becker, G. S. (1960), 'An Economic Analysis of Fertility', in *Demographic and Economic Change in Developed Countries*, National Bureau of Economic Research (ed.), Princeton University Press, Princeton, pp. 209–31.

Berman, E. and Z. Rzakhanov (2000), 'Fertility, Migration and Altruism', NBER Working Paper No. 7545, Cambridge, MA.

Boadway, R. W. and D. E. Wildasin (1989), 'A Median Voter Model of Social Security', *International Economic Review*, 30, 307–28.

Boeri, T., A. Börsch-Supan and G. Tabellini (2001), 'Would You Like to Shrink the Welfare State? A Survey of European Citizens', *Economic Policy*, 32, 9–44.

Bonin, H. (2001), 'Fiskalische Effekte der Zuwanderung nach Deutschland: Eine Generationenbilanz', *Beihefte der Konjunkturpolitik*, 52, 127–56.

Bonin, H. (2002), 'Eine fiskalische Gesamtbilanz der Zuwanderung nach Deutschland', *Vierteljahreshefte zur Wirtschaftsforschung*, 71, 215–29.

Bonin, H., B. Raffelhüschen and J. Walliser (2000), 'Can Immigration Alleviate the Demographic Burden?', *FinanzArchiv*, 57, 1–21.

Bonoli, G. (1997), 'Classifying Welfare States: A Two-Dimension Approach', *Journal of Social Policy*, 26, 351–72.

Borjas, G. J. (1995), 'Immigration and Welfare: 1970-1990', *Research in Labor Economics*, 14, 253–82.

Börsch-Supan, A. (2001), 'The German Retirement Insurance System', in *Pension Reform in Six Countries*, A. Börsch-Supan and M. Miegel (eds.), Springer, Berlin, pp. 13–38.

Börsch-Supan, A., A. Reil-Held and R. Schnabel (2001), 'Pension Provision in Germany', in *Pension Systems and Retirement Incomes Across OECD Countries*, R. Disney and P. Johnson (eds.), Edward Elgar, Cheltenham, pp. 160–96.

Breyer, F. (1990), *Ökonomische Theorie der Alterssicherung*. Vahlen, München.

Breyer, F. (1994), 'The Political Economy of Intergenerational Redistribution', *European Journal of Political Economy*, 10, 61–84.

Breyer, F. (2000), 'Kapitaldeckungs- versus Umlageverfahren', *Perspektiven der Wirtschaftspolitik*, 1, 383–405.

Breyer, F. and B. Craig (1997), 'Voting on Social Security: Evidence from OECD Countries', *European Journal of Political Economy*, 13, 705–24.

Breyer, F. and M. Kolmar (2002), 'Are National Pension Systems Efficient If Labor is (Im)perfectly Mobile?', *Journal of Public Economics*, 83, 347–74.

Breyer, F. and K. Stolte (2001), 'Demographic Change, Endogenous Labor Supply and the Political Feasibility of Pension Reform', *Journal of Population Economics*, 14, 409–24.

Breyer, F. and M. Straub (1993), 'Welfare Effects of Unfunded Pension Systems When Labor Supply is Endogenous', *Journal of Public Economics*, 50, 77–91.

Browning, E. K. (1975), 'Why the Social Insurance Budget is Too Large in a Democracy', *Economic Inquiry*, 13, 373–88.

Brücker, H. (2001a), 'Die Folgen der Freizügigkeit für die Ost-West-Migration: Schlussfolgerungen aus einer Zeitreihenanalyse der Migration nach Deutschland, 1967 bis 1998', *Beihefte der Konjunkturpolitik*, 52, 14–54.

Brücker, H. (2001b), 'The Impact of Eastern Enlargement on EU-Labour Markets', Deutsch-Französisches Wirtschaftsforum, ZEI Policy Paper B12-2001, Bonn.

Brücker, H., P. Trübswetter and C. Weise (2000), 'EU-Osterweiterung: Keine massive Zuwanderung zu erwarten', *Wochenberichte des Deutschen Instituts für Wirtschaftsforschung*, 67(21), 315–26.

Brunner, J. K. (1996), 'Transition from a Pay-as-You-Go to a Fully Funded Pension System: The Case of Differing Individuals and Intragenerational Fairness', *Journal of Public Economics*, 60, 131–46.

Bucovetsky, S. (1991), 'Asymmetric Tax Competition', *Journal of Urban Economics*, 30, 167–81.

Canova, F. and M. Ravn (1998), 'Crossing the Rio Grande: Migrations and the Welfare State', CEPR Working Paper No. 2040, London.

Casamatta, G., H. Cremer and P. Pestieau (2000a), 'The Political Economy of Social Security', *Scandinavian Journal of Economics*, 102, 503–22.

Casamatta, G., H. Cremer and P. Pestieau (2000b), 'Political Sustainability and the Design of Social Insurance', *Journal of Public Economics*, 75, 341–64.

Chand, S. K. and A. Jaeger (1996), 'Aging Populations and Public Pension Schemes', IMF Occasional Paper No. 147, Washington, DC.

Chlon, A., M. Góra and M. Rutkowski (1999), 'Shaping Pension Reform in Poland: Security Through Diversity', Pension Reform Primer Series, Social Protection Discussion Paper No. 9923, World Bank, Washington, DC.

Cigno, A., L. Casolaro and F. C. Rosati (2000), 'The Role of Social Security in Household Decisions: VAR Estimates of Saving and Fertility Behavior in Germany', CESifo Working Paper No. 394, München.

Cigno, A. and F. C. Rosati (1996), 'Jointly Determined Saving and Fertility Behavior: Theory, and Estimates for Germany, Italy, UK and USA', *European Economic Review*, 40, 1561–89.

Conde-Ruiz, J. I. and V. Galasso (2003 (forthcoming)), 'Positive Arithmetic of the Welfare State', *Journal of Public Economics*.

Cooley, T. F. and J. Soares (1999), 'A Positive Theory of Social Security Based on Reputation', *Journal of Political Economy*, 107, 135–60.

Cremer, H., V. Fourgeaud, M. Leite-Monteiro, M. Marchand and P. Pestieau (1996), 'Mobility and Redistribution: A Survey', *Public Finance/Finances Publiques*, 51, 325–52.

Cremer, H. and P. Pestieau (1998), 'Social Insurance, Majority Voting and Labor Mobility', *Journal of Public Economics*, 68, 397–420.

Dang, T. T., P. Antolin and H. Oxley (2001), 'Fiscal Implications of Ageing: Projections of Age-Related Spending', Economics Department Working Paper No. 305, OECD, Paris.

Dustmann, C. (1993), 'Earnings Adjustment of Temporary Migrants', *Journal of Population Economics*, 6, 153–68.

Dustmann, C. (1996), 'Return Migration: The European Experience', *Economic Policy*, 22, 215–50.

Dustmann, C. (2003), 'Children and Return Migration', *Journal of Population Economics*, 16, 815–30.

Dustmann, C. and I. Preston (2002), 'Racial and Economic Factors in Attitudes to Immigration', University College London, mimeo.

Ehrlich, I. and J.-G. Zhong (1998), 'Social Security and the Real Economy: An Inquiry Into Some Neglected Issues', *American Economic Review, Papers and Proceedings*, 88, 151–7.

European Integration Consortium (2001), 'The Impact of Eastern Enlargement on Employment and Labour Markets in the EU Member States: Final Report', Employment and Social Affairs Directorate General of the European Commission, Berlin and Milan.

European Union (2004), 'EUR-Lex: The Portal to European Union Law', download source: http://europa.eu.int/eur-lex/en/index.html.

Eurostat (2000), *Europäische Sozialstatistik - Wanderung*. Amt für amtliche Veröffentlichungen der Europäischen Gemeinschaften, Luxemburg.

Fassmann, H. and R. Münz (2002), 'Die Osterweiterung der EU und ihre Konsequenzen für die Ost-West-Wanderung', in *Migrationsreport 2002: Fakten-Analysen-Perspektiven*, K. J. Bade and R. Münz (eds.), Campus-Verlag, Frankfurt am Main, pp. 61–97.

Feldstein, M. (1974), 'Social Security, Induced Retirement, and Aggregate Capital Accumulation', *Journal of Political Economy*, 82, 905–26.

Fenge, R. (1995), 'Pareto-Efficiency of the Pay-As-You-Go Pension System with Intragenerational Fairness', *FinanzArchiv*, 52, 357–63.

Fenge, R. and V. Meier (2003), 'Pensions and Fertility Incentives', CESifo Working Paper No. 879, München.

Flaig, G. (2001), 'Die Abschätzung der Migrationspotentiale der osteuropäischen EU-Beitrittsländer', *Beihefte der Konjunkturpolitik*, 52, 55–76.

Franco, D., M. R. Marino and S. Zotteri (2004), 'Pension Expenditures Projections, Pension Liabilities and European Union Fiscal Rules', Economic Research Department, Banca d'Italia, mimeo.

Frederiksen, N. K. (2001), 'Fiscal Sustainability in the OECD. A Simple Method and some Preliminary Results', Danish Ministry of Finance, Working Paper No. 3/2001.

Friedberg, R. M. and J. Hunt (1995), 'The Impact of Immigrants on Host Country Wages, Employment and Growth', *Journal of Economic Perspectives*, 9, 23–44.

Gabszewicz, J. J. and T. van Ypersele (1996), 'Social Protection and Political Competition', *Journal of Public Economics*, 61, 193–208.

Galasso, V. and P. Profeta (2002), 'The Political Economy of Social Security: A Survey', *European Journal of Political Economy*, 18, 1–29.

Hagemann, R. P. and G. Nicoletti (1989), 'Ageing Populations: Economic Effects and Implications for Public Finance', OECD Department of Economics and Statistics Working Paper No. 61.

Hange, U. (2000), 'Unfunded Public Pension Systems in the Presence of Perfect Household Mobility', *FinanzArchiv*, 57, 77–88.

Hange, U. (2001), *Umlagefinanzierte Alterssicherung, Migration und Land.* Peter Lang, Frankfurt am Main.

Haupt, A. and W. Peters (1998), 'Public Pensions and Voting on Immigration', *Public Choice*, 95, 403–13.

Haupt, A. and W. Peters (2003), 'Voting on Public Pensions with Hand and Feet: How Young Migrants Try to Escape from Gerontocracy', *Economics of Governance*, 4, 57–80.

Hauser, R. (2001), 'Generationenverträge als Basis des Sozialstaates: Ökonomische Interpretationsmöglichkeiten und fiskalische Konsequenzen', in *Der Sozialstaat an der Jahrtausendwende*, E. Theurl (ed.), Physica, Heidelberg, pp. 31–51.

Hillman, A. L. (2002), 'Immigration and Intergenerational Transfers', in *Economic Policy for Ageing Societies*, H. Siebert (ed.), Springer, Berlin, pp. 213–26.

Homburg, S. (1990), 'The Efficiency of Unfunded Pension Systems', *JITE: Journal of Institutional and Theoretical Economics*, 146, 640–7.

Homburg, S. and W. F. Richter (1990), 'Eine effizienzorientierte Reform der GRV', in *Bevölkerung und Wirtschaft*, B. Felderer (ed.), Schriften des Vereins für Socialpolitik, N.F., Bd. 202,, pp. 183–91.

Homburg, S. and W. F. Richter (1993), 'Harmonizing Public Debt and Public Pension Schemes in the European Community', *Journal of Economics, Suppl.* 7, pp. 51–63.

Hu, S. C. (1982), 'Social Security, Majority-Voting Equilibrium and Dynamic Efficiency', *International Economic Review*, 23, 269–87.

Jägers, T. and B. Raffelhüschen (1999), 'Generational Accounting in Europe: An Overview', *European Economy, Reports and Studies*, No. 6, 1–16.

Jelínek, T. and O. Schneider (1999), 'An Analysis of the Voluntary Pension Fund System in the Czech Republic', in *Transformation of Social Security: Pensions in Central-Eastern Europe*, K. Müller, A. Ryll and H.-J. Wagener (eds.), Physica, Heidelberg, pp. 259–72.

Jousten, A. and P. Pestieau (2002), 'Labor Mobility, Redistribution and Pension Reform in Europe', in *Social Security Pension Reform in Europe*, M. S. Feldstein and H. Siebert (eds.), University of Chicago Press, Chicago, pp. 85–105.

Kanbur, R. and M. J. Keen (1993), 'Jeux Sans Frontieres: Tax Competition and Tax Coordination When Countries Differ in Size', *American Economic Review*, 83, 877–92.

Kemnitz, A. (2003), 'Immigration, Unemployment, and Pensions', *Scandinavian Journal of Economics*, 105, 31–47.

Kolmar, M. (1999), *Optimale Ansiedlung sozialpolitischer Entschei-dungskompetenzen in der Europäischen Union*. Mohr, Tübingen.

Konrad, K. A. (1995), 'Fiscal Federalism and Intergenerational Redistribution', *FinanzArchiv*, 52, 166–81.

Krieger, T. (2001), 'Intergenerational Redistribution and Labor Mobility: A Survey', *FinanzArchiv*, 58, 339–61.

Krieger, T. (2002), 'Chancen und Risiken für die nationalen Rentensysteme durch internationale Arbeitsmobilität', *Vierteljahrehefte zur Wirtschaftsforschung*, 71, 199–214.

Krieger, T. (2003), 'Voting on Unskilled Immigration under Different Pension Regimes', *Public Choice*, 117, 51–78.

Krieger, T. (2004), 'Fertility Rates and Skill Distribution in Razin and Sadka's Migration-Pension Model: A Note', *Journal of Population Economics*, 17, 177–82.

Krieger, T. and C. Sauer (2004), 'Will Eastern European Migrants Happily Enter the German Pension System After the EU Eastern Enlargement?', *Schmollers Jahrbuch*, 124, 1–30.

Krueger, A. B. and J.-S. Pischke (1997), 'A Statistical Analysis of Crime Against Foreigners in Unified Germany', *Journal of Human Resources*, 32, 182–209.

Kuné, J. B., W. F. M. Petit and A. J. H. Pinxt (1993), 'The Hidden Liabilities of Basic Pension Systems in the European Community', CEPS Working Document No. 80.

Lalonde, R. J. and R. H. Topel (1997), 'Economic Impact of International Migration and the Economic Performance of Migrants', in *Handbook of Population and Family Economics*, M. R. Rosenzweig and O. Stark (eds.), Elsevier, Amsterdam, pp. 799–850.

Laursen, T. (2000), 'Pension System Viability and Reform Alternatives in the Czech Republic', IMF Working Paper WP/00/16, Washington, DC.

Leers, T., L. Meijdam and H. A. A. Verbon (2004), 'Ageing, Migration and Endogenous Public Pensions', *Journal of Public Economics*, 88, 131–59.

Lejour, A. M. and H. A. A. Verbon (1996), 'Capital Mobility, Wage Bargaining, and Social Insurance in an Economic Union', *International Tax and Public Finance*, 3, 495–514.

Licht, G. and V. Steiner (1994), 'Assimilation, Labour Market Experience and Earnings Profiles of Temporary and Permanent Immigrant Workers in Germany', *International Review of Applied Economics*, 8, 130–56.

Lindbeck, A. and M. Persson (2003), 'The Gains from Pension Reform', *Journal of Economic Literature*, 41, 74–112.

Lindert, P. H. (1996), 'What Limits Social Spending?', *Explorations in Economic History*, 33, 1–34.

Mansoorian, A. and G. M. Myers (1993), 'Attachment to Home and Efficient Purchases of Population in a Fiscal Externality Economy', *Journal of Public Economics*, 52, 117–32.

Mayda, A. M. (2003), 'Who is Against Immigration?', Harvard University, mimeo.

Mueller, D. C. (2002), *Public Choice III*. Cambridge University Press, Cambridge.

Müller, K. (1997), 'Pension Reform in the Czech Republic, Hungary, and Poland: A Comparative View', in *Social and Economic Aspects of Ageing Societies: An Important Social Development Issue*, N. Stropnik (ed.), Institute for Economic Research, Ljubljana, pp. 224–34.

Müller, K. (2002), 'Between State and Market: Czech and Slovene Pension Reform in Comparison', in *Pension Reform in Central and Eastern Europe - Volume*, E. Fultz (ed.), International Labour Office, Budapest, pp. 113–46.

Musgrave, R. A. (1971), 'Economics of Fiscal Federalism', *Nebraska Journal of Economics and Business*, 10, 3–13.

Oates, W. E. (1972), *Fiscal Federalism*. Harcourt Brace Jovanovich, New York.

Palacios, R. and R. Rocha (1998), 'The Hungarian Pension System in Transition', Social Protection Discussion Paper Series No. 9805, World Bank, Washington, DC.

Pauly, M. V. (1973), 'Income Redistribution as a Local Public Good', *Journal of Public Economics*, 2, 35–58.

Persson, T. and G. Tabellini (1992), 'The Politics of 1992: Fiscal Policy and European Integration', *Review of Economic Studies*, 59, 689–701.

Persson, T. and G. Tabellini (2000), *Political Economics: Explaining Economic Policy*. MIT Press, Cambridge, MA.

Pischke, J.-S. (1992), 'Assimilation and the Earnings of Guestworkers in Germany', Centre for European Economic Research Discussion Paper No. 92.17, University of Mannheim.

Raffelhüschen, B. (1999), 'Generational Accounting: Method, Data and Limitations', *European Economy, Reports and Studies*, No. 6, 17–28.

Razin, A. and E. Sadka (1995), 'Resisting Migration: Wage Rigidity and Income Distribution', *American Economic Review, Papers and Proceedings*, 85, 312–16.

Razin, A. and E. Sadka (1996), 'Suppressing Resistance to Low-Skill Migration', *International Tax and Public Finance*, 3, 413–24.

Razin, A. and E. Sadka (1999), 'Migration and Pension with International Capital Mobility', *Journal of Public Economics*, 74, 141–50.

Razin, A. and E. Sadka (2000), 'Unskilled Migration: A Burden or a Boon for the Welfare State', *Scandinavian Journal of Economics*, 102, 463–79.

Razin, A. and E. Sadka (2001), 'Interactions Between International Migration and the Welfare State', in *International Migration: Trends, Policy and Economic Impact*, S. Djajic (ed.), Routledge, London, pp. 69–88.

Razin, A., E. Sadka and P. Swagel (2002), 'The Ageing Population and the Size of the Welfare State', *Journal of Political Economy*, 110, 900–18.

Richter, W. F. (2002), 'Social Security and Taxation of Labour Subject to Subsidiarity and Freedom of Movement', IZA Discussion Paper No. 490, Bonn.

Samuelson, P. A. (1958), 'An Exact Consumption-Loan Model of Interest With or Without the Social Contrivance of Money', *Journal of Political Economy*, 66, 467–82.

Schmidt, C. M. (1992), 'The Earnings Dynamics of Immigrant Labor', Münchener wirtschaftswissenschaftliche Beiträge No. 92-28, LMU München.

Schnabel, R. (2000), 'Opting Out of Social Security: Incentives and Participation in the German Public Pension System', SFB 504 Discussion Paper No. 99-42, University of Mannheim.

Schneider, O. (1996), 'The Harmonization of Public Pension Schemes – Perfect and Imperfect Labour Mobility Cases', CERGE-EI Working Paper No. 102, Prague.

Scholten, U. and M. Thum (1996), 'Public Pensions and Immigration Policy in a Democracy', *Public Choice*, 87, 347–61.

Sinn, H.-W. (1990), 'Tax Harmonization and Tax Competition in Europe', *European Economic Review*, 34, 489–504.

Sinn, H.-W. (1997), 'The Selection Principle and Market Failure in Systems Competition', *Journal of Public Economics*, 66, 247–74.

Sinn, H.-W. (1998), 'European Integration and the Future of the Welfare State', *Swedish Economic Policy Review*, 5, 113–32.

Sinn, H.-W. (2000), 'Why a Funded Pension System is Useful and Why It is Not Useful', *International Tax and Public Finance*, 7, 389–410.

Sinn, H.-W. (2001), 'The Value of Children and Immigrants in a Pay-As-You-Go Pension System: A Proposal for a Partial Transition to a Funded System', *Ifo Studien*, 47, 77–94.

Sinn, H.-W. (2002a), 'Die rote Laterne', *Ifo Schnelldienst*, 55(23), 3–32.

Sinn, H.-W. (2002b), 'EU Enlargement and the Future of the Welfare State', *Scottish Journal of Political Economy*, 49, 104–15.

Sinn, H.-W. (2003), *The New Systems Competition*, Yrjö Jahnsson Lectures. Basil Blackwell, Oxford.

Sinn, H.-W., G. Flaig, M. Werding, S. Munz, N. Düll, H. Hoffmann, A. Hänlein, J. Kruse, H.-J. Reinhard and B. Schulte (2001), 'EU-Erweiterung und Arbeitskräftemigration: Wege zu einer schrittweisen Annäherung der Arbeitsmärkte', Ifo Beiträge zur Wirtschaftsforschung, Bd. 2, München.

Sjoblom, K. (1985), 'Voting for Social Security', *Public Choice*, 45, 225–40.

Statistisches Bundesamt (2000), 'Löhne, Gehälter und Arbeitskosten im Ausland', Fachserie 16, Reihe 5, Wiesbaden.

Statistisches Bundesamt (2003), 'Bevölkerung Deutschlands bis 2050 – 10. koordinierte Bevölkerungsvorausberechnung', Wiesbaden.

Stigler, G. J. (1957), 'The Tenable Range of Functions of Local Government', in *Federal Expenditure Policy for Economic Growth and Stability*, Joint Economic Committee (Subcommittee on Fiscal Policy)(ed.), U.S. Government Printing Office, Washington, DC, pp. 213–19.

Storesletten, K. (2000), 'Sustaining Fiscal Policy Through Immigration', *Journal of Political Economy*, 108, 300–23.

Straubhaar, T. (2001), 'Migration Policies and EU Enlargement', *Intereconomics*, 36, 167–70.

Strömberg, D. (1999), 'Demography, Voting, and Public Expenditures: Theory and Evidence from Swedish Municipalities', Stockholm University, mimeo.

Tabellini, G. (2000), 'A Positive Theory of Social Security', *Scandinavian Journal of Economics*, 102, 523–45.

Tiebout, C. M. (1956), 'A Pure Theory of Local Expenditures', *Journal of Political Economy*, 64, 416–24.

Tiebout, C. M. (1961), 'An Economic Theory of Fiscal Decentralization', in *Public Finances: Needs, Sources and Utilization*, National Bureau of Economic Research (ed.), Princeton University Press, Princeton, pp. 79–96.

Übelmesser, S. (2004a), 'Political Feasilbility of Pension Reforms', *Topics in Economic Analysis and Policy*, 4, Article 20.

Übelmesser, S. (2004b), 'Harmonization of Old-Age Security Within the European Union', *CESifo Economic Studies*, 50, 717–43.

UNECE – United Nations Economic Commission for Europe (2005), 'Demographic Database', download source: http://w3.unece.org/stat/.

United Nations (2000), 'Replacement Migration: Is It a Solution to Declining and Ageing Populations', New York.

United Nations (2005), 'World Population Prospects: The 2002 Revision Population Data Base', download source: http://esa.un.org/unpp/.

US Department of Homeland Security (2003), *2002 Yearbook of Immigration Statistics*. US Government Printing Office, Washington, DC.

van den Noord, P. and R. Herd (1993), 'Pension Liabilities in the Seven Major Economies', OECD Economics Department Working Paper No. 142, Paris.

Veall, M. R. (1986), 'Public Pensions as Optimal Social Contracts', *Journal of Public Economics*, 31, 237–51.

Verband Deutscher Rentenversicherungsträger (2002), *Open Coordination of Old-Age Security in the European Union*, DRV-Schriften Bd. 35. Verband Deutscher Rentenversicherungsträger in Zusammenarbeit mit dem Bundesministerium für Arbeit und Sozialordnung und dem Max-Planck-Institut für ausländisches und internationales Sozialrecht, Frankfurt am Main.

Verbon, H. A. A. (1990), 'Social Insurance and the Free Internal Market', *European Journal of Political Economy*, 6, 487–500.

von Auer, L. and B. Büttner (2004), 'Endogenous Fertility, Externalities, and Efficiency in Old Age Pension Systems', *JITE: Journal of Institutional and Theoretical Economics*, 160, 294–310.

von Hagen, J. and U. Walz (1995), 'Social Security and Migration in Ageing Europe', in *Politics and Institutions in an Integrated Europe*, B. J. Eichengreen, J. A. Frieden and J. von Hagen (eds.), Springer, Berlin, pp. 177–92.

Wellisch, D. (1999), *Finanzwissenschaft III*. Franz Vahlen, München.

Werding, M. (1997), 'Pay-As-You-Go Public Pension Schemes and Endogenous Fertility: The Reconstruction of Intergenerational Trade', University of Passau, mimeo.

Werding, M. (2003), 'After Another Decade of Reform: Do Pension Systems in Europe Converge?', *DICE Report: Journal of Institutional Comparisons*, 1, 11–6.

Wildasin, D. E. (1991), 'Income Redistribution in a Common Labor Market', *American Economic Review*, 81, 757–74.

Wildasin, D. E. (1999), 'Public Pensions in the EU: Migration Incentives and Impacts', in *Environmental and Public Economics: Essays in Honor of Wallace E. Oates*, A. Panagariya, P. R. Portney and R. M. Schwab (eds.), Edward Elgar, Cheltenham, pp. 253–82.

Williamson, J. B. and M. Williams (2003), 'The Notional Defined Contribution Model: An Assessment of the Strengths and Limitations of a New Approach to the Provision of Old Age Security', Center for Retirement Research at Boston College, Working Paper No. 2003-18, Chestnut Hill, MA.

Wilson, J. D. (1991), 'Tax Competition with Interregional Differences in Factor Endowments', *Regional Science and Urban Economics*, 21, 423–51.

Wissenschaftlicher Beirat beim Bundesfinanzministerium (2000), 'Freizügigkeit und Soziale Sicherung in Europa', BMF-Schriftenreihe, Heft 69, Berlin.

World Bank (1994), *Averting the Old Age Crisis: Policies to Protect the Old and Promote Growth*. Oxford University Press, Oxford.

Index